D1218554

The American South and the Italian Mezzogiorno

Essays in Comparative History

Edited by

Enrico Dal Lago
National University of Ireland, Galway

and

Rick Halpern
University of Toronto

First published 2002 by
PALGRAVE
Houndmills, Basingstoke, Hampshire RG21 6XS and
175 Fifth Avenue, New York, N. Y. 10010
Companies and representatives throughout the world

PALGRAVE is the new global academic imprint of
St. Martin's Press LLC Scholarly and Reference Division and
Palgrave Publishers Ltd (formerly Macmillan Press Ltd).

ISBN 0–333–73971–X

This book is printed on paper suitable for recycling and
made from fully managed and sustained forest sources.

A catalogue record for this book is available
from the British Library.

Library of Congress Cataloging-in-Publication Data
The American South and the Italian Mezzogiorno : essays in comparative
history/edited by Enrico Dal Lago, Rick Halpern.
       p. cm.
    Includes bibliographical references and index.
    ISBN 0–333–73971–X
       1. Southern States—History. 2. Italy, Southern—History. 3. Southern
States—Historiography. 4. Italy, Southern—Historiography. 5. Southern
States—Social conditions. 6. Italy, Southern—Social conditions.   I. Dal
Lago, Enrico, 1966– II. Halpern, Rick.

F209 .A455 2001
945'.7—dc21
                                                                                2001036853

10   9   8   7   6   5   4   3   2   1
11 10 09 08 07 06 05 04 03 02

Printed and bound in Great Britain by
Antony Rowe Ltd, Chippenham, Wiltshire

Contents

v

Notes on the Contributors

Piero Bevilacqua is one of Italy's leading historians and public intellectuals. He teaches *Risorgimento* History at the University of Rome and is the editor of the journal *Meridiana*. He has written extensively on the economic and social history of Italy and the Mezzogiorno. His books include *Breve storia dell'Italia meridionale* (1997, 2nd edn), *Sull'utilità della storia* (1997), and, more recently, *Venezia e le acque* (1998). He is also co-editor of *La Calabria* (1985) and editor of *Storia dell'agricoltura italiana in età contemporanea*, 3 vols (1989–91).

Enrico Dal Lago is Lecturer in American History at the National University of Ireland, Galway. He completed his PhD at University College London on the comparative history of the American South and the Italian Mezzogiorno, and is working on a book manuscript entitled *Southern Elites: American Planters and Southern Italian Noblemen, 1815–1865*.

Giovanna Fiume teaches Modern History at the University of Palermo. Her publications include numerous articles and several books on Italian history and women's history, including *La crisi sociale del 1848 in Sicilia* (1982); and *Bande armate in Sicilia: Violenza e organizzazione del potere* (1984). More recently, she has published (with M. Modica) *S. Benedetto il Moro. Santità, agiografia e primi processi di canonizzazione* (1998) and *I processi di canonizzazione di Benedetto il Moro* (2000).

Richard Follett is Lecturer in American History at the University of Sussex. He is the author of the forthcoming *The Sugar Masters: Capitalism and Slavery in Louisiana's Cane World*. His current work focuses on the American sugar economy, 1845–1914, and he is presently researching slave fertility patterns in the antebellum South.

Donna Gabaccia is the Charles H. Stone Professor of American History at the University of North Carolina at Charlotte. She has written extensively on the international migration of Italians and on immigrant life in the United States. Her recent books include *Italy's Many Diasporas* (2000); *We Are What We Eat: Ethnic Food and the Making of Americans* (1998); and *From the Other Side: Women, Gender and Immigrant Life in the US* (1994).

Steven Hahn is Professor of History at Northwestern University. A specialist on the history of the American South and the comparative history of slave and postemancipation societies, he is author of *The Roots of Southern Populism: Yeoman Farmers and the Transformation of the Georgia Upcountry, 1850–1890* (1983), co-editor of *The Countryside in the Age of Capitalist Transformation: Essays in the Social History of Rural America* (1986), and co-author of *Freedom: A Documentary History of Emancipation, Land and Labor in 1865* (2001). He is completing a book on black politics in the rural South from slavery to the Great Migration.

Rick Halpern is the Bissell-Heyd-Associates Professor of American Studies at the University of Toronto. He has written extensively on race and labour in a number of national and transnational contexts. His publications include *Down on the Killing Floor: Black and White Workers in Chicago's Packinghouses* (1997) and a co-edited collection, *Racializing Class, Classifying Race: Labour and Difference in Britain the USA and Africa* (2000). Currently he is completing a comparative study of agricultural workers in the sugar industries of Louisiana and southern Africa.

J. William Harris is Professor and Chair in the History Department at the University of New Hampshire. He is the editor of *Society and Culture in the Slave South* (1992) and the author of *Plain Folk and Gentry in a Slave Society: White Liberty and Black Slavery in Augusta's Hinterlands* (1985) and of *Deep Souths: Delta, Piedmont, and Sea Island Society in the Age of Segregation* (2001).

Peter Kolchin is the Henry Clay Reed Professor of History at the University of Delaware. His work focuses on American slavery and emancipation in comparative perspective; recent books include *Unfree Labor: American Slavery and Russian Serfdom* (1987), and *American Slavery, 1619–1877* (1993). He is currently writing a comparative study of emancipation and its aftermath in the United States and Russia.

Bruce Levine is Professor of History at the University of California, Santa Cruz. Educated at the University of Michigan and the University of Rochester; he has also taught at Wayne State University, the University of Cincinnati and Columbia University. His books include *The Spirit of 1848: German Immigrants, Labor Conflict, and the Origins of the Civil War* (1992) and *Half Slave & Half Free: The Roots of Civil War* (1992).

Marta Petrusewicz is Professor of Modern European History at the City University of New York. Her books include *Latifundium: Moral Economy and Material Life in a European Periphery* (1996) for which she received the Sila Prize, and *Come il Meridione divenne Questione: Rappresentazioni del Sud prima e dopo il Quarantotto* (1998), which was awarded a Salvatore Valitutti Prize. She is currently working on a comparative history of alternative ideas of progress in Ireland, Poland and Italy.

Lucy Riall is Senior Lecturer in Modern European History at Birkbeck College, University of London. Her publications include *The Italian Risorgimento: State, Society and National Unification* (1994) and *Sicily and the Unification of Italy: Liberal Policy and Local Power, 1859–1866* (1998).

Part I

The Two Souths in Comparative Perspective

1

Two Case-Studies in Comparative History: The American South and the Italian Mezzogiorno

Enrico Dal Lago and Rick Halpern

The present volume arises from the 1999 Commonwealth Fund Conference in American History, held at University College London. The conference, entirely dedicated to exploring the prospects for comparison between the American South and the Italian Mezzogiorno,[1] originated from detailed reflection on the current state of the art of comparative studies involving the US South. For the past 50 years, American historians have utilized the comparative approach to southern history with different results: by viewing the South in a wider perspective they have tended to either refine the perception of its distinctiveness or, conversely, demolish the assumption of its uniqueness.[2] A growing body of scholarship increasingly sees the American South as simply one of many regions of the world with particular characteristics – a pre-eminently agricultural economy and a tendency to conservatism in society and politics – that have combined to produce a path to modernization dramatically different from northern American and European standards.[3]

Building upon these foundations, the contributors to the 1999 Commonwealth Fund Conference accepted the challenge of comparing the American South with another such region – the Italian Mezzogiorno – with similarities in its process of modernization, but also with striking differences in social and cultural terms. Historians at the forefront of the two regions' historiographical revolutions engaged in dialogues over specific topics and discovered the comparability of issues as diverse as the stereotypes relating to the two souths, the ideology of the landed elites, the treatment of labourers on the large landed estates, the importance of gender in the understanding of social relations, and the connections between progressive political forces and between migratory movements across the two sides of the Atlantic.

This collection of essays is a selection from those originally presented at the conference and then revised in light of critical discussion. The topics covered here are by no means exhaustive: the essays are intended to suggest lines of inquiry for future comparative studies of the American South and the Mezzogiorno through careful justaxposition of individual case-studies focused on specific issues. At the same time, the dialogue between scholars belonging to the two different fields is – in the words of Peter Kolchin – 'a step that is especially useful in creating what might be called a comparative consciousness'.[4] Piero Bevilacqua considers the nurturing of this sort of awareness the foundation of 'a "comparative culture"...a knowledge of different social realities grounded in comparative historical research'.[5] As such, this collection is at the same time an experiment and an invitation to pursue further comparison between the two souths as a way of building bridges between practitioners of the historical discipline in two countries that have more in common than has been acknowledged so far. In this sense, Kolchin's suggestion, supported by Piero Bevilacqua, of placing the comparison of the two souths in the wider context of comparison between the history of the USA and Italy, and American and Italian historiography, is particularly stimulating and points toward a promising way forward for future research on the two regions.[6]

Our point of departure is the definition of comparison and the designation of the units of study that are comparable. In his keynote lecture, reprinted here in expanded form, Peter Kolchin defines three approaches to the comparison of the American South: comparison between the South and the North, comparison between regions within the South, and comparison between the South and other societies. Kolchin goes on to say that while the first and the third approach have characterized most comparative studies, the second approach has been surprisingly neglected until relatively recently. Perhaps more important is the fact that several historians have used comparison with the North (the 'un-South') and comparison with other regions of the world (the 'other souths') to perpetuate the fallacy of a unique southern path to modernization.[7] It is important to note – as Kolchin does, citing Robert Fogel and Stanley Engerman – that, even though the nineteenth-century South lagged behind the North in terms of industrialization and economic development, in absolute terms it was one of the most prosperous regions of the world.[8] However, it is also important to put this statement in the context of the north–south divide in the USA. Absolute comparisons must not simply take into account economic factors, but social, political and cultural ones as well. The American South is a specific region within a nation-state, as Kolchin himself emphasizes in his historiographical survey of the literature on southern nationalism, and as such it should be compared with regions of other nations, whose recent history and historiography have been constructed in opposition to other norths, or 'un-Souths'.[9]

Following Kolchin's suggestions, Bevilacqua notices in his contribution that the historiographical perception of the North as 'un-South' is one of the strongest points of comparison between our two case-studies. Like the American South, the Mezzogiorno has been constructed, or perhaps imagined, in opposition to a supposedly more industrialized and economically developed north, or 'un-South'.[10] In both the USA and Italy, this construction has led to a paradigm of backwardness that has informed the historiographies of the two regions for most of the last 50 years. Both Kolchin and Bevilacqua notice the connection between the relatively recent reaction of American and Italian economic and social historians to this paradigm and the subsequent production of widely controversial works, such as Fogel and Engerman's *Time on the Cross* and Marta Petrusewicz's *Latifundium*.[11] Both in the USA and Italy, the reaction to a simplistic view of southern backwardness has led to a more sophisticated analysis of the actual economies of the two regions. This, in turn, has led to the discovery of a much more complex picture that has demonstrated the importance in both souths of particularly dynamic productive sectors dominated by agricultural operators who had a clear capitalist mentality.

The comparative approach between different regions within the souths – the 'many souths' – has characterized very few historical studies, and yet, as Kolchin notices, this is one of the most promising avenues for research.[12] Comparison between the historical development of the different regions that constituted the original American South – as in Ira Berlin's recent *Many Thousands Gone*[13] – has shown the importance of the diverse experience of slaves in relation to the shaping of different labour systems. In reality, this is not a wholly novel approach in slave studies, since historians of slavery have long been accustomed to thinking comparatively about slave life and labour systems across a whole range of different cultures in time and space. However, what is new here is the application of this method to a single slave society in order to show its internal differences, or rather its regional variations. It is certainly no accident that the two historians Kolchin credits for this

– Ira Berlin and Philip Morgan – are also the editors of major comparative collections on slavery in the Americas.[14]

As Piero Bevilacqua acknowledges, this second approach has enormous potential for the study of the Mezzogiorno.[15] The detailed analysis of the 'many souths' that formed the Italian South has been one of the most important characteristics of revisionist historiography. Beginning with the edited collections of essays on specific regions that appeared as volumes of the *Storia d'Italia Einaudi: Le Regioni*, and continuing with a series of major monographs focusing on particularly important centres of entrepreneurial activity (such as the Terra di Bari or the Conca d'Oro), regional analysis has been a defining feature of recent southern Italian historiography.[16] Yet what is missing is a comparative study between two or more of the 'many souths' that make up the Mezzogiorno following the methodological lead offered by Berlin and Morgan for the American South. While Piero Bevilacqua has written the best comparative synthesis available on the economic regions of the Mezzogiorno,[17] no historian has yet attempted to compare two areas of southern Italy in order to analyse similarities and differences in the historical development of their economies and social structures.

The third approach to the comparative history of the American South – comparison with 'other souths' – is, according to Kolchin, the most readily identifiable with the wider body of comparative studies.[18] This is in part because of the enormous popularity it has enjoyed among students of slave studies since the 1947 publication of Frank Tannenbaum's *Slave and Citizen*.[19] At the same time, more recent and highly praised works – such as Kolchin's own *Unfree Labour* and Shearer Davis Bowman's *Masters and Lords* – have pushed the boundaries of comparison between the nineteenth-century South and contemporary societies well beyond the confines of slave studies and have hinted at a breathtaking range of possibilities for future research. Central to these new comparative developments is the questioning of the simplistic dichotomy of slavery/free labour and its consequent replacement with a sophisticated scale of degrees of unfree labour, among which slavery is simply the strictest in legal terms.[20]

This new approach to slavery and unfree labour contains an implicit suggestion for comparison with other nineteenth-century agrarian societies such as the Italian Mezzogiorno. According to Piero Bevilacqua, even though in nineteenth-century southern Italy there was no slavery in legal terms, agrarian labourers were far from being free. They were exploited and abused, and overall were objects of 'specific forms of subordination which psychologically and morally tied the peasants to the landowners'. Bevilacqua extends this analogy by quoting an extract from an early twentieth-century parliamentary inquiry, according to which, 'At bottom, the landowners are convinced that the peasants are not men like them'.[21] This comment reminds one of the profound, almost racial, difference that the Russian landlords studied by Peter Kolchin felt towards their serfs well into the nineteenth century.[22] At the same time, it invites all sorts of comparisons between nineteenth-century agrarian societies in which a tiny elite dominated and exploited a large mass of mostly landless labourers (if not racially, certainly economically and socially). From this perspective, the comparison of the American South with 'other souths' certainly has many more implications than have been recognized so far.[23]

One of the most controversial debates in both the American and Italian historiographies has focused on the definition of the ideologies of the landed elites based in the two souths. To put it simply, the key issue has revolved around the opposite views of American planters and southern Italian landowners as either modern or pre-modern, capitalist or feudal, both in regard to their participation in economic activities and in regard to their implementation of social codes and rules of behaviour. In both cases, much of the debate has stemmed from the publication of key monographs, which have provocatively dismantled previous assumptions about the nature of the two master classes. In the USA, Fogel and Engerman's *Time on the Cross* and James Oakes's *The Ruling Race* seriously questioned Eugene Genovese's fundamental tenet regarding American planters (that they were neither feudal nor bourgeois), and argued persuasively for their capitalist character.[24] On the other hand, in Italy, Marta Petrusewicz's *Latifundium* displayed a similar preoccupation with understanding the mechanisms of capitalist rationality in the landowners' management of the agricultural estates which were once held as the symbol of southern Italian backwardness.[25] While these monographs received an intense critical reception upon publication, they have also been instrumental in prompting a reconsideration of the evidence regarding the ideology and behaviour of the two landed elites. In both cases, more recent studies have shown that capitalist behaviour was not at all uncommon among American planters and southern Italian landowners in those areas of the two souths where the implementation of commercial agriculture required entrepreneurial skills for the success of the enterprise in the world market. In this respect, William Dusinberre's analysis of the rice plantations of South Carolina and Salvatore Lupo's monograph on the citrus groves of Sicily and Calabria are particularly important examples of this new wave of scholarship.[26] Still, the most recent tendencies in both historiographies seem to move towards a common ground between the idea of American planters and southern Italian landowners as full-blown capitalists and the view that regards them as more akin to feudal aristocracies; scholars of both countries increasingly advocate an agreement on the co-existence of both pre-modern and modern characteristics in the behaviour of the two landed elites.[27]

Significantly, both Richard Follett's and Marta Petrusewicz's contributions in this collection look at elements of modernity in the otherwise pre-modern outlook of American planters and southern Italian landowners. Follett's study of Louisiana's plantations before the Civil War shows how 'the sugar masters...eagerly embraced the market revolution while simultaneously rejecting the liberal and democratic overtones of nineteenth-century progress'.[28] As promoters of one of the most successful economic enterprises of the antebellum south (the sugar industry), Louisiana planters stood as models of capitalist entrepreneurship; since the beginning of sugar cultivation, they had been able to transform the swamps of the lower Mississippi into plantations which, by the 1850s, were fully equipped with steam-powered sugar mills and capable of producing a quarter of the world's crop. Technological innovation and the implementation of 'modern' industrial practices – such as the assembly line – had been crucial in maximizing production; agricultural journals and documents written by the foremost Louisiana planters almost invariably pointed to good labour management and knowledge of agricultural techniques as the secrets of success in sugar production.[29]

Yet the 'sugar masters' achieved these stunning levels of productivity on their seemingly 'modern' agricultural enterprises by keeping their labour force unfree. Their factory-like plantations had slaves working according to a 'clock ordered labour regime', rather than being free labourers as in the northern plants; workers' discipline in the industrial sugar mills and on the assembly lines was maintained by drivers and overseers who frequently resorted to the whip. Yet Louisiana sugar planters found little discrepancy in the simultaneous implementation of capitalist technology and maintenance of non-capitalist relations of productions; they even went as far as asserting that 'free labour cannot compete, in the manufacture of sugar, with better organized labour'.[30] As a matter of fact, the plantations' successful economic performance depended largely on the slaves' acquiescence to their masters' demands for increasing productivity. Slaves, in turn, obtained from their masters greater autonomy, improved accommodation, and even financial remuneration in exchange for their crucial contribution to labour stability and efficiency. On Louisiana's sugar plantations, the 'pre-modern' paternalistic character of the master–slave relationship and its constant bargaining process co-existed with industrial capitalist practices and 'modern' technological innovations.

This mixture of 'modern' and 'pre-modern' elements in Louisiana is reminiscent of several areas of the nineteenth-century world in which increases in the quality and quantity of agricultural productivity were not accompanied by equally significant changes in the inequality of social relations or in the conservative ideology of the propertied classes. For example, in the Mezzogiorno, the production and trade of commercial crops – such as olive oil and citrus – increased exponentially during the nineteenth century. However, this measure of economic growth was not accompanied by any major structural or ideological change in the landowners' exploitation of peasants in the countryside. As in the American South, economic modernization did not necessarily imply the advent of more modern and egalitarian social relations between upper and lower classes.

Mirroring Follett's essay on the sugar masters, Marta Petrusewicz's contribution in Chapter 5 shows how the ideology of nineteenth-century southern Italian landed elites did have several modern characteristics. Much like Louisiana planters, nineteenth-century Neapolitan landowners were eager 'to respond to and to promote modernization' in their agricultural enterprises.[31] And just as Louisiana planters were one of many landed elites of the American South particularly concerned with agricultural profitability, Neapolitan landowners were one of many nineteenth-century European landed elites interested in agronomy and characterized by an 'entrepreneurial liveliness'. As Petrusewicz explains, in the Neapolitan case, entrepreneurial landowners mainly belonged to a recently formed class of landed proprietors (the *galantuomini*) whose origins dated back to the abolition of the feudal law, decreed in the early 1800s. They constituted a sort of 'landed *intelligentsia*', which gathered in liberal circles and secret societies and which drew its inspiration from European romantic and progressive movements.[32]

In economic terms, Neapolitan liberals advocated the agricultural modernization of the Kingdom of the Two Sicilies, whilst in political terms they 'identified with the constitutional monarchy' rather than with the absolutism practised by the Bourbon kings. Unlike what occurred in Louisiana, where planters were mainly concerned with economic improvements on an individual scale, in southern Italy, liberal landowners debated over economic development on a national scale.

Several of them wrote for government-sponsored periodicals or filled the highest ranks of government-sponsored economic societies; through both channels, they advocated the way to agricultural improvements through technological innovation and careful land and labour management. At the centre of this 'civilizing project' stood the propertied class, which perceived itself as 'the only social group that combined in itself tradition and modernity' and 'the only one capable of leading the country towards modernization'. Significantly, the landowners' conception of modernization included an improvement in the condition of the peasantry mainly through a paternalistic sort of education in agricultural matters. This type of education would have taught them how to work better and more efficiently, while at the same time holding sacrosanct 'the preservation of the hierarchical order'. Petrusewicz also points out the continuing paternalistic nature of relationships and of everyday transactions and negotiations on the nineteenth-century *latifondo*.[33] One can only conclude that, as in the case of Louisiana planters, the modern contents of the ideology of Neapolitan landed elites co-existed with the pre-modern character of the relations of productions on their landed estates.

Closely related to, and dependent upon, the definition of the ideology of the landed elites are the issues of implementation of land reform and the changing conditions of rural labourers. In both souths, momentous events brought about a sudden emancipation which dissolved the obligations that made the workers dependent on the juridical power of their masters. In the American South, Lincoln's 1863 Emancipation Proclamation and the Thirteenth, Fourteenth and Fifteenth Amendments to the Constitution – which abolished slavery, protected civil rights, and extended the right to vote to African-Americans – came as a result of the Union victory over the Confederacy during the Civil War. These legal measures were the background against which the transition from slavery to free labour occurred in the countryside, a process which radically changed the nature of social relations between ex-slaves and their former masters.[34]

On the other hand, the abolition of the feudal law in the continental Mezzogiorno was, to a certain extent, the result of military occupation, since it was decreed in 1806 by Joseph Napoleon during the so-called French *decennio* (1806–15). In Sicily, occupied by the British, it was implemented only in 1812 as a result of a compromise between the Bourbon king and the liberal nobility of the island.[35] The abolition of feudalism in southern Italy was certainly less consequential than the abolition of slavery in the American South in terms of changing the nature of social relations between rural labourers and their masters. Yet, if there is a similarity between the two processes, it lies in the fact that in both cases emancipation came through a legal revolution that brought little substantial land redistribution. Ex-slaves in the USA and peasants in southern Italy were left with 'nothing but freedom', to use Eric Foner's words.³⁶ Their economic emancipation was far from being established, and its achievement in both souths became the object of social and political unrest that shook the rural countryside throughout the following decades.

Both American and Italian historians have tried to establish the extent to which former masters managed to keep their control over lands and labourers after emancipation; at the same time, they have tried to establish the extent to which ex-slaves and peasants managed to assert their rights in spite of a persistent exploitation which manifested itself in the form of unequal sharecropping agreements, usurious land-lease, and other means of perpetuating dependence. The results of these studies have often been strikingly different; however, it is fair to say that in both cases the most recent scholarship has identified, through analysis of political struggles at the local level, the key to a deeper understanding of the social unrest on postemancipation plantations and *latifondi*.³⁷

The two essays by Steven Hahn and Lucy Riall in this collection are illuminating examples of analyses of the complex relationship between rural labourers' struggle to assert their rights and the local elites' battle to retain their power in the face of government intervention. Chapter 6 reflects Hahn's belief in the uniqueness of the 'process of emancipation and Reconstruction that set the American South apart from virtually all servile societies in Europe and the western hemisphere', and yet it contains plenty of stimulating thoughts for comparison with the situation of nineteenth-century peasants in the Mezzogiorno.³⁸ Hahn's focus is on black rural labourers and their political struggle to enforce their civil rights in spite of the landowners' continuous exploitation through labour obligations and contractual practices. Hahn makes clear that, after being defeated in the Civil War, southern planters 'did retain control of their estates and, therefore, wielded significant leverage over the newly liberated black labour force'. In spite of the work of the Freedmen's Bureau and the crucial pieces of legislation promoted by Radical Republicans (such as the 1867 Military Reconstruction Acts, which enfranchised African-American men in the former Confederacy), 'most prospective black voters still depended on white landowners for their livelihood'.³⁹ Still, particularly charismatic black leaders attempted to take full advantage of their new status as freedmen by building their own political communities. They did this by reconstituting families that had been dispersed under slavery and joining them with extended kinship networks, so to have effective means of resisting coercive acts from landowners. The kind of stability that families and kin networks provided freedmen with was an essential tool in the rural labourers' process of asserting their own rights. As with other rural societies, the labourers' communities became the most important social and political means of struggle against exploitation from landowners.

Disputes over land claims and labour obligations prompted not just the formation of communities of freedmen, but also of some of the earliest collective activities and formal organizations (such as drilling and militia companies) which equally were 'held together by sinews of kinship'.[40] In time, community organization became a political activity related to the protection of civil and voting rights through the formation of clubs and associations – the most important of which was the Union League – which hoped to influence local politics. Through a proliferation of councils which made their presence felt in the everyday life of freedmen in several counties, the Union League largely achieved its aim 'of mobilizing black support for the national government and the Republican Party' and also functioned as a vehicle for 'community development, defence and self-determination', especially in regard to the negotiation of labour contracts and in the defence of black rural labourers against the landowners' exploitative practices. It is certainly no wonder that white vigilantism and the Ku Klux Klan emerged both as responses to the activities of the Union League and as attempts at preventing African-Americans from enforcing their civil and political rights.

Significantly, Hahn proposes to use the term *'latifundist'* to describe politics in the postemancipation South; in fact, very like what took place in the large landed estates of nineteenth-century southern Italy, political struggles were waged by private armies attached to local bosses and landed proprietors against the claims to land and rights of an emerging landed peasantry whose communities were based on kinship.[41]

Chapter 7 implicitly responds to Steven Hahn's suggestions for comparison by clarifying the dynamics of the struggle over local politics in the nineteenth-century rural Mezzogiorno in reference to the repeated attempts to achieve a measure of land reform on the *latifondi*. Building upon the premises set by important revisionist works – such as Marta Petrusewicz's *Latifundium* – Riall analyses the nineteenth-century Sicilian *latifondo* as a relatively recent agricultural system that was tied to a peculiar type of social structure. Sicilian noblemen used to leave their estates in the hands of agents (*gabellotti*), who acted as both rent-collectors and 'middlemen, leasing land from the absentee landowners and sub-dividing it among the local peasantry'.[42] Sicilian peasants were mainly tenants who rented land on the *latifondo* and worked it as sharecroppers; however, the poorest of them worked as day-labourers (*braccianti*), especially during the crucial sowing and harvesting seasons. Peasants were exploited by both landowners and *gabellotti*, whose usurious practices of land-lease kept them 'in a permanent state of legal enslavement'.[43] As early as the eighteenth century, Sicilian economists had proposed agricultural reforms aimed at modernizing the *latifondo*, a system that they considered backward and unproductive. In 1812, the Sicilian noble parliament officially decreed the abolition of feudalism and the conversion of feudal estates into private properties. After 1815, the restored Bourbon government not only confirmed the change, but accelerated the process of land reform through further legislation aimed at breaking up the feudal *latifondi*, creating medium-sized commercial farms, and assisting the rural poor. Equally ambitious programmes of land reform were attempted during the 1848 revolution and during Garibaldi's dictatorship in Sicily, in 1860. According to Riall, none of these programmes succeeded and, as late as 1876, 'landed estates averaged 1000 to 2000 hectares'.[44]

To be sure, the effects of attempted land reform on the Sicilian *latifondo* were multifaceted. On one hand, even though the size of the *latifondi* remained the same, after 1812, the old nobility held increasingly less land and, therefore, had increasingly less control over the affairs of local government. Its power was challenged by a new class of landowners, who had been largely responsible for the creation of the nineteenth-century *latifondo* by profiting from the sale of noble land which had started after the abolition of feudalism. On the other hand, in spite of the government's efforts, the conditions of the peasantry had not improved. The reasons for this failure were partly due to the chaotic and vague nature of government legislation which exacerbated the already bitter struggle between the local elites and the former feudal lords over property rights. Caught in the middle of this struggle, peasants could do little to improve their lot, especially given the fact that 'both the Bourbon monarchy and its liberal successors relied on the support and compliance of local power-holders', who therefore had free hand to continue to exploit the peasantry.[45]

Similar to the situation described by Steven Hahn in the postbellum American South, family and kinship structures became an important element in the struggle for local power in nineteenth-century Sicily. However, rather than functioning to support rural labourers' struggle against exploitation, kinship ties gave the new elite stability and solidarity in their fight against former feudal landowners. At the same time, even though the new elites attempted to mobilize popular support through clientele networks, 'peasant anger over the appropriation and usurpation of common land' (perpetrated by the new landed proprietors) often exploded in prolonged unrest, attacks on landowners, and property crimes on the *latifondo*.

Like the postbellum American South, where the freedpeople's landlessness was a prime source of planters' power, 'poverty and land hunger was necessary to the power and wealth of the new elite on the *latifondo*'.[46] The difference between the two cases lies in the fact that this necessity made southern Italian nineteenth-century elites dependent on the central government for the enforcement of law and order against peasant unrest. In the USA, on the other hand, at least until 1876, planters had to rely far more on their own vigilantism, since the US central government supported the ex-slaves' struggle against exploitation, especially through the Freedmen's Bureau, the local Republican Party, and the military occupation of large parts of the South.

Study of the results of exploitation and inequality of power in the two souths opens the way to a comparative analysis of gender-related issues, and in particular to a comparative approach to the history of women. The study of the condition of women in the past has followed a radically different trajectory in the historiography of the American South and in the Italian Mezzogiorno. In the American South, since the 1970 publication of Ann Firor Scott's *The Southern Lady*,[47] the scholarship on women's history has increased exponentially. Significantly, the first wave of scholarship – which included, among others, Catherine Clinton's *The Plantation Mistress*[48] – was confined to the world of elite women and it was moving along the lines of a feminist deconstruction of the figure of Scarlett O'Hara in *Gone with the Wind*;[49] focusing their analysis on the plantation household, these early studies were primarily concerned with the definition of the antebellum South as a patriarchal system in which mistresses were unable to escape the oppression of a male-dominated society. It was only in 1985, with the publication of Deborah Grey White's *Ar'n't I a Woman?* and Jacqueline Jones's *Labor of Love, Labor of Sorrow*,[50] that scholars began to extend the analysis of the South's patriarchal system to the conditions of oppression of slave women on the plantations. Since then, the picture of gender relations in the slave South has become increasingly complex, revealing the importance of the agency of slave women in fighting against the 'double exploitation' of white patriarchs; at the same time, an increasing number of studies has pointed to the importance of evidence of elite women's activities away from the household as a means of escaping the rigidity of patriarchal roles.[51] The latest scholarship has extended the analysis of gender relations to previously understudied categories – such as the yeomen – and has looked at slavery and patriarchy as two intimately linked factors in the discourse of white male power in the antebellum south.[52]

This last historiographic development in southern historiography is the richest in suggestion for comparison with the Mezzogiorno, since there is no doubt that – as in most agrarian societies – a comparable discourse of power justified subordination of women and subordination of the lower strata of the population as strictly related practices; however, since there was no slavery in the nineteenth-century Italian south, the discourse of power was based on the construction of inequalities based on gender and class, rather than on gender and race. Unlike American historians, Italian historians have begun relatively recently to look at gender-related issues in the history of the Mezzogiorno. Until not long ago, the history of southern women in Italy was identified with a chapter of the much larger history of southern backwardness; in marked contrast with the American South, the stereotype of southern Italian women was one of illiterate peasants, subordinated to their fathers and husbands and permanently locked in the household.[53] The process of deconstruction and correction of this distorted image has paralleled the activity of deconstruction of the 'southern question' carried on by southern Italian historians in the past 15 years, yet it has produced not nearly as large and complex a literature as the one by scholars of the American South. However, the concerns of the continuously growing scholarship on women in the Mezzogiorno seem to move along some of the same lines, since the process of deconstruction of the traditional stereotype emphasizes women's agency and women's active opposition to patriarchal oppression. In reverse process to the path taken by American historiography, Italian historians have moved from the analysis of peasant women to the analysis of elite women. Scholars have focused especially on the active role of noble women in family strategies and in the transmission of property and on the importance of religious life as a different avenue of expression; at the same time, they have rediscovered the importance of peasant women's activities and work outside the household. The latest scholarship is moving towards an analysis of the political implications of the crucial role of women in the family and also of the many forms of their struggle against patriarchal oppression, both subjects which await further study.[54]

Chapters 8 and 9 by J. William Harris and Giovanna Fiume in this volume reflect the different state of scholarship in women's history in the USA and Italy. Each piece attempts to summarize and critically treat a large and rapidly increasing body of material. In Harris's case, it is fair to say that, given the particularly difficult task that the author faced in dealing with the enormous literature on gender in the American South, the essay represents the proverbial 'tip of the iceberg'. Harris traces the beginnings of women's history in the South back to the feminism of the 1960s, of which he sees Anne Firor Scott's *The Southern Lady* as a typical product.[55] At the same time, he acknowledges the affinities between Scott and Catherine Clinton in their common project of defining southern patriarchy. However, Harris sees much of the historiography of the following decade as an attempt – exemplified by Elizabeth Fox-Genovese's *Within the Plantation Household* – to take issue with 'Scott's and Clinton's claims that many southern women consciously resented their constraints' within the patriarchal system.[56] Harris considers the mid-1980s a turning point because by that time several scholarly works 'were already using an explicit gender analysis to shape their approach to women's historical experience'.[57] Influenced by Joan Scott's groundbreaking work, much scholarship shifted attention to the social construction of ideas of masculinity and femininity in the nineteenth-century South; through this kind of analysis, several feminist historians endeavoured to show that women's subordination was itself a historical construction.

Inevitably, gender analysis has led to analysis of the relationship between constructions of inequalities of power within the family and in society at large. Numerous recent studies have emphasized the political aspects of gender relations, the links between patriarchy and slavery in the antebellum South, and the strong ties between patriarchy and racism in the postbellum era. Harris sees much potential for comparison with the Italian Mezzogiorno in some of the current concerns of southern historiography; in particular, he points to historians' attention to issues relating to women's place within the family, the centrality of work outside the household, and the importance of women's religious activities in society.[58]

Giovanna Fiume's essay implicitly responds to Harris' suggestions and contributes in a major way to showing that there is, indeed, a potential for comparison of gender issues in the two souths. Fiume's essay is particularly important because it is the first attempt at synthesizing a large body of very recent and not particularly well-known scholarship on women's history in the Mezzogiorno. Fiume maintains that throughout the 1960s and 1970s, southern women were studied either in relation to the stereotype of southern family (an institution which was supposed to represent an essential backwardness), or as objects of anthropological curiosity. In the 1970s and 1980s, as a result both of foreign suggestions and of the development of the Italian women's movement, women's historians reacted against the stereotype of southern women and emphasized 'the rebellious female figures of the past', while at the same time beginning the 'rediscovery of extra-domestic work'.[59]

By the early 1980s, scholars had started to analyse and understand the importance of networks of relations and systems of kinship. As part of this development, they increasingly replaced an older concern with female oppression with an emphasis upon female agency. In Chapter 9, study of the family regularly surfaces as being intimately related to the analysis of women in society. One of the effects of this new scholarly departure has been an explosion of demographic studies which has refined historians' thinking about the structure of the household in the Mezzogiorno.

Equally important is the study of female labour and its versatility 'according to the necessity and the circumstances of the job market and the life cycle in both the private and the public spheres'.[60] There is no doubt that the study of the household as a social system and as a locus of the reproduction of values and behaviours has breathed new life into the old history of the family. At the same time, it has also opened new avenues of research on the workings of the patriarchal system, such as the study of the control of female honour, female transgression and female patrimonies, all of which are rich with suggestions for comparison with the American South. According to Fiume, the next step in southern Italian historiography should be a reflection on the nature of the family as a political institution and on the 'history of women in relation to the political history of the family', two themes that have enormous potential for comparison with the American South.[61]

The three topics of comparison outlined above – landed elites' ideologies, the conditions of rural labourers, and women's strategies of resistance – are fields of research which can be treated independently from one another and, at the same time, form the objects of specific comparative analyses of the two souths. In looking at similarities and differences between the two case-studies in regard to each of these topics, we have sketched guidelines for future research that simultaneously address both sides of the Italian–US comparison. However, we believe that before proceeding with specific comparisons, we need to understand how individual topics fit into the larger discourse of comparison; in other words, we need to build a background, a sort of grand narrative, of comparison between the history of the American South and the history of the Mezzogiorno in which to insert specific comparative topics. In this respect, it is particularly useful to bear in mind Peter Kolchin's suggestion that we refrain from limiting our approach to comparison of the two southern regions, and see how this project relates to the larger comparison between American and Italian history. If we take this suggestion to heart, we can begin thinking of comparable broad historical processes that unfolded in both the nineteenth-century USA and Italy into which could be inserted the comparison between the American South and the Italian Mezzogiorno.

The most important historical process which occurred in both countries was the formation of the nation-state. Both the USA and Italy emerged as unified nations in the course of the 1860s as a result of ideological and military conquests waged by the two norths against the two souths.[62] It is no accident that the most recent historiography in the USA links the American Civil War to contemporary national unifications in Europe; the assumption behind these studies is that the Union was characterized by a nationalist ideology no less than Prussia or Piedmont, and that it fought a war against the Confederacy in order to build a nation, rather than simply to restore it.[63] On the other hand, the most recent Italian historiography has been moving in the direction of re-evaluating the importance of the experience of military confrontation and the memory of defeat in the North–South divide during the process of Italian Unification. In particular, the expression 'civil war' is increasingly used by Italian historians in order to describe the military operations in which the Piedmontese army fought against the brigands in southern Italy between 1861 and 1865.[64]

Seen from the perspective of nation-building, the entire issue of historiographic construction and deconstruction of the idea of southern backwardness and its corollaries in the USA and Italy seems to be intimately linked to comparable historical trajectories that the two souths underwent in the process of forming two nation-states. Similarly, the specific topics of comparison between the two souths proposed in this volume emerge in a much clearer light if we relate them to the specific causes and consequences of these dual processes of nation-building. Even though the American Civil War and Italian Unification have far more differences than similarities in the specificity of their actual historical experiences, their outcomes have both contributed in a major way to crystallizing the traditionally negative notions of the two souths in modern American and Italian historiographies. Moreover, the outcomes of the American Civil War and Italian Unification set in motion comparable historical processes that radically altered the shape of economic and social relations between the norths and the souths of the two countries. At the same time, in the long run, these same processes contributed to the reciprocal knowledge of regions which had been largely ignorant of each other's culture and society for most of the period that preceded the process of nation-building. In this respect as well, the American Civil War and Italian Unification were crucial events at the heart of the historical processes that shaped the 'invention' of national traditions in the two countries during the nineteenth century.[65]

Starting from these assumptions, the two chapters by Enrico Dal Lago and Donna Gabaccia (both explicitly comparative contributions) reflect the authors' belief in the importance of looking at general historical processes as indispensable backgrounds for the comparison of specific themes in the two souths. Dal Lago's contribution in Chapter 10 focuses on the 30-year period before the American Civil War and Italian Unification and draws a comparison between the ideologies of radical northern politicians in the USA and Italy in respect to their perceptions of the two souths. According to Dal Lago, in the years between 1830 and 1860, American abolitionists and Italian Democrats 'sought to resolve two distinct, but related national problems'.[66] In the USA, the national problem was represented by the presence of slavery in the southern part of the country, an institution which abolitionists considered backward and inconsistent with the ideals of the American republic. In Italy, the national problem was constituted by the presence of reactionary regimes – first and foremost the Bourbon kingdom in the south – which stood in the way of the creation of a progressive Italian nation.

Throughout the 30 years preceding the American Civil War and Italian Unification, abolitionists and Democrats implemented both propaganda and direct action to convince public opinions that the time was ripe for an overthrow of the reactionary regimes that dominated the two souths. Throughout this extended period, 'they constructed an image of themselves as "liberators", while at the same time constructing an image of the southern masses as helpless victims longing for help coming from outside, particularly the North'.[67] According to Dal Lago, this construction was instrumental in creating the background for the development of subsequent ideas of the two souths as dependent upon the respective norths for social change. At the same time, these constructions helped create a stereotype of southern helplessness and lack of initiative that contributed in a major way to justifying subsequent discriminatory northern attitudes towards southern labourers in both countries.

Picking up chronologically roughly from where Chapter 10 stops, Donna Gabaccia's contribution adds an important dimension to the comparison between the history of the two souths in the period after the American Civil War and Italian Unification. As a historian of diasporas, Gabaccia focuses her study on the comparison of migratory movements of southern labourers from the two countries in the period between 1870 and 1930. During these 60 years, roughly 3.5 million Italian southerners went to America; at the same time, approximately 1.5 million African-Americans left the USA's south. In both cases, but not contemporaneously, a migration of southerners converged on the large industrial cities of the American north, such as Chicago, Pittsburgh, Philadelphia, Cleveland and New York. In comparing these two processes, Gabaccia reminds us of the contrast between the 'immigrant paradigm' of American history, with its stress on assimilation, and the 'racial paradigm', with its emphasis on the limits of the American idea of pluralism. According to Gabaccia, this contrast, and the effect it had on immigrants and blacks, seems to 'suggest two national narratives, at odds with each other'.[68]

In spite of this discordancy, when analysing the role of regionalism in the experiences of American and Italian southern migrants, Gabaccia finds that in both cases race became intimately connected to the migrant group's region of origin in each national history. According to Gabaccia, 'both black migrants from the American South and migrants from Italy's south experienced racial transformations as they entered northern cities'.[69] However, northern whites perceived both migrant southern blacks and resident northern blacks as one racially distinct group of 'black Americans'. At the same time, they perceived migrant southern whites as 'southerners', revealing a difference between the discourse of racial subordination of all blacks and the propensity to ascribe regional distinctions among whites. Southern Italians, on the other hand, were perceived both by northern Italians and outsiders as a 'distinctive and troublesome group both attached to, yet apart from, the Italian nation'. As Italian southerners started to develop a collective 'southern' identity and, at the same time, fought to dissociate themselves from the negative qualities related to their region of origin,

Americans came to perceive them as a single group of Italians, 'broadening what had been a racialized regional to a racialized national stigma'.[70]

In the essay that concludes this collection, Bruce Levine analyses the comparative potential of some of the major themes that have run throughout the contributions of both Americanists and Italianists. Significantly, he identifies these themes in the dichotomies 'old/new', 'backward/modern', 'capitalist/non-capitalist' and in the long-established perceptions of the two souths as 'different from their respective norths'.[71] As Levine observes, the deconstruction of these simplistic views – long established in both American and Italian historiography – has been a guiding principle in most of the essays in this volume. Through the prism of comparative analysis, the authors have pushed forward the revisionist process and have challenged previously held assumptions about the two souths. At the same time, they have opened new avenues of research for future comparative studies of the two regions. In this respect, it is vitally important to reiterate – as Levine does – that comparative inquiry not only has the advantage of shedding new light on previously understudied issues, but it also has the potential of raising a host of new questions, questions that are bound to be left unanswered until new specific empirical studies take on the burden of addressing them. In this regard, the project of comparing the American South and the Italian Mezzogiorno is only in its infancy; the field is as open as it can be to possible future developments. Joining Bruce Levine – who in his contribution rightly advocates additional comparative studies of subordinated groups[72] – we hope that the stimuli provided by the comparative discussion of the diverse themes treated in this volume will serve as a background for future comparative monographs and essays on the two regions.

Notes

This collection would not have been possible without the assistance of numerous individuals and institutions. First and foremost, thanks are due to all of the participants in the 1999 Commonwealth Fund Conference. Crucial to the success of that conference and this volume was the financial support of the British Academy, the University College London Graduate School, the Departments of History and Italian at University College London, and the History Faculty of Cambridge University. The editors are deeply grateful for the generous and cheerful assistance provided by Nazneen Razwi, Rachel Cutler, Laura Canzano and Frank Deserino during the 1999 conference.

1   *Mezzogiorno* is the term used by Italian historians to describe the southern part of the country.
2   For a reappraisal of the tradition of comparative studies of the American South and its relation to the notion of southern distinctiveness, see E. Dal Lago,

'Southern Elites: A Comparative Study of the Landed Aristocracies of the American South and the Italian South, 1815–1860', PhD Thesis, University of London, 2000, pp. 13–25.

3   Among the most important recent works, see I. Wallerstein, *The Modern World-System*, 3 vols (New York, 1974–1989); G. Fredrickson, *White Supremacy: A Comparative Study in American and South African History* (New York, 1981); P. Kolchin, *Unfree Labor: American Slavery and Russian Serfdom* (Cambridge, MA, 1987); S. D. Bowman, *Masters and Lords: Mid-Nineteenth-Century U.S. Planters and Prussian Junkers* (New York, 1993); A. Marx, *Making Race and Nation: A Comparison of the United States, South Africa, and Brazil* (New York, 1998).

4   P. Kolchin, Chapter 2 in this volume.

5   P. Bevilacqua, Chapter 3 in this volume.

6   Kolchin, Chapter 2 below.

7   Kolchin, Chapter 2 below.

8   Kolchin, Chapter 2 below.

9   Kolchin, Chapter 2 below.

10 Bevilacqua, Chapter 3 below.

11 R. W. Fogel and S. N. Engerman, *Time on the Cross: The Economics of American Negro Slavery* (New York, 1974); M. Petrusewicz, *Latifundium: Moral Economy and Material Life in a Nineteenth-Century Periphery* (Ann Arbor, MI, 1996).

12 Kolchin, Chapter 2 below.

13 I. Berlin, *Many Thousands Gone: The First Two Centuries of American Slavery* (Cambridge, MA, 1998); see also P. D. Morgan, *Slave Counterpoint: Black Life in Eighteenth-Century Chesapeake and the Low Country* (Chapel Hill, NC, 1998).

14 See especially I. Berlin and P. D. Morgan (eds), *Cultivation and Culture: Labor and the Shaping of Slave Life in the Americas* (Charlottesville, VA, 1993).

15 Bevilacqua, Chapter 3 below.

16 For two overviews of recent developments on southern Italian historiography, see J. Morris, 'Challenging *Meridionalismo*: Constructing a New History for Southern Italy', in R. Lumley and J. Morris (eds), *The New History of the Italian South: The Mezzogiorno Revisited* (Exeter, 1997); and J. A. Davis, 'Casting Off the "Southern Problem": Or the Peculiarities of the South Revisited' in J. Schneider (ed.), *Italy's Southern Question: Orientalism in One Country* (New York, 1998).

17 See P. Bevilacqua, *Breve storia dell'Italia meridionale dall'Ottocento a oggi*, 2nd edn (Rome, 1997).

18 Kolchin, Chapter 2 below.

19 Tannenbaum, *Slave and Citizen* (New York, 1946).

20 Two recent collections of essays are indicative of these new developments in slavery studies: M. L. Bush (ed.), *Serfdom and Slavery: Studies in Legal Bondage* (London, 1996); and S. L. Engerman (ed.), *Terms of Labor: Slavery, Serfdom, and Free Labor* (Stanford, CA, 1999).

21 Bevilacqua, Chapter 3 below.

22 See Kolchin, *Unfree Labor*.

23 This is a point clearly stated in I. Wallerstein, 'What Can One Mean by "Southern Culture"?', in N. Bartley (ed.), *The Evolution of Southern Culture* (Athens, GA, 1985).

24   See Fogel and Engerman, *Time on the Cross*; and J. Oakes, *The Ruling Race: A History of American Slaveholders* (New York, 1982). Genovese's most unambiguous articulation of his thoughts on this matter are in E. D. Genovese, *The Political Economy of Slavery: Studies in the Economy and Society of the Slave South* (New York, 1965); and E. Fox-Genovese and E. D. Genovese, *The Fruits of Merchant Capital: Slavery and Bourgeois Property in the Rise and Expansion of Capitalism* (New York, 1983).

25   See Petrusewicz, *Latifundium*; see also, along similar lines, B. Salvemini, *L'innovazione precaria. Spazi, mercati e società nel Mezzogiorno tra Sette e Ottocento* (Catanzaro, 1995).

26   See W. Dusinberre, *Them Dark Days: Life in the American Rice Swamps* (New York, 1995); and S. Lupo, *Il giardino degli aranci. Il mondo degli agrumi nella storia del Mezzogiorno* (Venice, 1990).

27   See, for example, M. M. Smith, *Debating Slavery: Economy and Society in the Antebellum South* (New York, 1998) for the American South; and G. Montroni, *Gli uomini del Re: La nobiltà napoletana dell'Ottocento* (Catanzaro, 1996), for the Italian South.

28   R. Follett, Chapter 4 in this volume; see also his forthcoming *The Sugar Masters: Capitalism and Slavery in Louisiana's Cane World, 1820–1860* (Baton Rouge, LA, 2002).

29   Follett, Chapter 4 below.

30   Follett, Chapter 4 below. On this point, see also M. M. Smith, *Mastered by the Clock: Time, Slavery, and Freedom in the American South* (Chapel Hill, NC, 1997).

31   M. Petrusewicz, Chapter 5 in this volume.

32   Petrusewicz, Chapter 5 below; these points are expanded in Petrusewicz, *Come il Meridione divenne Una Questione: Rappresentazioni del Sud prima e dopo il Quarantotto* (Catanzaro, 1998).

33   Petrusewicz, Chapter 5 below. For a comparison between paternalism on southern Italian *latifondi* and American plantations, see Dal Lago, 'Southern Elites', pp. 144–80.

34   On Emancipation and Reconstruction in the American South, see I. Berlin *et al.*, *Slaves No More: Three Essays on Emancipation* (New York, 1993); and E. Foner, *Reconstruction: America's Unfinished Revolution* (New York, 1988).

35   On the abolition of the feudal law in the continental Mezzogiorno and in Sicily, see A. Spagnoletti, *Storia del Regno delle Due Sicilie* (Bologna, 1997), pp. 38–44; and G. Giarrizzo, 'La Sicilia dal Cinquecento all' Unità d'Italia', in V. D'Alessandro and G. Giarrizzo, *La Sicilia dal Vespro all'Unità d'Italia* (Turin, 1989), pp. 557–668.

36   See E. Foner, *Nothing but Freedom: Emancipation and its Legacy* (Baton Rouge, LA, 1983).

37   On the American South, see, for example, L. F. Edwards, *'Gendered Strife and Confusion': The Political Culture of Reconstruction* (Urbana, IL, 1997); and J. Saville, *The Work of Reconstruction: From Slave to Wage Laborer in South Carolina, 1860–1870* (Cambridge, MA, 1994). On the Italian South, see especially P. Pezzino, 'Local Power in Southern Italy', in Lumley and Morris, *The New History of the Italian South*; and S. Lupo, 'Tra centro e periferia. Sui modi dell' aggregazione politica nel Mezzogiorno contemporaneo', *Meridiana* 2 (1988).

38 S. Hahn, Chapter 6 in this volume. See also, for important comparative suggestions, S. Hahn, 'Class and state in Postemancipation Societies. Southern Planters in Comparative Perspective', *American Historical Review* 95:1 (1990).

39 Hahn, Chapter 6 below.

40 Hahn, Chapter 6 below.

41 Hahn, Chapter 6 below. The reference here is to the Sicilian Mafia; see, for example, S. Lupo, *Storia della Mafia dalle origini ai giorni nostri*, 2nd edn (Rome, 1997).

42 L. Riall, Chapter 7 in this volume.

43 Sidney Sonnino, quoted in Riall, Chapter 7 below.

44 Riall, Chapter 7 below.

45 Riall, Chapter 7 below.

46 Riall, Chapter 7 below.

47 A. F. Scott, *The Southern Lady from Pedestal to Politics, 1830–1930* (Charlottesville, VA, 1970).

48 C. Clinton, *The Plantation Mistress: Woman's World in the Old South* (New York, 1982).

49 See M. Mitchell, *Gone with the Wind* (New York, 1936).

50 See D. Gray White, *Ar'n't I a Woman? Female Slaves in the Plantation South* (New York, 1985); and J. Jones, *Labor of Love, Labor of Sorrow: Black Women, Work, and the Family from Slavery to the Present* (New York, 1985).

51 See, among the most recent studies, L. Schwalm, '*A Hard Fight for We': Women's Transition from Slavery to Freedom in South Carolina* (Urbana, IL, 1997); and C. A. Kierner, *Beyond the Household: Women's Place in the Early South, 1700–1835* (Ithaca, NY, 1998).

52 See, for example, S. McCurry, *Masters of Small Worlds: Yeoman Households, Gender Relations, and the Political Culture of the Antebellum South Carolina Low Country* (New York, 1995); and B. E. Stevenson, *Life in Black and White: Family and Community in the Slave South* (New York, 1996).

53 On some of these issues, see G. Gribaudi, 'Images of the South. The Mezzogiorno as seen by Insiders and Outsiders', in Lumley and Morris, *The New History of the Italian South*.

54 On some of these issues, see G. Calvi and I. Chabot (eds), *Le ricchezze delle donne. Diritti patrimoniali e poteri familiari in Italia (XIII-XIX secc.)* (Turin, 1998); P. Nava (ed.), *Il lavoro delle donne nell'Italia contemporanea, continuità e rotture* (Turin, 1992); G. Fiume (ed.), *Madri. Storia di un ruolo sociale* (Venice, 1995); and G. Gribaudi, *A Eboli. Il mondo meridionale in cent'anni di trasformazione* (Venice, 1990).

55 See Scott, *The Southern Lady*.

56 E. Fox-Genovese, *Within the Plantation Household: Black and White Women in the Old South* (Chapel Hill, NC, 1988).

57 J. W. Harris, Chapter 8 in this volume.

58 Harris, Chapter 8 below.

59 G. Fiume, Chapter 9 in this volume.

60 Fiume, Chapter 9 below.

61 Fiume, Chapter 9 below.

62 This reflection owes much to the intuitions of David Potter and Raimondo Luraghi, who were the first historians who put in relation to one another the

American Civil War and the Italian Risorgimento. See especially D. Potter, 'The Civil War in the History of the Modern World: A Comparative View', in D. Pottes, *The South and Sectional Conflict* (Baton Rouge, LA, 1967); and R. Luraghi, *The Rise and Fall of the Plantation South* (New York, 1978).

63   See, for example, S. M. Grant, *North over South* (Lawrence, KS, 2000); and C. Degler, 'The American Civil War and the German Wars of Unification: The Problem of Comparison', in S. Forster and J. Nagler (eds), *On the Road to Total War: The American Civil War and the German Wars of Unification, 1861–1871* (New York, 1997).

64   See, for example, R. Martucci, *L'invenzione dell'Italia unita, 1855–1864* (Milan, 1999); and J. Dickie, 'A World at War: The Italian Army and Brigandage', in J. Dickie, *Darkest Italy: The Nation and Stereotypes of the Mezzogiorno, 1860–1900* (London, 1999).

65   On the 'invention' of national traditions in the nineteenth century, see E. J. Hobsbawm, 'Inventing Traditions', in E. J. Hobsbawm and T. Ranger (eds), *The Invention of Tradition* (Cambridge, 1983).

66   E. Dal Lago, Chapter 10 in this volume.

67   Dal Lago, Chapter 10 below.

68   D. Gabaccia, Chapter 11 in this volume.

69   Gabaccia, Chapter 11 below.

70   Gabaccia, Chapter 11 below.

71   B. Levine, Chapter 12 in this volume.

72   Levine, Chapter 12 below.

2
The American South in Comparative Perspective

Peter Kolchin

Historical study of the American South exhibits a curiously dualistic character. On the one hand there is its longstanding parochialism, its preoccupation with celebrating details of the past that are of interest mainly to southerners themselves; on the other there is the promise – and increasingly the reality – of an exceptionally innovative history providing insights into subjects far removed from sectional antiquarianism. Long the province of southern white men, southern history draws increasing attention from non-southerners, and is increasingly central to the study of American history in general. It is hardly surprising, then, that as part of a broadened effort to come to grips with the South's past, revisionist work on the region exhibits a growing comparative dimension. The South has become not just Americanized but globalized.

As both a southern and a comparative historian, I cannot but welcome this development. At the same time, it is important for us to think carefully about what we hope to learn from a widened focus, so as to control comparative history rather than let it control us. In this essay, I would like to consider the benefits of providing a comparative framework for southern history, looking at how historians have approached the subject and considering some of the ways we might best conceptualize the study of the South comparatively. Although historians have differed sharply in their definitions of 'comparative history', here I use the concept loosely to cover a variety of approaches designed to accentuate context.[1] I will set forth three different comparative approaches: (1) comparisons between the South and the North (the 'un-South'); (2) internal comparisons among various components of the South ('many souths'); and (3) comparisons between the South and other societies sharing some of the same attributes ('other souths'). My examination is necessarily sketchy and selective; I will pay special attention to the nineteenth-century South, which encompasses a set of topics – slavery, emancipation, the Civil War – that lend themselves particularly well to the comparative elucidation of important questions such as sectional distinctiveness and the extent of continuity versus change.

Although scholars have differed sharply over what has made the South southern, from white supremacy to celtic heritage and honour, however one defines the South, it has meaning only in terms of distinguishing it from what it is *not*: the *un*-South.[2] Two kinds of comparison with the North underlie efforts to understand the South's past. The first of these involves attempts to make broad societal comparisons, typically characterizing the sections as either basically similar or basically different. The second involves focusing on a specific theme – for example, economic growth – and seeking to determine its relation to particular sectional conditions.

Persistent observations of basic differences between North and South date from the late eighteenth century, when substantial numbers of northerners and southerners were first thrust together. Writing in 1785, Thomas Jefferson proclaimed that 'In the North they are cool, sober, labourious, persevering, independent, jealous to their own liberties, and just to those of others, interested, chicaning, superstitious and hypocritical in their religion'; by contrast, 'In the South they are fiery, Voluptuary, indolent, unsteady, independent, zealous for their own liberties, but trampling on those of others, generous, candid, without attachment or pretentions to any religion but that of the heart.'[3] With the exception of his observations on religion, which were soon rendered obsolete by the evangelical revivals that reshaped the South's religious landscape, Jefferson's characterizations entered the conventional wisdom as antebellum Americans adopted the familiar stereotypes of the southern 'Cavalier' and the northern 'Yankee'.[4]

The debate among historians has taken a somewhat different turn. Although some have addressed the question of southern versus northern character,[5] most have been leery of assigning a universal, homogenized personality to either northerners or southerners, preferring to focus on the two sections' social, economic, and political orders. Because the Civil War constituted a war for southern independence, it inevitably emerged as a central object of interest among those who would explore southern distinctiveness.

Scholars have disagreed sharply over the extent to which the War was a product of fundamental differences between North and South. During the first half of the twentieth century, most historians believed that it was; especially influential was the economic argument – which received its most famous enunciation in Charles and Mary Beard's classic *Rise of American Civilization* – that the Civil War constituted a 'Second American Revolution' in which northern masters of capital seized control of the country from the South's slave-based plantation aristocracy.[6] Beginning in the 1920s and drawing increasing support in the 'consensus' years after the Second World War, however, 'revisionist' historians played down differences between North and South and insisted that had it not been for extremist agitators, southerners and northerners would have been able to work out whatever minor differences they had. The new mood was caught well by publication in 1960 of a volume entitled *The Southerner as American* in which nine prominent historians rejected what they regarded as exaggerated claims for southern distinctiveness. 'The traditional emphasis on the South's differentness and on the conflict between Southernism and Americanism is wrong historically', explained the volume's editor. 'We all agree that the most important fact about the Southerner is that he has been throughout his history also an American.'[7]

Since the 1960s, a growing number of historians have reasserted the importance of differences between North and South, even as others have continued to minimize those differences. While some scholars updated the idea of a Second American Revolution, others developed a more sophisticated version of the 'blundering generation' thesis and argued that the War resulted not from differences between northerners and southerners but from their shared commitment to 'liberty' and 'republicanism'.[8] Two prominent essays illustrate the continuing divisions over this question. Asking 'How different from each other were the antebellum North and South?', Edward Pessen came down squarely on the side of similarity. Maintaining that 'Southern planters had the attitudes and goals ... of capitalistic businessmen', he argued that 'the South's political system ..., like its hierarchical social structure, conformed closely to the prevailing arrangements in the North' and concluded that 'the antebellum North and South were far more alike than the conventional scholarly wisdom has led us to believe'. But James M. McPherson reached a diametrically opposite conclusion. 'Antebellum Americans certainly thought that North and South had evolved separate societies', he noted, 'with institutions, interests, values, and ideologies so incompatible, so much in deadly conflict that they could no longer live together in the same nation'. Pointing to contrasts in 'urbanization, industrialization, labour force, demographic structure, violence and martial values, education, and attitudes toward change', he suggested that contemporary perceptions of difference were largely accurate.[9]

At the heart of this debate is the question of to what extent slavery set the antebellum South off from the rest of the country. Here, too, long-standing disagreements remain unbridged. On one side are historians such as Stanley L. Engerman, Robert W. Fogel and James Oakes, who stress the profit-orientation of slaveholders and portray southern slavery as pre-eminently capitalistic. On the other is a group of historians represented most prominently by Eugene D. Genovese, who note the non-market relationship between master and slave and see southern slavery as a non-capitalist social formation that produced an increasingly distinctive economy, social order and set of values.[10] Partially grounded in different understandings of capitalism, this debate is of more than semantic significance, because it has important interpretive implications. Those who stress slavery's capitalistic nature typically base their argument on the masters' *commercial* orientation. In their formulation, slavery emerges as simply another business – in Fogel's words, 'a flexible, highly developed form of capitalism' – and southern slave-owners emerge as particular variants of American businessmen; as Oakes put it, in 'fundamental ways, the slaveholding experience coincided with the American experience at large'. Those on the other side point to the non-market nature of southern *productive* relations, and almost invariably move on to explore how this distinctive master–slave relationship brought with it a distinctive social order. Clearly, the comparative historian needs to pay careful attention to how terms are used.[11]

Aside from definitions, two other considerations deserve attention as historians seek to make sense of conflicting claims concerning the extent of southern distinctiveness. First, there is the question of emphasis. Everyone can agree that in some ways the South resembled the North and in others it did not, but how does one determine whether it is 'more important' that southerners and northerners had different labour systems, demographic patterns, and levels of urbanization or that they spoke the same language (more or less), belonged to the same religious denominations (more or less), and believed in the same constitution (more or less)?[12] The comparativist needs to consider carefully which criteria should be used in establishing basic similarities and differences.

Second, scholars must come to grips with contextual variations. Here, two historical commonplaces work at cross-purposes. If historians like to understand a problem as contemporaries would, rather than 'ahistorically' imposing on the past the values or perceptions of another time and place, they also believe that distance lends perspective and that hindsight affords the historian a crucial advantage over contemporaries

in making sense of the past. Taken together, these two apparently contradictory commonplaces show how context shapes historical judgements. The nearer one gets to something, the easier it is to recognize
complexity and variation; the farther one gets, the clearer the common
patterns. To a Muslim cleric, the theological differences between southern and northern Baptists might appear insignificant, but to Baptists in
antebellum America they loomed large. And a foreign observer would
find it easier to see the common 'Americanness' of antebellum northerners and southerners than would those Americans, caught up in the
passions of the moment. It is therefore significant that so many foreign
observers, even while seeking to explain what Americans shared in
common, were struck by the differences between North and South. If
such differences were apparent from afar, how much more pronounced
must they have seemed to Americans themselves.[13]

More common than broad societal comparisons have been those
focusing on particular features of North and South. Historians have
compared a variety of subjects across North–South lines – from economy, social structure and political behaviour, to gender relations, family
life and social values – and even more await comparative study.[14] An
examination of two specific comparisons illustrates the practice and the
promise of this kind of study.

Few subjects have received as much comparative attention within the
confines of one country as that of southern economic growth; indeed,
this subject seems ready-made for comparative analysis. Not only is it
quantifiable, but it is also closely linked to the study of two questions of
persistent historical interest: slavery and the Civil War. How better can
one measure the impact of slavery than by comparing the economic
growth of the 'slave' South and the 'free' North? And how better to
measure the impact of the Civil War than by following the course of
the South's post-war economic development?

The consensus of most historians, that slavery was a 'backward'
system which impeded southern economic growth, was upset by a
spate of econometric studies that reached full fruition in Fogel and
Engerman's *Time on the Cross* (1974) and Fogel's *Without Consent or
Contract* (1989). Rebutting notions that the southern economy was
stagnant and slavery was increasingly unprofitable, these scholars
stressed the peculiar institution's economic viability, suggested that
slave-based agriculture was more productive than that using free labour,
and argued that between 1840 and 1860 the southern economy grew
faster than the northern. Such arguments were closely linked to the
theme discussed above, that slavery was a 'highly developed form of

capitalism' under which slaves were turned into 'metaphoric clock punchers' who internalized the work ethic.[15]

Although most historians have accepted the conclusion that antebellum slavery was economically profitable, they have been less willing to buy the proposition that it in no way retarded or distorted southern economic development, for if the antebellum southern economy was growing rapidly, based on increased cultivation and export of staple crops (especially cotton), it did not undergo the kind of qualitative transformation experienced by the North during the late antebellum years. Virtually every index of economic modernization – from urbanization and industrialization to mechanization, scientific endeavour and education – indicated what contemporaries believed: the antebellum South was lagging further and further behind the North. Fogel and his supporters tacitly acknowledged this lag, attributing the South's failure to urbanize and industrialize at the North's pace to the 'comparative advantage' enjoyed by southern agriculture and the more inelastic rural than urban demand for labour. At least, then, there is widespread agreement that the southern economy was growing *differently* from that of the North.[16]

Much the same is true when it comes to analysing the South's *post*-war economic development. Belying expectations of free-labour spokesmen that the destruction of slavery would usher in an era of southern prosperity, the South remained economically underdeveloped. Whereas in 1860 southern per capita income stood at 80.5 per cent of the national average, by 1880 it had plunged to 50.1 per cent, a level that remained essentially unchanged over the next generation.[17] An avalanche of historical writings has addressed the question of 'what went wrong' in the postwar South, and why the South suffered from continued poverty and exploitation rather than enjoying the free-labour paradise that many contemporaries and subsequent scholars felt 'should' have emerged. If many early scholars blamed the tremendous destruction caused by the War,[18] recent social historians have pointed to the failure to distribute land to former slaves and poor whites, and more generally to the failure to revolutionize the hierarchical social structure, while economic historians have typically stressed the postbellum South's various institutional imperfections.[19]

I have questioned elsewhere the utility of this 'tragic era' paradigm of the postwar South, with its emphasis on things gone wrong. For one thing, it is based on a tacit assumption that things usually go 'right', that poverty, exploitation and oppression are aberrations to be explained rather than normal features of human experience. For another, it is based on an implicit judgement that developments in the post-war South were *unusually* bleak, a judgement that I think does not stand up in a comparison with other postemancipation societies.[20] Still, despite their differences over the reasons, most scholars *have* agreed that the post-war southern economy, like the pre-war, followed a fundamentally different course from that of the North. All of this suggests that what is at issue is less *whether* the South differed from the North than how it did so, and why.

One of the most interesting ways of grappling with southern distinctiveness involves exploring the subject of southern identity. Of course, southerners (like everyone else) have felt numerous overlapping ties and loyalties: they have defined themselves in terms of their beliefs, values, associations and occupations and have identified with others in terms of family, friendship, ethnicity, locality, region and country. On the whole, however, many southerners have felt a stronger sense of *regional* attachment than most Americans. Local and national chauvinism may be prevalent virtually everywhere in America, but most non-southerners have felt a relatively weak sense of *regional* loyalty; few people spend much time thinking of themselves as 'midwesterners' or 'mid-Atlantic coasters'.[21]

Any such regional identification carries with it an implicit non-identification with what is outside the region, especially when regions are defined bipolarly, as South versus North. Being a southerner means being a non-Yankee. It does not, however, necessarily imply being a non-American. Indeed, according to a variety of indices, twentieth-century white southerners tended to be the *most* patriotic of Americans, volunteering disproportionately for military service, supporting military action abroad more enthusiastically and less questioningly than other Americans, and objecting most strenuously to assaults on the national honour such as flag-burning or draft-dodging. What may seem at first glance a logical contradiction – identifying more strongly than most Americans at *both* the regional and national levels – is possible only by implicitly separating Americanness from Yankeeness: if self-identification as a southerner requires use of northerners as a negative reference group, the self-identification of southerners as Americans requires minimizing the Yankee nature of Americanness, even though *most* Americans are northerners.

The second kind of comparison that I want to address is closely related to the first. Defining the South involves establishing not just how it has differed from the rest of the country, but also how much cohesion and variation has existed within its boundaries. In what sense should a suburb of Washington, DC, be regarded as part of the same section as a suburb of New Orleans? If a southern 'drawl' can be recognized as distinct from accents found in Philadelphia, Boston or New York, what unites the English spoken in southern Louisiana, tidewater Virginia, lowcountry South Carolina, and upcountry Georgia and makes them all recognizable as 'southern'? Clearly, there have been and continue to be many 'Souths'.

The most obvious form of variation within the South is geographical. Scholars have long recognized that the South was far from a monolithic region, even if they have not always agreed on how to divide it. Just as one can compare the South with the North, so too one can compare sub-regions of the South with each other: upper versus lower South, seaboard versus inland, blackbelt versus upcountry. And as with North–South comparisons, these can be of entire sub-regions as social entities, or of particular events, institutions and processes within these sub-regions: for example, comparing slavery in upper and lower Souths, or the economic growth of the cotton and tobacco Souths, or Reconstruction in Georgia and South Carolina. The possibilities are practically limitless.

Two new books illustrate some of the opportunities afforded by such internal comparison. In *Many Thousands Gone: The First Two Centuries of Slavery in North America*, Ira Berlin provides a sweeping survey of slavery in four regions of colonial and Revolutionary-era North America: the Chesapeake, the low country, the lower Mississippi Valley, and the North. Although the book is in some ways a series of juxtaposed 'parallel' histories, comparative themes inevitably emerge as Berlin develops the ways in which his four regions experienced common trends even as specific historical conditions shaped variations among them. More explicitly comparative is Philip D. Morgan's *Slave Counterpoint: Black Culture in the Eighteenth-Century Chesapeake and Lowcountry*. This almost encyclopaedic study lacks the dynamic sweep of Berlin's but offers in its stead a nuanced delineation of the similarities and differences between two slave societies, in the process providing an authoritative statement of our current understanding of slavery in the colonial South.[22]

A very different sort of comparison is evident in a type of history that is usually not considered comparative at all: local history. Because such history invariably raises questions of typicality, it is implicitly comparative. Take, for example, my current home state: Delaware. Every state to its north abolished slavery during the late eighteenth and early nineteenth centuries; in every state to its south, a significant proportion of the population remained enslaved until the Civil War. But Delaware followed neither the southern nor the northern pattern: by 1860, the state's 1798 slaves constituted under 1 per cent of its population and under 10 per cent of its black population; it had become practically a free state. Nevertheless, Delaware's lawmakers stubbornly refused to abolish slavery, even when offered the possibility of compensated emancipation during the Civil War, and after the War they refrained from ratifying the Thirteenth Amendment until 1901. Any examination of the history of slavery in Delaware inevitably becomes an exercise in comparative history, an attempt to explain why the state followed the course that it did instead of that pursued either to the north or south.[23]

A second form of internal variation within the South involves variation over time. Of course, in one sense, all history involves comparison over time. But just as the attempt to make variations over space explicit can turn non-comparative into comparative history, so too can conscious attention to change over time. It has been a commonplace, for example, that most studies of antebellum slavery provide what is essentially a 'snapshot' of the last (atypical) years of the peculiar institution rather than tracing the ways in which it changed – or did not – over the generations. Because most of the slave sources we have date from the late antebellum period, those sources have tended to dominate the historical recreation of slavery in America. It is therefore important to emphasize that the slavery described in those sources was not necessarily the slavery that existed for most of the peculiar institution's 250-year history.[24]

There are at least two ways in which scholars can focus on change over time. The most common is to study a subject over a broad chronological span; this is the approach that I took, for example, in my book *American Slavery*, which traces slavery's evolution from its establishment through the postemancipation struggle over Reconstruction.[25] More explicitly comparative is a second approach, involving comparison across two different chronological eras: for example, Chesapeake slavery (or social structure, or political ideology) of the mid-eighteenth century and that of the mid-nineteenth century. This second approach, which is just as truly comparative as is comparison over space, strikes me as especially promising, and I believe that its application could make important contributions to our understanding of a wide range of historical problems.

A central preoccupation of many southern historians – grappling with the perennial question of change versus continuity – is implicitly comparative in the sense that I have just been discussing. Although the dichotomy is too neat, and obscures a range of positions, historians have divided into two camps, one of which emphasizes elements of continuity in southern history and the other sharp turning points or discontinuities. Those falling into the first camp have varied, of course, over precisely what it was that provided the basis for southern continuity; two well-known versions include emphasis by U. B. Phillips on white supremacy and by W. J. Cash on the South's pre-modern 'mind'. On the other side, C. Vann Woodward has lobbied strenuously against the notion of an unchanging South, pointing to the sharp break between the Old South and the New and arguing that the supposedly time-honoured southern tradition of racial segregation was in fact largely a product of the 1890s and early years of the twentieth century.[26] More recently, historians have engaged in an intense debate over how 'revolutionary' the Civil War, emancipation and Reconstruction were, with some stressing the basic continuity between the Old South and the New, and others describing a bourgeois revolution that led to a halting, uneven, but unstoppable transformation of a slaveholding into a capitalistic society.[27] Any effort to come to grips with the impact of the Civil War and emancipation on the South must be at least implicitly comparative, because determining their impact makes sense only in terms of what had existed before.

A third kind of internal variation within the South is that among groups of southerners, whether those groups are defined in ideological, ethnic or class terms. Despite the proclivity of many people to think in monolithic terms – it is hard, for example, to break students of the habit of saying 'the South felt' this or 'the South wanted' that – the prototypical 'southerner' does not exist. In dealing with the 'character' of the South, one must continually confront the question of *which* southerners one is considering.[28]

Perhaps the clearest enunciation of this simple point is to be found in a book called *The Other South*, in which Carl N. Degler focused on those whom he termed the 'losers' who dissented from the South's dominant ethos: southern whites who opposed slavery, remained Unionists during the Civil War, and sought to forge a more egalitarian society in the late nineteenth century.[29] Although Degler's 'other southerners' were limited to whites who questioned prevailing norms concerning race and slavery, there are many other notable variations: over the centuries southerners have included women as well as men, blacks as well as whites, poor whites as well as yeomen farmers and planters, immigrants, mechanics, Jews, socialists, populists, racists, democrats (both with capital and small d), republicans (with capital and small r), shopkeepers, accountants, secretaries, waiters, conservatives, liberals, Catholics, Baptists, soldiers, airline pilots, Hispanics and prostitutes, and that is just a start. To generalize about the 'southernness' of these diverse southerners is indeed a herculean task.

Since the Civil War led to the formation of a southern 'nation', the behaviour and beliefs of southerners during that conflict is especially pertinent to efforts to explore the question of southern unity and disunity. From the beginning, two competing myths surfaced, one proclaiming the solidarity of the southern 'people' in the wake of Yankee aggression and the other portraying the Confederacy as the product of a 'slave power conspiracy' foisted on 'loyal' southerners by a small but powerful planter class. If the starkest versions of these competing interpretations no longer find much support among historians, scholars continue to disagree over the degree of southern support for the Confederacy, the nature of Confederate nationalism, and the viability of the Confederacy as a 'nation'. Some, such as the authors of a recent book entitled *Why the South Lost the Civil War*, have seen insufficient nationalism as the cause of Confederate defeat. Others, such as James M. McPherson and Drew Gilpin Faust, have cautioned against working backwards from what eventually happened to argue that Confederate defeat was pre-ordained. In *The Creation of Confederate Nationalism*, Faust warned that nationalism was 'not a substance available to a people in a certain premeasured amount' so much as a 'dynamic of ideas and social realities' that needed to be *created*; 'Comparative inquiry reminds us', she noted, 'that nationalism is more often than not "insufficient" at the time of its first expression'. (In another work, however, Faust suggested that lack of support among white women *was* fatal to the Confederacy; tackling head-on one of the most enduring myths associated with the Confederacy (that of the selfless loyalty of its women), she concluded that 'it may well have been because of its women that the South lost the Civil War'.)[30]

The most recent case for southern wartime unity has been made by Gary W. Gallagher in his book *The Confederate War*. Complaining that 'historians employing the analytical prism of class, gender, and race have focused almost exclusively on sources of division', he countered that far from collapsing as a result of internal weaknesses, the Confederacy survived for so long because it aroused an extraordinary level of popular support. Noting that more than three-quarters of the South's white men of military age served in the Confederate military, Gallagher stressed the patriotic devotion of white southerners – male and female – to the Confederacy.[31]

Gallagher's case is a strong one, within narrow confines. Clearly, millions of southern whites believed passionately in the Confederate cause, and many continued for decades after the War to be consumed by bitter hatred of their Yankee conquerors. But the intensity of such feelings among many southerners cannot negate their absence among others and does not speak to the question of southern unity or disunity. I will return shortly to the question of creating southern nationalism, a question that I think is best approached in comparison with similar efforts elsewhere, but it is worth noting that the degree of support one finds for the Confederacy is closely related to how one frames this question. If the majority of white southerners can be described as identifying strongly with the Confederacy *at some point* in time, many of them expressed serious reservations either earlier or later.[32] And counting all southerners, black as well as white, it is likely that in no state with the possible exception of Texas did secession ever represent the will of the majority.[33]

In this context, it is important to emphasize that the term 'southerner' encompasses blacks as well as whites. In 1860, one-third of all southerners were slaves, yet in the conventional terminology of both contemporaries and historians, to be pro-slavery was to be 'pro-southern' and to be anti-slavery was to be 'anti-southern'. If it was second nature for contemporaries to describe abolitionists as anti-southern, there is no reason for *us* to accept such usage: from the point of view of many southerners, the abolitionists were *pro*-southern, as were the proponents of a radical Reconstruction policy in the 1860s or a sweeping civil rights programme in the 1960s. Use of the conventional terminology pre-defines the South as conservative, racist, and unchanging – something that *one* South was, but that others were not.

The third kind of comparison, between the South and regions outside the USA, is the kind that people identify most readily as comparative. Indeed, some scholars, such as George Fredrickson, consider them the only real form of comparison.[34] Although I do not share this judgement, I regard this kind of comparison as exceptionally fruitful. Of course, given the nature of my own work, some may suspect that I am not entirely unbiased on this question.

What is 'comparable'? Although anything *can* be compared with something else, utility is the key to comparison's desirability. Comparison can serve at least three major functions. First, it can lead to a reduction of parochialism, through an awareness of alternatives and a clarification of significance.[35] Second, it enables the historian to form generalizations, based upon discovering common patterns; indeed, strictly speaking, it is *only* through comparison that such generalizations can be made. Third, it makes it possible to disprove a generalization or hypothesis by showing that in at least one case it is not accurate. These second and third functions, although apparently very different, in fact represent opposite sides of the same coin: through comparison, the scholar hopes to weigh the impact of specific historical conditions on the objects being compared, thereby distinguishing the particular from the general. Far from constituting a simple listing of similarities, successful comparison requires the existence of significant differences. The most useful comparisons are likely to involve common items or processes – such as labour systems, revolutions, families, industrialization – in different historical environments; it is the resulting interplay between similarities and differences that provides the comparison's utility. As Donna Gabaccia suggests, although scholars have typically warned that comparing the experiences of European immigrants and American blacks amounts to 'comparing apples and oranges', the experiences of African-Americans and Italians as 'migratory southerners' are eminently comparable.[36]

By far the largest body of comparative work on the American South has focused on the closely-related questions of slavery and race relations. Much of the early comparative literature appeared in direct response to a controversial book published in 1959 in which Stanley M. Elkins contrasted slavery in the southern USA with that in Latin America. Elkins stressed the uniquely harsh conditions that prevailed in the American South, where, unlike Latin America, no Church or Crown existed to limit the masters' arbitrary authority and the slaves were reduced to a state of infantile dependence or, as he termed them, 'Sambos'.[37]

During the 1960s and 1970s, at the same time that historians of the South demonstrated that most American slaves were in fact far from Sambos,[38] a largely different group of comparative historians challenged the notion of a uniquely harsh American slavery. Some of these scholars emphasized the extent to which – despite very different legal traditions – actual master–slave relations in the American South had much in common with those in Latin America, while others argued that in some ways slavery in the American South was *less* oppressive (at least in material terms) than that in Brazil and the Caribbean. But whether historians stressed common patterns or differences, most agreed that when one looked at how concrete historical conditions shaped actual slave relations, Elkins's interpretation did not hold up. The need to differentiate between the character of a slave regime and that of its

race relations also became clear, for if American *slavery* was not unusually harsh, historians continued to find American *race relations* unusually rigid, whether measured in terms of slaves' access to freedom or
in terms of the extent to which whites differentiated among people of
colour rather than lumping them all together as blacks.[39]

More recently, comparative historians of slavery have branched out in
new directions. Lacking a common target – Elkins – they have also
lacked the common thematic approach that united their predecessors,
but typically their comparisons have differed in focus from those of
earlier scholars in at least one of three ways. Some historians turned
the comparative lens on the slaves themselves, exploring topics such as
slave resistance and slave economic activity.[40] Others expanded their
geographical focus beyond the New World, including Africa and Eastern
Europe as well as generalizing broadly across time and space.[41] And still
others began to explore the end of slavery – emancipation and its
aftermath – in comparative perspective.[42] In short, whatever their disagreements, a wide variety of scholars have recognized that southern
slavery is best understood in the context of slavery and other forms of
unfree labour elsewhere in the modern world.

Although no other branch of southern history has been subjected to
such intensive comparative scrutiny as slavery, virtually every subject –
from the role of women to religion, patterns of settlement, and frontiers
– could benefit from an effort to put it in broader context, and some
have already seen promising (although usually less than systematic)
efforts at comparison.[43] The question of southern economic 'backwardness', for example, can be measured against the performance of other
economies as well as that of the North. Thus, in disputing the thesis that
slavery retarded southern economic development, Fogel and Engerman
argued that if the South had been a separate country in 1860, it would
have been the fourth richest in the world, behind only Australia, the
North, and Great Britain; 'indeed', they wrote, 'a country as advanced as
Italy did not achieve the southern level of per capita income until the eve
of World War II'. Similarly, in debunking the notion that the Civil War
was responsible for the poverty that gripped the postbellum South, Roger
L. Ransom and Richard Sutch pointed out that throughout history, most
other 'war-devastated economies' have recovered relatively quickly and
suggested, therefore, that 'a closer examination of the asserted connection between the physical destruction and the subsequent economic
performance of the South seems in order'. Other scholars, including
Jonathan Wiener, Steven Hahn and Barbara Fields, have debated the
extent to which the post-war South followed the so-called 'Prussian

Road' to capitalism, a formulation originally developed by Lenin to distinguish an authoritarian (Prussian) model, in which landed elites retained their political hegemony by allying with industrial capitalists, from a democratic (American) model.[44]

Comparative analysis is equally promising in elucidating southern political history. Take, for example, the question of the basic conservatism that, despite some important exceptions, has dominated southern politics from the antebellum years to the present. During the past 30 years the Democratic Party, which throughout most of the twentieth century enjoyed political hegemony in the South, has become an increasingly endangered species in the white South, even as conservative Republicans have become a sectional staple as prevalent as cotton used to be.[45]

Although this conservatism has usually been considered in a comparative context in which the South is contrasted with the North, southern politics can also be examined in the light of regional politics elsewhere. In many European countries, recent politics has also been marked by regional patterns, although these patterns defy easy generalization. In England, the more prosperous South has voted consistently Conservative, while the North, suffering from the effects of de-industrialization and high unemployment, has shown pro-Labour proclivities. In Italy, by contrast, in a trend bearing some resemblance to the USA, the poorer South has traditionally shown less support than the rest of the country for parties of the left and more support for Church-affiliated parties pledged to defend traditional values. And in post-Cold War Germany, the East, after first indulging in a reflexive anti-Communist surge that provided the bulwark for Helmut Kohl's re-election to a third term as Chancellor, in 1998 expressed its disillusionment with the new order by voting for candidates of the left and helping to bring about the replacement of Kohl's Christian Democrats by the current 'Red-Green' coalition.[46] Still, if regional voting patterns have existed elsewhere, they have been particularly strong in the American South, not only because of that section's distinctive history but also because of the unusual weakness of the central government under the American federal system. Most other countries have country-wide school systems, drivers' licences and levels of unemployment compensation; in the USA, however, the augmented authority of states *vis-à-vis* the Federal government makes possible an unusual degree of variation from the national political norm in regions where common interests, experiences and values also deviate from the national norm. The South has been pre-eminently such a region.[47]

Given the central importance of the Civil War to the very concept of the 'South', the section's Civil War experience must loom especially large in any comparative approach to southern history. Needless to say, the American Civil War is hardly the only civil war in history; dozens of others, from the English Civil War of the 1640s to the conflict that has raged in the Congo on and off from the early 1960s to the present, invite comparison.

Considering the American Civil War in international context can put all kinds of traditional assumptions in a new light.[48] One can begin with the number of casualties. The Civil War was by far the bloodiest confrontation in the history of the USA, a point sensitively explored in Drew Gilpin Faust's recent essay, 'A Riddle of Death'. It is therefore worth emphasizing that when compared with other countries' military experiences, the American Civil War ranks as a mid-level conflict, one in which death and destruction were widespread but of nowhere near record-breaking proportions. Sudan, for example, has about the same number of people today that the USA had in the 1860s, but the civil war which has beset that African country for the past 15 years has produced nearly 2 million deaths, more than three times the number killed in the American conflict. And as a proportion of the population, the number of Soviets who perished in the Second World War was about five times as great as the number of Americans in the Civil War.[49]

A broadened context is also useful in re-evaluating two longstanding debates about how to characterize the Reconstruction settlement that followed the War, one over its severity and one over its radicalism. For many years it was common to describe Reconstruction as 'harsh' or 'vindictive' to the South,[50] but in comparative terms the former Confederates fared remarkably well. Indeed, one would be hard pressed to find another example in which defeated combatants in a civil war were treated as gently as those in the American South. The Yankees imposed no mass executions or jailings on the vanquished South. A small number of high-ranking Confederates were disfranchised by the Fourteenth Amendment to the Constitution and the Reconstruction Act of 1867, but a series of amnesty acts (the most important of which was passed in 1872) restored their political privileges, and in the 1870s former Confederate leaders, including Vice President Alexander Stephens, served in the US Congress. One can imagine how relieved the losers in the Spanish Civil War – tens of thousands of whom were executed and hundreds of thousands jailed – would have been to receive such 'vindictive' treatment. Of course, harshness is in the eye of the beholder, but there is no reason for historians to judge Reconstruction from the particular perspective of former Confederates rather than from the broader perspective of other sequels to civil war.[51]

A comparative perspective also suggests that the unusual way in which slavery came to an end in the USA made possible a more radical sequel to slavery – Reconstruction – than was typical. Elsewhere in the modern Western world (with the exception of Haiti and the partial exception of Cuba) slavery ended peacefully. Although the masters sought to defend their prerogatives, they did not oppose abolition by force of arms. American slave-owners, unusually militant in elaborating arguments on behalf of the peculiar institution, were also unusually militant in taking up arms to defend their cause. The consequences of this slaveholders' rebellion were legion, but one of the most important was the extent to which it accentuated the revolutionary nature of emancipation. Widely regarded throughout the North as traitors, slave-holders lost the moral authority and political power to help shape the course of the postwar Reconstruction settlement. Elsewhere, former masters played an important role in setting the terms of the new, post-emancipation order. They typically received compensation for the loss of their human property and they often directed a gradual process of emancipation, lasting years or even decades. In the American South, by contrast, emancipation was immediate and uncompensated, and the former masters were largely excluded from setting the rules for the new order. The former slaves, meanwhile, were the beneficiaries of a remarkable body of legislation that gave them unusual access to civil rights and political power. In short, because of the distinctive way slavery died in the South, there occurred an unusually sharp break with the past. In *this* comparative context, Reconstruction appears notably 'radical'.[52]

An international context also provides a useful venue for returning to the question of southern national identity during the Civil War. The concepts of 'nation' and 'nationalism' have received increased attention in recent years, in part as a result of the explosion of nationalist violence that has rocked much of the world and in part as a consequence of the collapse of competing methods of conceptualizing human relationships. In an era in which ideals of socialist solidarity and class consciousness seem to have lost much of their salience, national and religious identity loom correspondingly larger as ways of explaining how people relate to each other.[53]

Considering the creation of southern nationalism, and of the Confederate nation, in an international context suggests some intriguing themes that so far as I know have not been explored. The very basis for Confederate identity is striking for its atypicality. Sense of nation-hood in the modern world has usually been built around one or more of language, religion and 'ethnicity'. Using these to create national identi-fication occurred both in countries that were already in existence – as in nineteenth-century France, where much of the country did not speak French and local attachments were usually stronger than national – and in those where independence or unity was forged in struggle, as in Italy, Germany, Poland and Ireland. The spreading sense of Polishness or Irishness (or, for that matter, more recently Croatian-ness and Serb-ness) depended on an accentuation of differences reconfigured as long-standing and immutable: we have our own language, religion, trad-itions, folklore and culture that have since time immemorial made us a people. It also depended on accentuating common elements that supposedly united a people at the expense of class differences that divided them: class consciousness and nationalism are historical en-emies.[54]

Despite the best efforts of Confederate propagandists, linguistic, reli-gious or ethnic identification were of minimal use in creating Confeder-ate nationalism; indeed, all three served to unite Confederates and Yankees more than to divide them. Instead, loyalty to the new nation rested on the defence of perceived *interests*, most particularly slavery. As Vice President Alexander Stephens put it, the 'great truth that the negro is not equal to the white man; that slavery... is his natural and moral condition' constituted the 'cornerstone' of the Confederacy. At the heart of the effort to forge a slaveholders' republic, and of Confederate self-identification, was not a shared religion, language or ethnicity, but a shared ideological vision.[55]

In the ideological basis of its nation-building – although not in the ideology itself – the Confederacy resembled two other countries born in revolution: the USA and the Soviet Union. In both of these countries, national identity initially rested on a common commitment to an ideal: in the former case to republicanism, in the latter to socialism. Both were widely spoken of as 'experiments' and received enthusiastic support elsewhere as beacons pointing the way to a better world. To 'friends of liberty' and supporters of the 'toiling masses', the USA and the USSR were worthy of support and emulation because their identity rested on general principles rather than on a particular language, religion or ethnicity. So too did the Confederacy's.[56]

In trying to create a sense of nationhood on the basis of a shared ideology, all three countries faced unusual difficulties, for ideological enthusiasm is notoriously hard to sustain over prolonged periods.

During the Second World War, when push came to shove, Soviet authorities played down socialism and appealed to old-fashioned Russian patriotism. More recently, of course, despite the apparent success of the
Soviet Union in forging a sense of super-nationality over three-quarters
of a century, nationalist, ethnic and religious loyalties have proved
surprisingly resilient, even as the socialist ideal has collapsed. There is
not time here to discuss how it occurred, but the successful creation of
an *American* sense of nationality – which appeared gravely threatened in
the Civil War – must stand as one of the world's most remarkable feats of
social engineering.

Viewed in this light, one can suggest that the architects of the Confederacy faced almost insuperable odds, not of a military but of a political nature. In the Confederate case, all of the problems associated with
creating a new sense of ideologically-driven national identity were com-
pounded by the nature of the ideology in question. Slavery – even when
dressed up with appeals to states' rights and honour – proved a poor
cornerstone on which to build national commitment at home or national support abroad. If the American and Soviet experiments drew
enthusiastic support around the world from republicans and socialists,
there were few 'friends of slavery' to rally to the Confederate cause.
Within the South, although I think that there is little evidence for the
widespread 'guilt' over slavery that some analysts have seen, slavery
represented an *interest* (and a minority interest, at that) more than a
glorious cause that could serve to forge a new national consciousness.
No wonder that after military defeat and the abolition of slavery, Confederate nationalism collapsed so quickly. Despite pride in their past and
mythical delineations of the 'Lost Cause', no one in the South seriously
proposed resurrecting the Confederacy at some future date, or fighting
on guerilla-style, until victory was eventually achieved. Instead, the
southern political elite immediately began arguing that their states
had never really been out of the Union, that they were Americans in
exactly the same sense that northerners were and should be able to
enjoy all the rights and privileges of American citizenship as if the War
had never occurred. In comparative context, the 'creation of Confederate nationalism' appears a more problematical venture than many
scholars have recognized.[57]

Finally, let me turn to comparison of the southern USA and southern
Italy. In what ways can and should they be compared? Although, as
Enrico Dal Lago points out, American abolitionists and Italian democrats considered themselves part of the same movement to expand
human liberty,[58] a meaningful comparison does not depend on any

assertion of identity – or even overwhelming similarity – between these 'two Souths'; obviously, in numerous respects they were radically different. Rather, the utility of the comparison stems from exploring specific subjects in the two regions for which the settings are partially similar and partially different, thereby providing a new context for familiar problems and encouraging new ways of thinking about them.

One of the most obvious bases on which to compare the two Souths is that of regional backwardness, together with a host of concomitant cultural characteristics. Both the American South and the Italian Mezzogiorno have been perceived – by contemporaries and subsequent scholars – as suffering from underdevelopment, poverty and an absence of 'modernization' in comparison with the two 'Norths'. Less urbanized, less industrialized, and less educated, they were supposedly marked by 'traditional' or 'pre-modern' values, seigneurialism, a hierarchical social structure, conservatism, a propensity for violence, an exaltation of honour; and also by poverty, poor health, intellectual isolation and massive emigration. Of course, such generalizations require (and have received) qualifications in terms of specific time and place, but in both Italy and the USA, the two souths appeared as laggards which even in the second half of the twentieth century were desperately trying to 'catch up' to national norms.[59]

This is not the place for an evaluation of these perceptions, which I think it safe to say are on both sides of the Atlantic based, as Susanna Delfino points out, on a combination of reality and self-serving stereotyping. What is interesting, however, is the parallel challenges that historians have recently raised to the orthodox portraits of the two souths, challenges that show remarkable similarities even though they appeared independently and in isolation from each other. Just as Fogel and Engerman insisted that slavery was a highly advanced form of capitalism and that the antebellum southern economy was dynamic, Marta Petrusewicz has rebutted the idea that the southern *latifondo* was backward, feudal or inefficient, stressing instead its flexibility, efficiency and market-orientation. 'For most of the nineteenth century', she maintained, 'it remained a model of rationality'.[60]

Meanwhile, scholars have joined in challenging other elements of the traditional stereotypes of the two Souths, in both countries stressing that supposedly monolithic societies were in fact marked by great diversity, making generalization about their 'character' extremely difficult. Although outsiders have been free with such generalizations, within the Souths local or sub-regional identification was usually stronger than regional: as John Dickie notes, 'at no point . . . did a significant group of interests in the Mezzogiorno mobilize by identifying with the banner of a neglected or oppressed "South" '. Similarly, although the Civil War sharply bolstered the concept of 'the South', local and state loyalty was typically stronger than sectional, except among the political and intellectual elite. On both sides of the Atlantic, abstract national and regional identification typically spread from the top down rather than from the bottom up.[61]

A related issue of considerable historiographical importance involves the way the two Souths fit into the highly-charged debate over historical continuity and change. Here, too, a 'traditional' story, in which the American Civil War and Italian unification represented decisive turning points, has come under attack from 'revisionist' scholars. The idea of these events as bourgeois revolutions – an idea that fitted comfortably with that of southern backwardness being overcome by progressive national forces – appears dubious to those more impressed by southern continuity than southern transformation and sceptical of either whiggish or Marxist versions of 'progress'. 'According to revisionist accounts of economic development, the idea of a united Italy was a purely political idea', wrote Lucy Riall in her recent book, *The Italian Risorgimento*. 'Revisionists seek to "de-privilege" national unification . . . [and to] stress the continuity between the political struggles of Restoration and Liberal Italy.' It does not take much imagination to recognize the parallel between this argument and the one playing down the impact of the American Civil War, or to recognize the shared ideological perspective of these arguments. As Riall pointed out, central to the new approach is dissatisfaction with the supposed 'teleology' of Marxist history and suspicion of the very concepts of modernization, class and nation.[62]

Yet neither the challenge to the idea of 'backward' Souths nor the assertion of basic continuity within the two Souths has entirely carried the day. Despite the sophisticated revisionism of the past two decades, it is clear that the two Souths *were* different in important ways from the rest of Italy and the USA, and it is legitimate to suggest that although the term 'backward' carries too much value-laden baggage, it captures many of the characteristics that set the Souths apart. In the USA, a more sophisticated version of the interpretation stressing the revolutionary character of the 1860s has gained increasing currency among a new generation of scholars dissatisfied with the emphasis on historical continuity. Although I am less familiar with the Italian historiography, I suspect that the same may be true in Italy as well. As Riall suggested, 'in practice, . . . [the revisionist] account is hard to sustain', in part because 'the new historiography, while challenging categories such as class and nation, has not developed an alternative means of conceptualising political action'. In short, the debate goes on.[63]

In comparing developments in southern Italy with those in the southern USA, one needs to keep in mind not only the obvious differences between them – southern Italy was not a slave society; the American South did not have a history going back thousands of years – but also the degree to which both were part of larger wholes. Any comparison must be to some extent not only between the two souths but also between Italy and America. But the situation is more complicated still, because there are in fact not just two but three comparisons at issue: one between the two souths, a second between Italy and the USA, and a third between Italian and American historiographies. Although these developed separately from each other, they have clearly been subject to some of the same intellectual and ideological currents. The overlapping nature of these comparisons creates both intellectual excitement and a caution: the methodology to be used in this kind of complex, tri-partite comparison requires careful attention and elaboration.

In concluding, I would like to note the distinction between true historical comparison, in which the historian actually compares two or more developments, events or geographical areas, and historical juxtaposition, in which these are set side by side but any comparison is left to the reader or listener. Typically, edited volumes and comparative conferences consist less of essays or talks that engage in actual comparison than of works on individual cases that when juxtaposed next to others invite historical comparison. While making a pitch for true comparison, I would suggest that juxtaposition is a first step towards such comparison, a step that is especially useful in creating what might be called a comparative consciousness. I think that the 'Two Souths' conference should be very useful, both in helping to create such a consciousness and in encouraging true works of comparative history.

Notes

1 I would like to thank Anne M. Boylan and Stanley L. Engerman for helpful comments on an earlier version of this essay. For some recent explorations of the nature and methodology of comparative history, see Raymond Grew, 'The Case for Comparing Histories', *American Historical Review*, 85 (October 1980), pp. 763–82; George M. Fredrickson, 'Comparative History', in Michael Kammen (ed.), *The Past Before Us: Contemporary Historical Writings in the United States* (Ithaca, NY, 1980), pp. 457–73; A. A. van den Braembussche, 'Historical Explanation and Comparative Method: Towards a Theory of the History of Society', *History and Theory* 28 (1989), pp. 1–24; Peter Kolchin, 'Comparing American History', *Reviews in American History* 10 (December 1982), pp. 64–81;

and Peter Kolchin, 'The Comparative Approach to the Study of Slavery: Problems and Prospects', delivered at the conference on *Les dépendances serviles*, Ecole des Hautes Etudes en Sciences Sociales, Paris, June 1996.

2   Ulrich B. Phillips, 'The Central Theme of Southern History', *American Historical Review*, 34 (1928), pp. 30–43; Grady McWhiney, *Cracker Culture: Celtic Ways in the Old South* (Tusealoosa, AL, 1988); Bertram Wyatt-Brown, *Southern Honor: Ethics and Behavior in the Old South* (New York, 1982); Kenneth S. Greenberg, *Honor and Slavery* (Princeton, NJ, 1996); and Greenberg, 'Honor and Sectional Conflict in America: "Something" Happened on May 22, 1856', paper presented at conference on the Two Souths, University College London, January 1999. On the attempt to define the South, see David L. Smiley, 'The Quest for the Central Theme in Southern History', *South Atlantic Quarterly*, 71 (Summer 1972), pp. 307–25. In this essay, unless otherwise indicated, I will consider the South to consist of the eleven states that fought for independence in the Civil War.

3   Jefferson to Chastellux, 2 September 1785, in *The Portable Thomas Jefferson*, edited by Merrill D. Peterson (New York, 1975), p. 387. Positing a sharp geographic gradation, Jefferson suggested (p. 388) that 'an observing traveller, without the aid of the quadrant may always know his latitude by the character of the people among whom he finds himself'. See also the observations in *Journal and Letters of Philip Vickers Fithian, 1773–1774: A Plantation Tutor of the Old Dominion*, edited by Hunter Dickinson Farish (Charlottesville, VA, 1957). For development of the argument that a self-conscious South first emerged during the American Revolution, see John Alden, *The First South* (Baton Rouge, LA, 1961).

4   On the evangelical transformation of southern Protestantism, see John B. Boles, *The Great Revival, 1787–1805: The Origins of the Southern Evangelical Mind* (Lexington, MA, 1972); and Christine Leigh Heyrman, *Southern Cross: The Beginnings of the Bible Belt* (New York, 1997). On the Cavalier versus Yankee stereotypes, see William R. Taylor, *Cavalier and Yankee: The Old South and American National Character* (New York, 1961).

5   One thinks, for example, of David Bertelson's designation of the 'lazy South' and John Hope Franklin's 'militant South': see David Bertelson, *The Lazy South* (New York, 1967); and John Hope Franklin, *The Militant South, 1800–1861* (Cambridge, MA, 1956).

6   Charles A. Beard and Mary R. Beard, *The Rise of American Civilization*, 2 vols (New York, 1928), II, ch. 18. Other versions of the 'difference' thesis stressed the gap between Yankee and Cavalier culture, the moral conflict between defenders and opponents of slavery, or the irreconcilable political struggle between those committed to states' rights and those who sought to impose a unified national state. For a thorough treatment of these arguments, see Thomas J. Pressly, *Americans Interpret Their Civil War* (New York, 1962; orig. pub. 1954), pp. 149–262.

7   Charles Grier Sellers, Jr (ed.), *The Southerner as American* (Chapel Hill, NC, 1960), pp. vi–vii. For examples of the revisionist thesis that the Civil War constituted a 'needless war' brought on by a 'blundering generation', see Charles W. Ramsdell, 'The Natural Limits of Slavery Expansion', *Mississippi Valley Historical Review*, 16 (September 1929), pp. 151–71; Avery O. Craven, *The Repressible Conflict, 1830–1861* (Baton Rouge, LA, 1939); and James G. Randall,

'The Blundering Generation', *Mississippi Valley Historical Review*, 27 (June 1940), pp. 3–28. See Pressly, *Americans Interpret Their Civil War*, esp. pp. 289–328.

8   'The term "revolution" has reappeared in the most recent literature as a way of describing the Civil War and Reconstruction', noted Eric Foner in *Reconstruction, 1863–1877: America's Unfinished Revolution* (New York, 1988), p. xxiv. For examples of the thesis that *shared* values rather than differences lay at the root of the conflict between North and South, see Michael F. Holt, *The Political Crisis of the 1850s* (New York, 1978); and William E. Gienapp, *The Origins of the Republican Party, 1852–1856* (New York, 1987). An earlier version of this thesis is evident in David Donald, 'An Excess of Democracy: the American Civil War and the Social Process', in his *Lincoln Reconsidered: Essays on the Civil War Era*, 2nd edn (New York, 1961), pp. 209–36. For an overview of recent historiography on Civil War causation, see Eric Foner, 'Slavery, the Civil War, and Reconstruction', in Eric Foner (ed.), *The New American History*, revised edn (Philadelphia, PA, 1997), pp. 86–92.

9   Edward Pessen, 'How Different from Each Other were the Antebellum North and South?', *American Historical Review*, 85 (1980), pp. 1119–49 (quotations: pp. 1146, 1147); James M. McPherson, 'Antebellum Southern Exceptionalism: A New Look at an Old Question', in *Drawn With the Sword: Reflections on the American Civil War* (New York, 1996), pp. 3–23 (quotations: pp. 7, 20). For a recent variant of Pessen's position, see Jonathan D. Wells, 'Class, Race and Nation in the Old South: the Origins of the Southern Middle Cass', paper presented at conference on the Two Souths, University College London, January 1999.

10   Examples of the first group include Robert William Fogel and Stanley L. Engerman, *Time on the Cross: The Economics of American Negro Slavery*, 2 vols (New York, 1974); Robert William Fogel, *Without Consent or Contract: The Rise and Fall of American Slavery*, with 4 supplementary volumes (New York, 1989); and James Oakes, *The Ruling Race: A History of American Slaveholders* (New York, 1982). Examples of the second include Eugene D. Genovese, *The Political Economy of Slavery: Studies in the Economy and Society of the Slave South* (New York, 1965); Genovese, *Roll, Jordan, Roll: The World the Slaves Made* (New York, 1974); Elizabeth Fox-Genovese, *Within the Plantation Household: Black and White Women of the Old South* (Chapel Hill, NC, 1988); and Peter Kolchin, *American Slavery, 1619–1877* (New York, 1993).

11   Fogel, *Without Consent or Contract*, p. 64; Oakes, *The Ruling Race*, p. 227. See Douglas R. Egerton, 'Markets Without a Market Revolution: Southern Planters and Capitalism', *Journal of the Early Republic*, 16 (Summer 1996), pp. 207–21. It is worth noting that scholars who contrast the coercive relationship between masters and slaves with the contractual one between employers and employees approach the question in much the same way that antebellum Americans did: rather than seeing entrepreneurialism as the essence of capitalism and stressing what southern planters and northern businessmen had in common, antebellum observers typically focused on the status of *labour*, distinguishing between the 'free-labour' North and the slave-labour South. See Eric Foner, *Free Soil, Free Labor, Free Men: The Ideology of the Republican Party Before the Civil War* (New York, 1970).

12   Even while arguing for the basic similarity between North and South, Pessen conceded in passing that 'the striking similarities of the two antebellum sections of the nation neither erase their equally striking dissimilarities nor detract from the significance of these dissimilarities'. Ticking off a lengthy list of contrasts, he suggested that 'an essay focusing on these rather than on the themes emphasized here would highlight the vital disparities between the antebellum South and North'. Then, however, he immediately reiterated his main point: 'the antebellum North and South were far more alike than the conventional scholarly wisdom has led us to believe': Pessen, 'How Different From Each Other Were the Antebellum North and South?', p. 1147.

13   'The South is seceding from the North because the two are not homogeneous', wrote Englishman Anthony Trollope at the start of the Civil War. 'They have different instincts, different appetites, different morals, and a different culture': Trollope, *North America*, edited by Robert Mason (London, 1992; orig. pub. 1862), p. 22. For a detailed examination of antebellum travel accounts, see Thomas D. Clark (ed.), *Travels in the Old South, a Bibliography*, 3 vols (Norman, OK, 1956).

14   See, e.g., Fox-Genovese, *Within the Plantation Household*; Michael S. Hindus, *Prison and Plantation: Crime, Justice, and Authority in Massachusetts and South Carolina, 1767–1878* (Chapel Hill, NC, 1980); Howard N. Rabinowitz, 'A Comparative Perspective on Race Relations in Southern and Northern Cities, 1860–1900, with Special Emphasis on Raleigh, N. C.', in Jeffrey J. Crow and Flora J. Hatley (eds), *Black Americans in North Carolina and the South* (Chapel Hill, 1984), pp. 137–59; William H. Pease and Jane H. Pease, *The Web of Progress: Private Values and Public Styles in Boston and Charleston, 1828–1843* (New York, 1985); Mark M. Smith, 'Old South Time in Comparative Perspective', *American Historical Review*, 101 (December 1996), pp. 1432–69.

15   Alfred A. Conrad and John R. Meyer, 'The Economics of Slavery in the Antebellum South', *Journal of Political Economy*, 66 (1958), pp. 95–130, and *The Economics of Slavery* (Chicago, IL, 1964); Fogel and Engerman, *Time on the Cross*; Fogel, *Without Consent or Contract*, (quotations: pp. 64, 162). For a recent work arguing for the increasing prevalence of modern 'time-consciousness' n the antebellum South, see Mark M. Smith, *Mastered by the Clock: Time, Slavery, and Freedom in the Antebellum South* (Chapel Hill, NC, 1997). There is a huge critical literature discussing the recent debate over the economics of slavery; for my perspective, see Peter Kolchin, 'Toward a Reinterpretation of Slavery', *Journal of Social History*, 11 (Fall 1975), pp. 99–113, and 'More *Time on the Cross*? An evaluation of Robert William Fogel's *Without Consent or Contract*', *Journal of Southern History*, 58 (August 1992), pp. 491–502. On the *earlier* debate over the economics of slavery, see Harold D. Woodman, 'The Profitability of Slavery: A Historical Perennial', *Journal of Southern History*, 29 (1963), pp. 303–25.

16   To some extent, what appeared to be the superior growth rate of the South reflected clever statistical manipulation, for Fogel and Engerman's figures indicated that although the southern economy as a whole was growing more rapidly than the northern, in every sub-region of the South the growth rate was *slower* than that in every sub-region of the North, an anomaly explained by interregional population shifts. For statistics on regional and sub-regional growth rates, see Fogel and Engerman, *Time on the Cross*, p. 248. For a few of

many challenges to the Fogel version of southern economic growth, see Harold D. Woodman, 'Economic History and Economic Theory: The New Economic History in America', *Journal of Interdisciplinary History*, 3 (1972), pp. 323–50; Gavin Wright, *The Political Economy of the Cotton South: Households, Markets, and Wealth in the Nineteenth Century* (New York, 1978), pp. 4, 44–55, 74–88, 90–127; and Fred Bateman and Thomas Weiss, *A Deplorable Scarcity: The Failure of Industrialization in the Slave Economy* (Chapel Hill, NC, 1981), esp. pp. 118–27, 157–63. For a summary of the 'comparative advantage' argument, see Fogel, *Without Consent or Contract*, 108–11; the argument received full elaboration in Claudia Dale Goldin, *Urban Slavery in the American South, 1820–1860* (Chicago, IL, 1976). But for a still largely persuasive exposition of the basic contradiction between slavery and urban life, see Richard C. Wade, *Slavery in the Cities: The South, 1820–1860* (New York, 1964).

17 Statistics are from Fogel, *Without Consent or Contract*, p. 89. As the persistence of this 50 per cent level indicates, the southern economy, far from stagnating, grew at about the same pace as the northern during the last third of the nineteenth century; what is more, between 1869 and 1899 *industrial* output in the ex-Confederate states grew at a faster pace than in the USA as a whole (7.8 per cent versus 5.8 per cent annually). See Gavin Wright, *Old South, New South: Revolutions in the Southern Economy Since the Civil War* (New York, 1986), p. 61.

18 For emphasis on the War's devastation of the South, see James L. Sellers, 'The Economic Incidence of the Civil War in the South', *Mississippi Valley Historical Review*, 14 (September 1927), pp. 179–91; E. Merton Coulter, *The South During Reconstruction, 1865–1877* (Baton Rouge, LA, 1947), ch. 1; Fogel, *Without Consent or Contract*, p. 89. But for the argument that – as in most other modern wars – the *physical* damage wrought by the Civil War was quickly overcome, see Roger L. Ransom and Richard Sutch, *One Kind of Freedom: The Economic Consequences of Emancipation* (Cambridge, 1977), pp. 40–55.

19 For the former approach, see Jonathan Wiener, *Social Origins of the New South: Alabama, 1860–1885* (Baton Rouge, LA, 1978); for the latter, see Ransom and Sutch, *One Kind of Freedom*; and Wright, *Old South, New South*.

20 Peter Kolchin, 'The Tragic Era? Interpreting Southern Reconstruction in Comparative Perspective', in Frank McGlynn and Seymour Drescher (eds), *The Meaning of Freedom: Economics, Politics, and Culture After Slavery*, (Pittsburgh, PA, 1992), pp. 291–311.

21 The most notable partial exception to this generalization involves the American West, an exception that suggests the utility of a historical comparison between South and West. Even westerners, however, have not usually invested the same symbolic meaning in region that southerners have, in part perhaps because virtually all westerners are descended from easterners, whereas most southerners are not descended from northerners. For a recent book that explores the intersection of South and West over more than 150 years of history, see Neil Foley, *The White Scourge: Mexicans, Blacks, and Poor Whites in Texas Cotton Culture* (Berkeley, CA, 1997). See Edward L. Ayers *et al.* (eds), *All Over the Map: Rethinking American Regions* (Baltimore, MD, 1996); Edward L. Ayers, 'The South, the West, and the Rest', *Western Historical Quarterly*, 25 (Winter 1994), pp. 473–6; and William Cronon, 'The West: A Moving Target', *Western Historical Quarterly*, 25 (Winter 1994) pp. 476–81. For

an early effort at West–South comparison, see Douglas F. Dowd, 'A Comparative Analysis of Economic Development in the American West and South', *Journal of Economic History*, 16 (December 1956), pp. 558–74.

22   Ira Berlin, *Many Thousands Gone: The First Two Centuries of Slavery in North America* (Cambridge, MA, 1998); Philip D. Morgan, *Slave Counterpoint: Black Culture in the Eighteenth-Century Chesapeake and Lowcountry* (Chapel Hill, NC, 1998).

23   Two new books trace the peculiar history of the peculiar institution in Delaware: William H. Williams, *Slavery and Freedom in Delaware, 1639–1865* (Wilmington, NC, 1996); and Patience Essah, *A House Divided: Slavery and Emancipation in Delaware, 1638–1865* (Charlottesville, VA, 1996).

24   To take one obvious example, although historians of late antebellum slavery have properly emphasized the central role that Christianity played in the slave quarters, the conversion of the slaves did not reach notable proportions until the late eighteenth and early nineteenth centuries. On the centrality of Christianity to antebellum slave life see, e.g., Genovese, *Roll, Jordan, Roll*, esp. pp. 161–284; and John B. Boles (ed.), *Masters and Slaves in the House of the Lord: Race and Religion in the American South, 1740–1870* (Lexington, MA, 1988). For recent recognition of the colonial contrast, see Morgan, *Slave Counterpoint*, who notes (p. 420) that 'the vast majority of eighteenth-century Anglo-American slaves lived and died strangers to Christianity'.

25   Kolchin, *American Slavery*.

26   Phillips, 'The Central Theme of Southern History'; W. J. Cash, *The Mind of the South* (New York, 1941); C. Vann Woodward, *Origins of the New South, 1877–1913* (Baton Rouge, LA, 1951); and Woodward, *The Strange Career of Jim Crow* (New York, 1955 and subsequent editions). Howard N. Rabinowitz has noted the announcement of at least three 'New Souths' since 1920, in addition to the most commonly cited ('first') New South of 1877–1919; see Rabinowitz, *The First New South, 1865–1920* (Arlington Heights, IL, 1992), pp. 1–2.

27   For examples of works emphasizing continuity, see Carl N. Degler, *Place Over Time: The Continuity of Southern Distinctiveness* (Baton Rouge, LA, 1977); Wiener, *Social Origins of the New South*; and Jay R. Mandle, *The Roots of Black Poverty: The Southern Plantation Economy after the Civil War* (Durham, NC, 1978), recently reissued with slight revisions as *Not Slave, Not Free: The African American Economic Experience Since the Civil War* (Durham, NC, 1992). Those exploring 'transformation' include Foner, *Reconstruction*; and Barbara Jeanne Fields, 'The Advent of Capitalist Agriculture: The New South in a Bourgeois World', in Thavolia Glymph and John J. Kushma (eds), *Essays on the postbellum Southern Economy* (College Station, TX, 1985), pp. 73–94. For a discussion of some of these issues, see Peter Kolchin, 'Slavery and Freedom in the Civil War South', in James M. McPherson and William J. Cooper, Jr (eds) *Writing the Civil War: the Quest to Understand* (Columbia, SC, 1998), esp. pp. 254–7.

28   On conflicting versions of 'southern' interests, see Chapter 6 in this volume.

29   Carl N. Degler, *The Other South: Southern Dissenters in the Nineteenth Century* (New York, 1974), p. 1 (quotation).

30   Richard E. Beringer, Herman Hattaway, Archer Jones and William N. Still, Jr, *Why the South Lost the Civil War* (Athens, GA, 1986); James M. McPherson, 'Why Did the Confederacy Lose?' in *Drawn With the Sword*, pp. 113–36; Drew

Gilpin Faust, *The Creation of Confederate Nationalism: Ideology and Identity in the Civil War South* (Baton Rouge, LA, 1988), quotation: p. 6; Faust, 'Altars of Sacrifice: Confederate Women and the Narratives of War', in her *Southern Stories: Slaveholders in Peace and War* (Columbia, MO, 1992), pp. 113–40 (quotation: p. 140).

31 Gary W. Gallagher, *The Confederate War* (Cambridge, MA, 1997), quotation: p. 27; statistic: p. 28. For a similar argument based on a statewide study, see William Blair, *Virginia's Private War: Feeding Body and Soul in the Confederacy, 1861–1865* (New York, 1998).

32 For evidence of disunity among southern whites *during* the Civil War, see, *inter alia*, Stephen Ambrose, 'Yeomen Discontent in the Confederacy', *Civil War History*, 8 (1962), pp. 259–68; Paul D. Escott, *After Secession: Jefferson Davis and the Failure of Confederate Nationalism* (Baton Rouge, 1978); William W. Freehling, 'The Divided South, the Causes of Confederate Defeat, and the Reintegration of Narrative History', in his *The Reintegration of American History: Slavery and the Civil War* (New York, 1994), pp. 220–52; and David Williams, *Rich Man's War: Class, Caste, and Confederate Defeat in the Lower Chattahoochie Valley* (Athens, GA, 1998).

33 This calculation is based on the propositions that (1) virtually no slaves and relatively few free blacks supported secession, and (2) support among whites for secession ranged from overwhelming in some plantation districts of the deep South to a minority position in much of Appalachia. For the more extreme judgement that 'at no time during the winter of 1860–1861 was secession desired by a majority of the [*white*] people of the slave states', see David M. Potter, *Lincoln and his Party in the Secession Crisis* (New Haven, CT, 1942), p. 208. Important works on the secession of southern states include Steven A. Channing, *Crisis of Fear: Secession in South Carolina* (New York, 1970); William L. Barney, *The Secessionist Impulse: Alabama and Mississippi in 1860* (Princeton, NJ, 1974); Michael P. Johnson, *Toward a Patriarchal Republic: the Secession of Georgia* (Baton Rouge, 1977); Daniel W. Crofts, *Reluctant Confederates: Upper South Unionists in the Secession Crisis* (Chapel Hill, NC, 1989); and Peyton McCrary, Clark Miller and Dale Baum, 'Class and Party in the Secession Crisis: Voting Behavior in the Deep South', *Journal of Interdisciplinary History*, 8 (1978), pp. 429–57. Of the seven deep-South states that seceded before the firing on Fort Sumter, Texas had by far the smallest concentration of African-Americans (about 30 per cent of its population); on secession politics in Texas, see Dale Baum, *The Shattering of Texas Unionism: Politics in the Lone Star State During the Civil War Era* (Baton Rouge, LA, 1998), esp. pp. 42–81.

34 Fredrickson proposes that the term 'comparative history' be reserved for scholarship that 'has *as its main objective* the systematic comparison of some process or institution in two or more societies that are not usually conjoined within one of the traditional geographical areas of historical specialization'; Fredrickson, 'Comparative History', p. 458. See also Fredrickson, 'From Exceptionalism to Variability: Recent Developments in Cross-National Comparative History', *Journal of American History*, 82 (September 1995), pp. 587–604.

35 For example, historians of the USA knew for a long time that the American slave population grew very rapidly, more than tripling between 1810 and

1860 even though the legal importation of slaves ended in 1808, but the significance of this natural population growth became clear only when they realized that it did *not* occur in Brazil, Jamaica, Cuba, or most other new world slave societies. For an exploration of the significance of this now widely-recognized contrast, see C. Vann Woodward, 'Southern Slaves in the World of Thomas Malthus', in Woodward, *American Counterpoint: Slavery and Racism in the North-South Dialogue* (Boston, MA, 1971), pp. 78–106.

36   See Chapter 9 in this volume.

37   Stanley M. Elkins, *Slavery: A Problem in American Institutional and Intellectual Life* (Chicago, IL, 1959). Elkins built on sociologist Frank Tannenbaum's *Slave and Citizen: The Negro in the Americas* (New York, 1946), but whereas Tannenbaum stressed the contrast in race relations between Latin America and the United States, Elkins shifted the focus to the severity of slave treatment. For a study that largely supported the Tannenbaum–Elkins conclusions, see Herbert Klein, *Slavery in the Americas: A Comparative Study of Virginia and Cuba* (Chicago, IL, 1967).

38   There is a vast literature from the 1970s focusing on slave agency in the antebellum South. See, e.g., John W. Blassingame, *The Slave Community: Plantation Life in the Antebellum South* (New York, 1972; rev. edn, 1979); Genovese, *Roll, Jordan, Roll*; Herbert G. Gutman, *The Black Family in Slavery and Freedom, 1750–1925* (New York, 1976); and Lawrence W. Levine, *Black Culture and Black Consciousness: Afro-American Folk Thought From Slavery to Freedom* (New York, 1977).

39   For some of the many comparative works challenging Elkins's interpretation, see Marvin Harris, *Patterns of Race in the Americas* (New York, 1964), esp. ch. 6; David Brion Davis, *The Problem of Slavery in Western Culture* (Ithaca, NY, 1967), ch. 8; Carl N. Degler, *Neither Black Nor White: Slavery and Race Relations in Brazil and the United States* (New York, 1971); Eugene D. Genovese, 'The Treatment of Slaves in Different Countries: Problems in the Application of the Comparative Method', in Laura Foner and Eugene D. Genovese (eds), *Slavery in the New World: A Reader in Comparative History* (Englewood Cliffs, NJ, 1969), pp. 202–210; Genovese, *The World the Slaveholders Made: Two Essays in Interpretation* (New York, 1969), pt I; Woodward, 'Southern Slaves in the World of Thomas Malthus'; Richard S. Dunn, 'A Tale of Two Plantations: Slave Life at Mesopotamia in Jamaica and Mount Airy in Virginia, 1799 to 1828', *William and Mary Quarterly*, 3rd ser., 34 (January 1977), pp. 40–64.

40   Eugene D. Genovese, *From Rebellion to Revolution: Afro-American Slave Revolts in the Making of the New World* (Baton Rouge, LA, 1979); Peter Kolchin, 'The Process of Confrontation: Patterns of Resistance to Bondage in Nineteenth-Century Russia and the United States', *Journal of Social History*, 11 (Summer 1978), pp. 457–90; Roderick A. McDonald, *The Economy and Material Culture of Slaves: Goods and Chattels on the Sugar Plantations of Jamaica and Louisiana* (Baton Rouge, 1993); Ira Berlin and Philip D. Morgan, 'Labor and the Shaping of Slave Life in the Americas', in Ira Berlin and Philip D. Morgan (eds), *Cultivation and Culture: Labor and the Shaping of Slave Life in the Americas* (Charlottesville, VA, 1993), pp. 1–45.

41   George M. Fredrickson, *White Supremacy: A Comparative Study in American and South African History* (New York, 1981); Peter Kolchin, *Unfree Labor: American Slavery and Russian Serfdom* (Cambridge, MA, 1987); Shearer Davis Bowman,

Masters and Lords: Mid-Nineteenth Century U.S. Planters and Prussian Junkers (New York, 1993); and Orlando Patterson, *Slavery and Social Death: A Comparative Study* (Cambridge, MA, 1982).

42 Eric Foner, *Nothing But Freedom: Emancipation and its Legacy* (Baton Rouge, LA, 1983); Stanley L. Engerman, 'Economic Adjustments to Emancipation in the United States and British West Indies', *Journal of Interdisciplinary History*, 13 (Autumn 1982), pp. 191–220; Steven Hahn, 'Class and State in Postemancipation Societies: Planters in Comparative Perspective', *American Historical Review*, 95 (February 1990), pp. 75–98; Rebecca J. Scott, 'Defining the Boundaries of Freedom in the World of Cane: Cuba, Brazil, and Louisiana After Emancipation', *American Historical Review*, 99 (February 1994), pp. 70–102; Peter Kolchin, 'Some Thoughts on Emancipation in Comparative Perspective: Russia and the United States South', *Slavery and Abolition*, 11 (December 1990), pp. 351–67; and Kolchin, 'Some Controversial Questions Concerning Nineteenth-Century Emancipation From Slavery and Serfdom', in Michael Bush (ed.), *Serfdom and Slavery: Studies in Legal Bondage* (London, 1996), pp. 42–67.

43 See, e.g., the essays in Kees Gispen (ed.), *What Made the South Different?* (Jackson, MI, 1990); Norbert Finzsch and Jurgen Martschukat (eds), *Different Restorations: Reconstruction and 'Wiederaufbau' in Germany and the United States: 1865, 1945, and 1989* (Providence, RI, 1996); Smith, 'Old South Time in Comparative Perspective'; and Marc Egnal, *Divergent Paths: How Culture and Institutions Have Shaped North American Growth* (New York, 1996).

44 Fogel and Engerman, *Time on the Cross*, pp. 249–51 (quotation: p. 249); Ransom and Sutch, *One Kind of Freedom*, p. 41; Wiener, *Social Origins of the New South*, *passim*, esp. pp. 71–3; Hahn, 'Class and State in Postemancipation Societies', and 'Emancipation and the Development of Capitalist Agriculture: The South in Comparative Perspective', in Gispen, *What Made the South Different?*, pp. 71–88, 166–71; Fields, 'The Advent of Capitalist Agriculture', pp. 84–9; Barrington Moore, Jr, *Social Origins of Dictatorship and Democracy: Lord and Peasant in the Making of the Modern World* (Boston, MA, 1966), *passim*, esp. pp. 111–55, 413–508; V. I. Lenin, *The Development of Capitalism in Russia: The Process of the Formation of a Home Market for Large-Scale Industry* (Moscow, 1974; orig. pub. in Russian, 1899), pp. 32–3.

45 On southern conservatism and the growing Republican hegemony in the contemporary white South, see especially Earle Black and Merle Black, *Politics and Society in the South* (Cambridge, MA, 1987), and *The Vital South: How Presidents are Elected* (Cambridge, MA, 1992). In 1996, southern whites voted for Bob Dole over Bill Clinton by 56 to 36 per cent, while southern blacks voted for Clinton over Dole by 87 to 10 per cent. The disparity in voting for members of the House of Representatives was even greater: southern whites voted Republican by 64 to 36 per cent, while southern blacks voted Democratic by 85 to 15 per cent. In 1998, the split in voting for House members was still more pronounced: whites voted Democratic by 65 to 35 per cent, while blacks voted Republican by 89 to 11 per cent. Voting statistics are from the *New York Times*, 10 November 1996, p. 28, and 9 November 1998, p. A20.

46 For a regional breakdown by party of seats in British Parliament following the elections of 1974, 1979, 1983 and 1987, see J. Denis Derbyshire and Ian Derbyshire, *Politics in Britain from Callaghan to Thatcher* (n.p., 1988), p. 191.

Denis Mack Smith notes that 'in 1946 a referendum showed 76 per cent at Naples and 85 per cent at Lecce in favor of retaining the monarchy, while the North voted heavily for a republic': see his *Modern Italy: A Political History* (Ann Arbor, MI, 1997), p. 432. On the shift in east German voting patterns, see the *New York Times*, 28 September 1998, p. A10 and 29 September 1998, p. A1.

47   For emphasis on continued southern cultural distinctiveness in the post-1945 era, a distinctiveness rooted in 'localism, violence, and a conservative religion', see, *inter alia*, John Shelton Reed, *The Enduring South: Subculture Persistence in Mass Society* (Lexington, MA, 1972), *passim* (quotation: p. 89); and Jeanne S. Hurlburt and William B. Bankston, 'Cultural Distinctiveness in the Face of Structural Transformation: The "New" Old South', in R. Douglas Hurt (ed.), *The Rural South Since World War II* (Baton Rouge, LA, 1998), pp. 168–88. For varied judgements on this question, see Robert P. Steed, Lawrence W. Moreland and Tod A. Baker (eds), *The Disappearing South? Studies in Regional Change and Continuity* (Tuscaloosa, AL, 1990).

48   For an early speculative effort at comparison, see Eric McKitrick's imaginative but questionable use of the post-1945 behaviour of defeated German and Japanese powers to suggest that if the Confederates had accepted their defeat with more humility in 1865, they would have been spared the imposition of a vindictive Reconstruction settlement: McKitrick, *Andrew Johnson and Reconstruction* (Chicago, IL, 1960), pp. 21–41. McKitrick's suggestion that the Germans and Japanese, in unconditionally repudiating their wartime goals, met the 'symbolic needs' of the victors and thereby undercut anti-German and anti-Japanese sentiment among the Allies after the war, ignores the largely diplomatic reason for the absence of a 'harsh' post-1945 reconstruction programme – the imperatives of an emerging Cold War policy – as well as the very real persistence of bitter anti-German and anti-Japanese sentiment in Allied countries that had suffered most heavily in the war (especially the Soviet Union, Poland, China and Korea). See, also, David M. Potter, 'The Civil War in the History of the Modern World: A Comparative View' reprinted in his *The South and Sectional Conflict* (Baton Rouge, LA, 1968), pp. 287–99; and Carl N. Degler, 'One Among Many: The Civil War in Comparative Perspective', 29th Annual Robert Fortenbaugh Memorial Lecture (Gettysburg, PA, 1990).

49   Drew Gilpin Faust, ' "A Riddle of Death": Mortality and Meaning in the American Civil War', 34th annual Robert Fortenbaugh Memorial lecture (Gettysburg, PA, 1995). About 620 000 Americans were killed in the Civil War, or roughly 2 per cent of the population of 31 million. (About 1.7 per cent of northerners and 2.9 per cent of southerners died in the War.) The Sudanese Civil War has so far claimed about 6 per cent of the population, including 'one in five southern Sudanese'; *New York Times*, 12 December 1998, p. A6. Estimates of the number of Soviet deaths in the Second World War are imprecise, but typically fall in the 20–25 million range; for a recent suggestion of 8.6 million Soviet soldiers and 'at least 17 million civilians' killed in the War, see William C. Fuller, 'The Great Fatherland War and Late Stalinism, 1941–1953', in Gregory L. Freeze (ed.), *Russia, A History* (Oxford, 1997), pp. 319–46 (quotation: p. 334).

50   Of course, this terminology implicitly identifies *part* of the South as *the* South; it would be hard to argue that most *black* southerners found Reconstruction harsh or vindictive.

51   See Jonathan T. Dorris, *Pardon and Amnesty Under Lincoln and Johnson: The Restoration of the Confederates to Their Rights and Privileges* (Chapel Hill, NC, 1953), and 'Pardoning the Leaders of the Confederacy', *Mississippi Valley Historical Review*, 15 (1928), pp. 3–21; Harold Hyman, *The Era of the Oath: Northern Loyalty Tests During the Civil War and Reconstruction* (Philadelphia, PA, 1954); William A. Russ, 'Registration and Disfranchisement Under Radical Reconstruction', *Mississippi Valley Historical Review*, 21 (1934), pp. 163–80; and James A. Rawley, 'The General Amnesty Act of 1872', *Mississippi Valley Historical Review*, 47 (1960), pp. 480–4. Although precise statistics are lacking, Stanley G. Payne has estimated that the victorious Spanish Nationalists executed 70 000–72 000 Republicans during and after the Spanish Civil War (the Republicans may have executed a similar number of Nationalists *during* the War), and jailed hundreds of thousands more; see Payne, *The Franco Regime, 1936–1975* (Madison, WI, 1987), pp. 216–23.

52   For elaboration of this point, see Kolchin, 'The Tragic Era?', 294–7.

53   In exploring the concepts of 'nation' and 'nationalism', it is useful to begin with Benedict Anderson's idea of nation as 'imagined community': that is, a body of humans whose shared sense of identity makes them seem a 'people'. Despite common assumptions that national identity, nationalism and national animosities are usually the products of centuries-old traditions, they appear to be relatively recent phenomena in human history and to be more often imposed from the top down than reflections of immutable popular folkways. Rather than constituting natural phenomena, nations and a sense of nationality are *created*. See Anderson, *Imagined Communities: Reflections on the Origin and Spread of Nationalism*, 2nd edn (London, 1991); E. J. Hobsbawm and Terence Ranger (eds), *The Invention of Tradition* (Cambridge, 1983); E. J. Hobsbawm, *Nations and Nationalism since 1780: Programme, Myth, Reality* (Cambridge, 1990); and William Pfaff, *The Wrath of Nations: Civilization and the Furies of Nationalism* (New York, 1993).

54   Rather than nations making states, wrote E. J. Hobsbawm, 'states...created "nations"....The Italian kingdom...did its best, with mixed success, to "make Italians" through school and military service, after having "made Italy"': Hobsbawm, *The Age of Empire: 1875–1914* (London, 1987), p. 150.

55   Stephens quoted in Michael Perman (ed.), *Major Problems in the Civil War and Reconstruction* (Lexington, MA, 1991), p. 280. On the extent to which Confederate leaders and slave-owners saw the war as one for slavery, see Faust, *The Creation of Confederate Nationalism*, pp. 59–60; and James L. Roark, *Masters Without Slaves: Southern Planters in the Civil War and Reconstruction* (New York, 1978), pp. 1–32, 68–108. But see Drew Faust's discussion of religion 'as a source of legitimation for the Confederacy', in Faust, *The Creation of Confederate Nationalism*, pp. 22–40 (quotation: p. 22); and Paul D. Escott's discussion (in *After Secession*, pp. 35–52) of how Jefferson Davis deliberately de-emphasized slavery in his public statements, in order to win the allegiance of non-slaveholding whites. Many modern African 'nations' – based on the legacy of European colonial administration – also lack linguistic, religious or ethnic bases, and face exceptional difficulties in forging national consciousness; see Basil Davidson, *The Black Man's Burden: Africa and the Curse of the Nation-State* (New York, 1992).

56   For a recent essay noting the ways in which nineteenth-century American nationalism departed from European models, and criticizing theorists of nationalism for ignoring the USA, see Peter J. Parish, 'An Exception to Most of the Rules: What Made American Nationalism Different in the Mid-Nineteenth Century?', *Prologue: Quarterly of the National Archives*, 27 (Fall, 1995), pp. 219–29. For the suggestion that perceived interest rather than shared culture lay at the heart of southern nationalism, see David M. Potter, 'The Hstorian's Use of Nationalism and Vice Versa', reprinted in *The South and Sectional Conflict*, pp. 34–83.

57   Catherine Clinton, 'Remembrance of Things Imagined: Southern Reconstructions from 1865–1936', paper presented at conference on the Two Souths, University College London, January 1999; and David Blight, 'Reunion and Race: Did the South Win the Struggle Over the Memory of the American Civil War?', paper presented at conference on the Two Souths, University College London, January 1999. In 'Why the Confederacy did not Fight a Guerilla War after the Fall of Richmond: A Comparative View', 35th annual Robert Fortenbaugh Memorial Lecture (Gettysburg, PA, 1996), George M. Fredrickson argued that 'Afrikaner nationalism [in South Africa] was self-evidently stronger and deeper than the Confederate variety and thus able to sustain a more desperate and costly struggle, one that included facing up to the agonies and cruelties of full-scale guerilla war' (p. 23). It is also worth suggesting that with the abolition of slavery, the principal basis of Confederate nationalism had vanished. But for evidence of widespread attachment to the Confederate cause in the current South, see Tony Horwitz, *Confederates in the Attic: Dispatches From the Unfinished Civil War* (New York, 1998).

58   See Chapter 10 in this volume.

59   For a stereotypical portrait of southern Italian backwardness, see Joseph Lopreato, *Peasants No More: Social Class and Social Change in an Underdeveloped Society* (San Francisco, CA, 1967). On perceptions of the South, see Gabriella Gribaudi, 'Images of the South: The *Mezzogiorno* as seen by Insiders and Outsiders', in Robert Lumley and Jonathan Morris (eds), *The New History of the Italian South: The Mezzogiorno Revisited* (Exeter, 1997), pp. 83–113; John Dickie, 'Stereotypes of the Italian South, 1860–1900', ibid., pp. 114–47; Dickie, '"The Ancient Fiery Matter": Representations of the South in Post-Unification Italy (1860–1900)', paper presented at conference on the Two Souths, University College London, January 1999; and Martin Clark, 'Sardinia: Cheese and Modernization', in Carl Levy (ed.), *Italian Regionalism: History, Identity and Politics* (Oxford, 1996), pp. 81–106. On the role on 'honour' in the traditional South, see Pino Arlacchi, *Mafia Business: The Mafia Ethic and the Spirit of Capitalism*, transl. Martin Ryle (London, 1986), pp. 4–38; and E. J. Hobsbawm, *Primitive Rebels: Studies in Archaic Forms of Social Movement in the 19th and 20th Centuries* (New York, 1965; orig. pub. 1959), esp. pp. 30–56. On the conservatism of the southern Italian peasantry, see E. J. Hobsbawm, *The Age of Revolution: Europe, 1789–1848* (London, 1962), p. 159, and *Primitive Rebels*, pp. 13–29. On southern emigrations in comparative perspective, see Chapter 11 in this volume and Heather Ann Thompson, 'Southern Migrants and the Transformation of Shop Floor Politics in Detroit, 1945–1980', paper presented at conference on the Two Souths, University College London, January 1999, pp. 1–2.

60   Susanna Delfino, 'Deconstructing Economies, Constructing Ideas of Southern Backwardness in Italy and the United States', paper presented at conference on the Two Souths, University College London, January 1999; Fogel and Engerman, *Time on the Cross*; Fogel, *Without Consent or Contract*; Marta Petrusewicz, *Latifundium: Moral Economy and Material Life in a European Periphery*, transl. Judith C. Green (Ann Arbor, MI, 1996), quotation: p. 217; see also Chapter 5 in this volume. Jonathan Morris, 'Challenging *Meridionalismo*: Constructing a New History for Southern Italy', in Lumley and Morris, *The New History of the Italian South*, pp. 1–19. Although her perception is different from Petrusewicz's, Lucy Riall also emphasizes that 'the association of the *latifondo* with feudalism is a tenuous one ... Despite appearances to the contrary, the nineteenth-century Sicilian *latifondo* was largely a nineteenth-century creation': see Chapter 7 in this volume.

61   Dickie, ' "The Ancient Fiery Matter" '. For challenges to the idea of a backward or monolithic American South, see many of the sources cited above in notes 7–10 and 22–33. On similar challenges concerning the *Mezzogiorno*, see Lucy Riall, *The Italian Risorgimento: State, Society, and National Unification* (London, 1994), pp. 51–9; Pino Arlacchi, *Mafia, Peasants, and Great Estates: Society in Traditional Calabria*, transl. Jonathan Steinberg (Cambridge, 1983; orig. pub. Bologna, 1980); Morris, 'Challenging Meridionalismo'; and John A. Davis, 'Changing Perspectives on Italy's Southern Problem', in Levy, *Italian Regionalism*, pp. 53–68. On the top-down emergence of national consciousness, see especially Hobsbawm, *Nations and Nationalism since 1780*, who notes (pp. 60–1) that although the Italian language 'united the educated elite of the peninsula ... , at the moment of unification (1860) only $2\frac{1}{2}$% of the population used the language for everyday purposes'.

62   Riall, *The Italian Risorgimento*, pp. 61, 65, 5–7.

63   Riall, *The Italian Risorgimento*, 65, 9. 'The value of the new historiography lies not in a denial of the particularities of the history of the Mezzogiorno, but its preparedness to rethink ways of explaining this', suggests Jonathan Morris; see his 'Challenging Meridionalismo', p. 17. In his recently-published *Modern Italy*, Denis Mack Smith refers unapologetically to 'the backward South' (p. 432) when discussing the post-1945 era. Similarly, in *The First New South*, Howard N. Rabinowitz notes (p. 4) that 'Despite the New South rhetoric, southern reality in 1920 meant widespread poverty, continued dependence on single-crop agriculture, limited industrialization and urbanization, and racial oppression. As a result, the South was economically the nation's most underdeveloped region, and politically and socially, its most benighted. The legacies of that reality still confront and confound us today.' For examples of recent American works emphasizing the revolutionary character of the 1860s, see many of the sources cited in notes 8, 27 and 44.

3

Peter Kolchin's 'American South' and the Italian Mezzogiorno: Some Questions about Comparative History

Piero Bevilacqua

Three different approaches

I have read with interest and true pleasure Peter Kolchin's chapter, 'The American South in Comparative Perspective'. It is full of acute analysis and written with rare clarity. At first glance, Kolchin's piece runs the risk of being taken for a brilliant historiographic survey of different points of view among historians and of various issues which have emerged in the last few decades in the burgeoning scholarship on the American South. But this would be a superficial reading, one for which Kolchin cannot be held responsible; indeed, on the contrary, he must be lauded for combining a richness of information and detail with a clear analysis that keeps the non-specialist reader from losing his way by becoming preoccupied with one or other of the numerous suggestive paths and byways that Kolchin sketches.

No, Kolchin's is much more than an historiographic essay; it is a true and telling application of the comparative method to a significant yet understudied case, albeit a case about which a large and innovative body of research has accumulated in the last few years. It is an essay which shows, in a persuasive way, the fertility of the comparative method and, at the same time, makes a critical contribution to the analytical tools of comparison. This is an aspect of our craft to which historians must devote original and sustained effort in the future.

Kolchin maintains programmatically that he wants to pursue three different comparative approaches: (1) the comparison between the South and the North; (2) internal comparison between different regions, social formations, and components of the South; and (3) comparison between the American South and the other 'Souths' in the world. As one might expect, given my expertise as a scholar of Southern Italy, I would prefer, of course, to concentrate upon the third approach proposed by Kolchin. But I note immediately that I do not wish to neglect the first two approaches as insignificant or unimportant for, so to speak, an 'outside' historian like myself. On the contrary, reading Kolchin's reflections on the comparative possibilities of the American South, I was repeatedly struck by a number of deep affinities with the Italian Mezzogiorno.

As an example, let us consider the problem of the definition of 'the South'. Kolchin tells us that for a long period American historians, for the most part, tried to say what the South was *not*: an '*un*-South', to use his words. In Italy, even historians of the Mezzogiorno, who in recent years have gained no small degree of scholarly notoriety for their questioning of traditional historiographical values, have grappled with a similar problem of definition. What was the Mezzogiorno then? An '*un*-North', one might say, adapting Kolchin's phrase; that is, an unconscious, ideological comparison.

In the last 15 years historians and other scholars of contemporary southern Italy have had to develop analyses of a society which was, actually, an enigma: its most distinguishing feature was that of being something deeply different – politically, economically and culturally – from northen Italy. Insofar as history and 'progress' were identified with economic development and capitalistic modernization, these were exclusive prerogatives of northen society. Consequently the South seemed to be a region *without* history. Indeed, traditional scholarship portrayed this area of Italy as a society whose history was 'exhausted', so to speak, in its efforts to be similar to the North and, in any case, a history that existed only in its struggles, strains and attempts to reach the economic level of the North.

In this case, we can speak, paradoxically, of an unconscious form of comparative approach. Indeed, our way of forming judgements is always, intrinsically, comparative. We estimate situations, facts and events through implicit comparison with a precedent or contemporary experience. But the judgement passed upon the Italian South, in this case, was expressed on the basis of an indistinct and summary condemnation of the region's relatively recent history: a condemnation tinged with moralism for the terrible fault of backwardness. The analytical tools for this sort of implicit comparison were not detailed empirical understandings of the two societies: that is, they did not employ the methods of rigorous scientific or historiographic scholarship. Instead, a general ideology was at work, that of capitalistic development, an ideology which takes as its task the pushing of all western societies towards modernization. Serge Latouche wrote sharply on this phenomenon: 'Non appena l'Occidente ha posto il Progresso come pietra angolare della modernità, tutti i paesi vittime della sua presenza e per cominciare quelli nella sua prossima vicinanza si sono ritrovati colpiti dal male incurabile del ritardo.'[1]

Furthermore, the Italian historians of the Mezzogiorno who first wanted to analyse in new ways the social realities of the South had to make a preliminary effort to focus and redefine their own object of study. I certainly do not mean to imply that the innovative scholarship they produced came as a result of a comparative strategy and approach. At the time we certainly did not have a clear and conscious awareness of doing anything like that. However, without doubt at the beginning of this historiographic revision there was an implicit, but determining, comparative effort: one of investing the social realities investigated with an analytical dignity by accepting their diverse and multifaceted nature and, at the same time, resisting the subtle influence of the ideology of modernization that had so distorted earlier analyses.

In addition, Italian historians, like American ones, had to face the problem of the internal diversity of their South. At a certain point in the development of the new scholarship on the Mezzogiorno it became no longer possible to state 'the South did' or 'the South decided'. Indeed, today, precisely because the Mezzogiorno is recognized to be such a large and varied subject of study, it easily repels any neat or easy historiographical consensus.

To take this point further, one can observe that as the revision gathered scholarly momentum, it became necessary to make analytic distinctions between the different social classes in the South, between different geographic areas, among different economies, and so on. This was our own discovery of 'many Souths', to paraphrase the second comparative approach proposed by Kolchin. So we discovered an urban South near a rural South, a dynamic South near one sleeping, an entrepreneurial South near one that was largely rentier-based. For example, Sicily – traditionally represented as a rural society, the country of the large estate, or *latifondo* – was also the region most dominated by towns and cities of late medieval and especially early modern history: Palermo, Catania, Messina, Agrigento, Siracusa, Trapani, Enna, Caltanissetta and so on have histories stretching back into antiquity. Agriculture in the South was, indeed, characterized by 'backward' methods of production (relatively stagnant and undynamic large estates), but also by intensive, market-oriented cultivation in both the coast of Campania and in the citrus groves (*giardini di agrumi*) of Sicily and Calabria. Also, industry emerged at a relatively early date in the regions around Naples (*Napoletano* and *Salernitano*), where there was a long tradition of manufacturing.[2]

In order to question traditional forms of self-representation – or the features of representation used by contemporaries in their social and political struggles – it is necessary to know the actual social reality. In this case it is mostly the knowledge of other similar and different realities (that is, an explicit or even implicit comparative approach) that is the most powerful tool for discovering the secret mechanisms that work together to construct social identity. In comparing different societies we come to understand that the representation and the idea which a given society has of itself is the result of social interests, conflicts, political and ideological struggles: in short, a historical construction which the scholar must decode and interpret. Certainly, for the historian and social scientist this is a new frontier of research.[3]

Let us now turn and consider the third comparative approach pursued by Peter Kolchin, comparison between the American South and 'other souths' of the world. As a matter of fact, the starting point of the Italian historians' criticism of traditional assumptions about the Mezzogiorno has a great deal in common with Kolchin's suggestions. In fact, Italian historians started their own process of dismantling traditional stereotypes by considering southern Italy as 'a region like any other in the world', or, to paraphrase Kolchin, one of 'many souths'.[4] The Mezzogiorno, then, was a case study calling for scholarly analysis rather than a social pathology to be judged according to a preconceived hierarchy of values. This starting point had the prime advantage of considering the Italian South as a region defined by its relation to other regions, a relative rather than an absolute; therefore, it implicitly opened the way for future comparison with 'other souths'.

What is backwardness?

One of the most immediate and evident results of comparison of the South with 'other souths' is vigorous criticism of the concept of backwardness. How do we define backwardness? In comparison to what, to which other society? Peter Kolchin reminds us – referring back to the work of Fogel and Engerman – that 'if the South had been a separate country in 1860, it would have been the fourth richest in the world, behind only Australia, the North, and Great Britain'.[5] This is a very important assertion because it reveals a truth which is generally ignored;

at the same time, this assertion challenges the connection, mostly taken for granted, between the South and poverty.

The fact of moving beyond the simplistic dichotomy North–South – a dichotomy loaded with political and ideological meanings – provides us with a much larger horizon for analysis and allows us to understand a particular society at a more sophisticated level. The American South was backward compared to the American North; however, from a purely economic point of view, its wealth in the late antebellum period placed it in a position akin to the North when compared to most of the other countries in the world. In a similar manner, one can ask how southern Italian backwardness should be defined. Was the South at the time of the *Risorgimento* at a level of development akin to some countries in Africa or Latin America? In other words, was the backwardness of the Mezzo-giorno the same as what we used to call a 'Third World' country? Only a comparison – no matter how implicit – between a wide range of profoundly different societies can give us the actual measurement of southern Italian backwardness. Given this premise, we need to take into account the different levels and, especially, the forms of development in Italy and western Europe; a difference arising from the particular path to industrialization followed by Italy in the modern era. Yet, even with this in mind, we still need to argue against the simplistic view of a North–South dichotomy. The fact that even now there remains an important difference in the level of per capita income between the North and the South of Italy prompts several contemporary scholars to talk about southern backwardness. Nevertheless, between 1951 and 1992, southern Italy's Gross Domestic Product increased 551 per cent, while northern Italy's Gross Domestic Product increased only 473 per cent.[6] This data strongly suggests that the Mezzogiorno has undergone quite a dramatic change in economic terms. However, the paucity of comparative study of the South and North inhibits our understanding of the depth and magnitude of social change which accompanied the economic transformation of both regions. The scholars' obsession with the idea of proving an enduring diversity between North and South through macro-statistics has prevented them from making real efforts at discovering and comparing the history of the two regions hidden behind the numbers.

In his comparison of the American South with 'other souths', Kolchin achieves remarkably cogent results, particularly when he deals with questions related to the supposed uniqueness of the American Civil War. To what extent was the Civil War exceptionally brutal, bloody or destructive compared to other wars? According to Kolchin, 'the Civil

War was by far the bloodiest confrontation in the history of the USA'. However, 'compared with other countries' military experiences, the American Civil War ranks as a mid-level conflict, one in which death and destruction were widespread but nowhere near record-breaking proportions'. Correctly, Kolchin reminds us that the civil war that has ravaged Sudan in the past 15 years has caused nearly 2 million deaths; equally instructive as well is his reference to the Spanish Civil War, one of the bloodiest conflicts of the twentieth century.[7] Through these 'external' comparisons between the American case and other cases, Kolchin shows how it is possible to reach an idea of the actual dimension of the American Civil War; this, in turn, allows him to avoid preconceived ideas and to reach a colder and more detached historical judgement of the case under review.

Slavery and 'free labour'

I wholeheartedly agree with Kolchin that 'far from constituting a simple list of similarities, successful comparison requires the existence of significant differences. The most useful comparisons are likely to involve common items or processes – such as labour systems, revolutions, families or industrialization – in different historical environments; it is the resulting interplay between similarities and differences that provides the comparison's utility.'[8] He further adds that 'the utility of the comparison stems from exploring specific subjects in the two regions for which the settings are partially similar and partially different.'[9] Certainly, the differences cannot be too deep or too radical; otherwise, one has to conclude that the case-studies are not comparable. This last observation is very important; it also shows how difficult an exercise comparative history is.

In any case, I would add a general point about the meaning of comparison between different case-studies. Comparison is an operation that leads us to scrutinize the conceptual means of analysis, to open the box of our analytical tools and make use of them. This is the reason why comparison produces an effect of detachment towards the object of study, an object that at the end of the analysis appears under a new light.

As an example let us consider the feature which distinguishes most drastically the American South from the Italian South: the presence of slavery in the former and its absence in the latter. There is no doubt that the labour performed by southern Italian peasants was an extremely different social and political reality from the one performed by black slaves in the American South. Nevertheless, if we were to describe labour systems and labour relations in the nineteenth-century southern Italian countryside, we would have to make several generalizations. We know that peasants worked hard and that they were exploited and badly paid. However, we know very little about the forms of recruitment, organization and division of labour on the farms, and about skilled jobs, methods of payment, seasonal rhythms and working hours. We know equally little about conflicts between landowners and workers and about tensions between different groups of workers. This lack of detailed knowledge – in spite of an impressive number of works on southern Italian rural society produced in the last two decades[10] – clearly shows some of the deleterious consequences of the absence of genuine and rigorous comparative study in Italian historiography; only comparative research allows us to discover similarities and differences within our own society and to investigate it with new insight, fresh questions and novel theoretical tools.

In the case of similarities and differences related to labour systems, we must consider another factor. When we speak of free labour, we usually refer to what is considered formally and legally 'free'. Certainly, the formal and legal aspect of the relations between master/landowner and worker/peasant are very important, if not essential. However, between slavery and real free labour there are several intermediate steps that only a sustained comparison can discover and elucidate. For example, we usually consider nineteenth-century and early twentieth-century peasants as free labourers. Even though this is true, by making this consideration, we do not take into account the complexity of social relationships and, above all, the specific forms of subordination which psychologically and morally tied the peasants to the landowners. In this respect, a particularly revealing episode regarding an Apulian agricultural village (*agrotown*) was reported in the 1909 Parliamentary Inquiry on the Southern Italian Peasants:

> At bottom, the landowners are convinced that the peasants are not men like them. *Commendatore* Dalmazzo, the general inspector from the Ministry of the Interior sent to break last May's strike at Cerignola, told me about the landowners' amazement at the equality in formal treatment given to the peasants; this stemmed from the fact that he had asked both landowners and peasants to sit beside him.[11]

This episode gives us a glimpse of the kind of severe subordination suffered by many southern Italian peasants in spite of their formal legal freedom as late as the beginning of the twentieth century. At the same time, the episode shows us that our analysis does not allow us to fully understand the much more subtle kind of slavery that character-ized the oppression of workers within formally free labour relations. We can reach this sophisticated level of understanding only through a comparative approach.

Some questions about comparative history

Let us now return to some general problems related to comparative historical inquiry and the methods employed by its practitioners. In chapter 2, Peter Kolchin has posed general questions – such as 'What is comparable?' – when considering both the object and the goals of comparison. According to him, although we can compare almost any-thing, we should focus on those comparisons that are truly useful. Comparison for Kolchin serves three major functions. First, it leads to a reduction of parochialism, through an awareness of alternative histor-ical paths and through an understanding of the particular significance of the case studies. Second, it enables historians to form generalizations based upon the discovery of common patterns; and finally, 'it makes it possible to disprove a generalization or hypothesis by showing that in at least one case it is not accurate'.[12]

It is difficult not to agree with Kolchin about these statements. I would also add that comparison is the forgotten soul of the social sciences, since from the very beginning social science drew inspiration from a comparative dimension. How else could Tocqueville write *Dem-ocracy in America* (1832) if not with a comparison between New World's society and European society in mind? Tocqueville was particularly aware of the importance of comparison in the making of generalizations – or, to paraphrase Kolchin, escaping parochialism – over one of the greatest events in modern history: the French Revolution. He wrote that 'whoever has seen and studied only France will never be able to under-stand anything about the French Revolution'.[13]

Comparison, then, is the leavening of research, and as such it should constantly be utilized in our approaches to the study of the past. One of the major historians of the twentieth century, Marc Bloch, elaborated an ambitious programme of comparative research, which he entit-led *Toward a Comparative History of European Societies* (1928). Bloch was persuaded that the comparative method was the historians' key to a deeper understanding of social phenomena and, at the same time, the future of historical research. The comparative method, he wrote, 'can, or rather, must influence the specific types of research. Its future, and perhaps the future of our science [history] as a whole, has this price.'[14]

To be honest, Bloch was not a good prophet; he thought that comparative history would have been widely practised in Europe because of the existence of so many different countries. However, only a handful of European historians have made use of the comparative method in a systematic way. Yet, in today's world, Bloch's ideas are particularly relevant. There is nowadays a host of historiographical, cultural and political reasons which urge the implementation of a comparative approach to history. Europe and the rest of the world need a 'comparative culture', intended as a knowledge of different social realities grounded in comparative historical research. In this respect, Kolchin's final observation about the necessity of comparing not only the two Souths but also the USA and Italy and their respective historiographies points to the direction in which future comparative studies must move. We need to compare the different ways of making history if we want to exploit the method and the practice of comparison to its fullest and richest potential. By doing this, we will not only acquire a deeper historiographical and conceptual understanding, but we will also reach a new level of scientific awareness. This is the first step in the direction of creating a new cultural territory of communication and confrontation.

The creation of a 'comparative consciousness', as Kolchin calls it, is a goal to pursue. It is a new frontier of historical research. Through the implementation of the comparative method, we come to realize that our knowledge of the past is inadequate and rough, and, at the same time, we feel compelled to make deeper and more detailed investigations. Also, only through comparison can we reach a reciprocal understanding of different countries and different cultures.

Notes

1   'As soon as the West considered Progress as the cornerstone of modernity, all the countries affected by its existence, starting from the ones closest to it, found themselves hit by the incurable disease of backwardness': S. Latouche, *L'occidentalizzazione del mondo: Saggio sul significato, la portata e i limiti dell'uniformazione planetaria* (Turin, 1994), 84. On the influence of progressive ideology in the formation of southern Italian identity, see P. Bevilacqua, 'Riformare il Sud', *Meridiana* 31 (1998), pp. 19–44.

2   On these issues, see G. Barone, 'Mezzogiorno ed egemonie urbane', *Meridiana* 5 (1989); C. Donzelli, 'Mezzogiorno tra "questione" e purgatorio. Opinione commune, imagine scientifica, strategie di ricerca', *Meridiana* 9 (1990); S. Lupo, *Il giardino degli aranci: Il mondo degli agrumi nella storia del Mezzogiorno* (Venice, 1990); P. Bevilacqua, *Breve storia dell'Italia meridionale dall'Ottocento* (Rome, 1993). For a brief survey of recent southern Italian historiography, see

P. Bevilacqua, 'Corsi e ricorsi della storiografia sul Mezzogiorno', in P. Macry and A. Massafra (eds), *Fra storia e storiografia. Studi in onore di pasquale Villani* (Bologna, 1994), 131–50.

3 Significantly, most of the studies on the demystification of the traditional image of southern Italy have been written by non-Italian historians. See, for example, N. Moe, '"Altro che Italia." Il Sud dei Piemontesi (1860–1861)', *Meridiana* 15 (1992), pp. 53–89; and N. Moe, *The View from Vesuvius: Geographies of Cultural Production in Nineteenth-Century Italy* (forthcoming). See also J. Dickie, 'La "sicilianità" di Francesco Crispi. Contributo a una storia degli stereotipi del Sud', *Meridiana* 24 (1995); and J. Dickie, *Darkest Italy: The Nation and Stereotypes of the Mezzogiorno, 1860–1900* (London, 1999).

4 See C. Donzelli, 'Presentazione', *Meridiana* 1 (1987), 9–16.

5 Peter Kolchin, Chapter 2 in this volume.

6 CENSIS (*Istituto Centrale di Statistica*), *Rapporto sulla situazione sociale del Paese* (Milan, 1999), p. 427.

7 Kolchin, Chapter 2 above.

8 Kolchin, Chapter 2 above.

9 Kolchin, Chapter 2 above.

10 In the past 15 years, Italian historians have analysed the condition of labour mainly as part of the wider social historical context of their investigation. See, for example, P. Bevilacqua, 'Uomini, Terre, Economie' in P. Bevilacqua and A. Placanica (eds), *La Calabria*, (Turin, 1985), pp. 117–362; M. Petrusewicz, *Latifundium: Moral Economy and Material Life in a Nineteenth-Century Periphery* (Ann Arbor, MI, 1996), pp. 143–84.

11 See Bevilacqua, *Breve storia dell'Italia meridionale*, p. 72.

12 Kolchin, Chapter 2 above.

13 Quotation in L. Cafagna, 'La comparazione e la storia contemporanea', *Meridiana* 6 (1989), p. 19.

14 Quotation in C. Fumian, 'Le virtù della comparazione', *Meridiana* 4 (1988), p. 201.

Part II
Landed Elites and Rural Workers

4

On the Edge of Modernity: Louisiana's Landed Elites in the Nineteenth-Century Sugar Country*

Richard Follett

With Union and Confederate troops massing in northern Virginia, William Howard Russell hurried upstream after his sojourn in New Orleans. Anxious to visit the plantations of the Louisiana sugar country, Russell promptly arrived at John Burnside's expansive sugar holdings some 30 miles south of the state capital, Baton Rouge. Climbing the bell tower of the plantation house, Russell's eyes cast over a vast agricultural kingdom:

> The view from the belvedere ... was one of the most striking of its kind in the world. If an English agriculturist could see six thousand acres of the finest land in one field, unbroken by hedge or boundary, and covered with the most magnificent crops of ... sprouting sugar-cane ... he would surely doubt his senses. But there is literally such a sight – six thousand acres, better tilled than the finest patch in all the Lothians, green as Meath pastures, which can be turned up for a hundred years to come.[1]

Like Russell, those who visited south Louisiana left the region impressed by the superior slave workmanship, advanced horticulture and industrial productivity of the late antebellum sugar estates. His fellow Briton, James Robertson, similarly marvelled at the 'enterprise and energy' with which Louisianans committed themselves to improved methods of sugar production, while a travelling planter from the French cane island of Guadeloupe lauded the superior 'intelligence and skill manifested in the cultivation and manufacturing of sugar'.[2] International praise found its domestic reflection in Frederick Law Olmsted, who noted upon visiting the sugar country 'that intelligence, study, and enterprise had seldom better claims to award'.[3] Echoing these accolades, Louisianans proudly charged that 'there are but few estates either in Mexico, Cuba, or any of the West India Islands which equal...the average plantations in Louisiana'.[4] These enthusiastic and ambitious declarations of economic modernity, however, masked profound incongruities as planters and slaveholders eagerly embraced the market revolution while simultaneously rejecting the liberal and democratic overtones of nineteenth-century progress.

Preaching the doctrine of economic evolution, the sugar masters exhibited a marked discrepancy as they vigorously advocated modernity while simultaneously conserving an archaic form of social organization that suppressed the emergence of an integrated capitalist society in the sugar country. Responding to Mark Smith's recent injunction that future research in slave studies should tease out 'the dialectical relationship between the doses of capitalism and pre-capitalism in southern society', this study establishes that sugar planters embraced the capitalist ideology of the burgeoning market revolution, yet simultaneously retained a commitment to the organic ties of paternalism.[5] Recasting the master–slave relationship to ensure optimal productivity, the sugar masters discovered that capitalist economic predilections co-existed quite harmoniously with pre-capitalist social relations of production. While previous historians found these tensions irreconcilable, this analysis interrogates the dynamic interplay between capitalism and archaic social values to illustrate the evolution of plantation capitalism and the articulation of an economic culture that broached modernity while remaining anchored within arcane modes of societal construction. By rendering alternative matrices for the study of slave-based capitalism, this chapter builds upon the seminal work of Eugene Genovese and James Oakes to suggest that modernizing tendencies and patriarchal paternalism pulsed through the rhythms of southern society as planters forged a novel route to modernity where slavery and capitalism progressed in concert.[6]

In Louisiana, as in Italy, the road to modernization did not guarantee comprehensive development as planters assimilated aspects of individualistic, capitalist and market-oriented thought into a political economy and holistic social ethic that emphasized primordial concepts of reciprocal and mutual equality, personal integrity, social standing, human mastery and autonomous self-definition. Originating in the societal and economic values of the slave plantation complex, southern planter-politicians utilized an ideological vocabulary where capitalist modernity fused with paternalism and a regional commitment to the preservation of liberty, slavery, independence and virtue. Drawing on aspects of the liberal and republican traditions, antebellum southerners defined a singular economic culture that condoned market and entrepreneurial behaviour while concurrently depicting regional development through the prism of non-capitalist social relations. The alluvial sugar lords of south Louisiana exhibited these internal dualities, for although they spoke a *lingua franca* of rationality and modernization, their discourse remained wedded to a pre-modern labour structure, an antiquated form of societal construction, and an ideology that remained bound by the organic ties of paternalism and honour. Neither capitalist nor precapitalist, ancient nor modern, the antebellum sugar masters bisected categorization and collapsed historical definitions on the nature of southern society. The emerging matrix of economic and social identity provides an opportunity to probe the articulation of the slaveholder's twin commitment to chattel bondage and modern economic and managerial values. The resulting admixture indicates that slaveholding sugar planters embraced truncated concepts of nineteenth-century modernity, for while they managed their estates acquisitively, rationally and efficiently, they found little that was contradictory in slavery and modernization. Indeed, as they strove toward the creation of industrialized vertically integrated plantation units, the sugar masters encountered few incongruities in the use of bonded labour for profit and productivity maximization. Culturally distinct, yet sharing an economic universe with their free labour brethren in the North, the antebellum sugar masters stood at the edge of modernity where the market and its related *laissez-faire* order beckoned the slaveholder.

The emergence of a discrete sectional culture did not operate in polar opposition to the development of a national economic ideology, as southerners enveloped interregional notions of economic progress and embraced the cross-fertilization of mercantile thought. Deconstructing classical and Smithian critiques of slavery, the plantation elite resolved the modernist–traditionalist tension by forging models of development where slavery meshed with modernization and economic development. Amongst the myriad of southern planters, Louisianans considered themselves and their industry as exemplary models of southern economic progress. Ever eager to praise, the prominent New Orleans journalist and publisher, James De Bow, announced in an early edition of his *Commercial Review* that 'we congratulate our country on the spirit of enterprise which prevails. The competition evinced in the improvement of the manufacture of sugar shows energetic feelings amongst our planters.'[7]

These claims carried more than the hollow ring of antebellum boosterism, for the Louisiana sugar industry underwent a profound transformation in the early nineteenth century. Following the successful
production of sugar in 1795, the nascent Louisiana industry spread
swiftly from its original core in New Orleans and, by 1810, sugar occupied a premier position amongst agriculturalists on the lower reaches of
the Mississippi river. Secure behind the lofty walls of federal tariff protection, the gilt-edged appeal of sugar farming drew successive waves of
Anglo-American settlers who extended sugar cultivation beyond the
Mississippi and on to the alluvial rich soils of central and western
Louisiana. Conspicuous geographical expansion paralleled climbing
productivity as masters and slaves 'converted waste lands into verdant
fields and reaped . . . stores of gold and silver from the glebe they turned
up'.[8] Clearing land, draining swamps and erecting plantation com-
plexes, the sugar masters oversaw a flourishing trade where both the
scale and scope of production advanced briskly. Less than a decade after
De Bow's celebrated realization of Louisiana sugar, 70 estates pioneered a
small but dynamic industry where the locus of success lay in the lucrative combination of land, capital and slavery.[9] Stimulated by federal
tariffs and depressed cotton prices, production expanded keenly as the
number of estates increased more than three-fold from 193 in 1824 to
691 in 1830.[10] Remaining relatively constant during the Jacksonian era,
production increased significantly in the 1840s when Whig tariff support and lean cotton prices stimulated new sugar concerns from the Gulf
Coast to central Louisiana. While the industry qualitatively increased
from 1245 sugar houses in 1845 to over 1500 in 1849, Louisiana's
nascent sugar interest experienced quantitative gains in productivity
despite a comprehensive decline in the total number of sugar plantations in the 1850s.[11]

The economic success of the cane industry rested primarily on the
swift expansion of the internal slave trade and on the mass importation
of African-American bondspeople to Louisiana.[12] Astutely characterized
as 'sugar machines' and 'the engines of wealth', the slave population on
the sugar estates grew briskly and, by 1830, over 36 000 slaves laboured
on the cane fields.[13] By mid-century, the slave population had almost
quadrupled as 125 000 men and women toiled in the oppressive heat of
Louisiana's sugar bowl.[14] The evolution of slave labour in the sugar
industry underpinned agricultural expansion as farm output similarly
multiplied from a mean of 108 hogsheads in 1830, to 269 hogsheads in
1844, and 310 hogsheads during the bumper crop of 1853. Production
furthermore experienced a comparable expansion as the number of

acres cultivated per hand rose from approximately 2 acres in 1802 to 3.5 in 1822. This figure climbed to 5 acres by the latter years of the ante-bellum era and, on the largest estates, planters confidently expected their slaves to cultivate 6.6 acres of sugar per hand.[15] While man–land ratios rose, so did individual productivity as estate managers measured appreciable increases in plantation efficiency from the 1830s to the Civil War. In 1831, efficient sugar masters cultivated and manufactured ap-proximately 2.5 hogsheads per slave or 4 per plantation worker.[16] Six-teen years later, planter Valcour Aime estimated that the average yield of sugar per hand in the late 1840s varied between 5 and 8 hogsheads of sugar. Edward Forstall concurred, noting that on favourably managed estates, sugar producers could manufacture 7 hogsheads of sugar per slave whilst their competitors in Cuba struggled to cultivate 5 hogsheads per hand.[17]

Despite these indices of economic progress, the plantation elite en-countered a series of overlapping dilemmas that imposed rigid labour and production criteria upon slaves and planters alike. In resolving these difficulties, the sugar masters fused slavery and plantation capitalism and underscored the immediate association between chattel bondage and modernization in the cane country. Of principal concern to Loui-siana's farming community was the region's sporadically icy climate that delimited the agricultural calendar and threatened destructive frost damage. Following an extensive eight-month growing season during which the slaves tended the crop, planters entered the annual harvest in a frenetic rush to cut, strip and grind the cane before the first killing frosts descended in early December.[18] While frost damage, followed swiftly by a warming front, irreversibly diminished the plant's commercial value, estate managers encountered additional ecological pressures as they proved understandably reluctant to order the harvest while the sucrose content swiftly increased in the growing canes. Botan-ical obstacles further impelled plantation urgency, for once the cane was cut, crop deterioration quickly advanced to the detriment of the su-crose-rich juice. Under these climatically and agronomically trying con-ditions, sugar planters embarked upon a six-week long grinding season where speed and labour stability were held at a premium. Telescoping the experience of the sugar masters illustrates that in resolving these production difficulties, Louisiana's slaveholding elite modernized their estates while concurrently yielding to the bondspeoples' desire for greater personal autonomy and financial independence. Reweaving the paternalist web, masters and slaves fashioned a mutual set of recip-rocal obligations that accommodated the machine age, ensured labour stability and transformed the dynamics of agro-industrial slavery in the sugar country.

Beyond the crop and climate specific difficulties of sugar production in Louisiana, domestic and global economic forces stimulated the planters to transform the manufacturing stage of their industry from its reliance on primitive horse-drawn sugar mills to costly steam-powered equipment that increased both the scale and scope of industrial sugar production.[19] As Peter Coclanis observes, the key to economic growth lies in rising aggregate demand and the internal capacity of a regional economy to supply that market.[20] In antebellum America, the growth of personal income, combined with declining real and relative costs of sugar, profoundly altered the position of sucrose within the US diet.[21] Consumer demand, in turn, rose keenly from 161 million pounds in 1837 to almost 900 million pounds of sugar in 1854.[22] Per capita consumption paralleled broader national developments as sugar emerged as a widely purchased and income-elastic condiment that found a vigorous market niche as antebellum wages gradually rose. In 1831, for instance, every American consumed 13 pounds of sugar every year, yet by mid-century, US consumption multiplied three- fold as per capita consumption surpassed 30 pounds of sugar annually.[23] With a burgeoning market available for those who sought to tap the nation's savoury appetite, Louisiana planters intensified cultivation, enlarged production facilities, and modernized their grinding equipment to maximize yields. Responding to shifting domestic demand, the sugar planting elite increased production ten-fold and, by 1853, Louisiana produced a quarter of the world's sugar. Enthusiastically fanning re-gional pride, Representative Miles Taylor announced that such progress 'is without parallel in the United States, or indeed in the world in any branch of industry'.[24] While Taylor's exhortations carried the familiar ring of antebellum boosterism, agrarian commentators lauded the plan-tation elite as expanding yields matched Louisiana's improved status as the nation's principal sugar supplier.

Technological innovation and economic evolution emerged at the vanguard of a commercial transformation that guaranteed regional pri-macy in the prosperous market for crystalline sucrose. The rapid intro-duction of steam-powered technology further boosted the productive capacity of the mills and ensured that planters could expand cultiva-tion, confident that their machinery would grind the crop before the first hard freeze struck. With 80 per cent of the sugar estates utilizing steam power by 1860, cane farmers resolved the combined exigencies of speed and productivity while concurrently minimizing the risk of crop deterioration and cane oxidization. Breaking the technological bottle-neck to advanced production and unlocking the potential for econ-omies of scale and speed, steam power resolved diverse climate and crop specific production problems while equipping the Louisiana sugar masters with superior facilities to those utilized in the Caribbean. The urgency to compete with foreign competition appears contradictory given federal protection of domestic sugar, but throughout the antebel-lum era, Louisianans vied for control of the US sugar market against a technologically inferior yet agriculturally superior industry in the West Indies. Cuban sugar, in particular, challenged Louisiana's privileged position within the domestic market, for although the Washington administration retained a high tariff upon refined sugar, Cuban planters exported raw and unprocessed sugar that refiners subsequently purified in the North-east for domestic consumption. Trapped within a limited geographic area with scarce room for significant expansion, the Louisi-ana sugar lords had little choice other than to intensify their operations and bring science to the art of agronomy, and the tools of capitalist industrialization to antebellum labour management.

While regional and international pressures account for the modern-ization of the Louisiana sugar industry, the introduction of novel tech-nology modified work patterns and recast the matrix of entrepreneurial management in the sugar country. As William Dusinberre, Shearer Davis Bowman, Carville Earle and others have suggested, slavery and entre-preneurial capitalism advanced in tandem as planters fashioned agricul-tural enterprises that approached the organizational complexity of modern factories.[25] To this extent the sugar masters proved similarly entrepreneurial, yet, as Eugene Genovese suggests, their truncated notions of modernization encompassed diverse concepts emblematic of traditionalism: slavery, honour, an aversion to centralized authority, and profound misgivings over the democratic countenance of liberal capitalism.[26] In Louisiana, however, the slaveholders resolved this para-dox by advocating qualitative economic growth and by synthesizing aspects of slave and wage labour to develop productive work crews for the grinding season. Interlacing the disparate and frequently discordant threads of the master–slave relationship, the sugar masters proved sin-gularly effective in merging their pre-modern labour system into a commercial network of plantation economies.

Progress in the nineteenth-century sugar country fused colossal in-vestment in land, labour and machinery. To ensure maximum product-ivity, the labour lords financed a tri-partite division of capital where investment in the primary factors of production dwarfed those of the cotton South.[27] Funnelling assets into a capitalized labour system that transformed the productive capacity of the Louisiana swamps, the sugar masters sponsored a technological revolution which bore profitable fruit in higher yields and enhanced sugar quality. Charles Fleischmann, for instance, concluded before the US Commissioner of Patents that 'there is no sugar growing country, where all the modern improvements have been more fairly tested in Louisiana'. Attributing their success to 'enterprise and high intelligence', Fleischmann, like other contemporary agronomists, warmly praised the sugar masters for 'fulfilling all the conditions... for obtaining a pure and perfect crystalline sugar'.[28] Effusive in commendation but representative in their findings, editorialists and visiting commentators endorsed Louisiana's technical primacy, noting that the state appeared 'far superior to most sugar growing regions... in the intelligence and skill manifested in both the cultivation and manufacturing of sugar'.[29] Suitably equipped with the latest steam-powered production facilities, one correspondent concluded that the planter 'will reap his harvest in half the time, and with half the labour and expense' than he had previously achieved with primitive agronomy and animal-powered mills.[30] Benefiting from time- and labour-saving techniques, steam power emerged as a technical panacea to the sugar planters' harvest difficulties and as an integral means for boosting production standards. Those planters who sought to tap the growing demand for white sugar, and circumvent refining costs, additionally invested in costly vacuum pans and clarification facilities that produced 'large and brilliant crystals... [of] any size required by the caprice of the customer'.[31] While the Rillieux apparatus and allied vacuum evaporators proved too expensive for most planters, over 65 prominent sugar cultivators pioneered these new technologies and produced, on average, 475 hogsheads of crystalline and snowy sugar that Princeton chemist R. S. McCulloh praised as 'equal to those of the best double-refined sugar of our northern refineries'.[32] Frederick Olmsted echoed Professor McCulloh's enthusiastic endorsement, applauding the sugar planters as 'among the most intelligent, enterprising, and wealthy men of business in the United States'.[33]

While the introduction of expensive steam-powered machinery in the 1840s dramatically increased the pace, capacity and cane-crushing efficiency of the sugar mills, escalating costs forced the smaller and less competitive out of the burgeoning sugar industry.[34] Those who remained, however, found that steam power established an exacting mechanical rhythm that transformed labour relations on the plantations. Frequently equipped with constantly moving conveyor belts that slaves fed with a constant supply of cane, the late antebellum sugar estate established an early form of assembly line production where the industrial sugar mill imposed an inflexible, persistent and unforgiving labour discipline on the slaves. Striving towards operational efficiency and productivity maximization, the assembly line inaugurated new management practices where each operative, Thorstein Veblen notes, keeps 'pace with the machine process...and adapts his movements with mechanical accuracy to its requirements'.[35] In their quest to establish a disciplined work force that would labour at the measured cadence of the steam age, overseers and owners sub-divided their labourers' tasks, instituted systematized shift work and imposed the regimented order of the mechanical clock. Partisan in both content and readership, the *Planter's Banner* echoed the view that regional economic success rested upon 'good management on the improved principle adopted in Louisiana'.[36] Correspondent Edward Forstall similarly observed that on favourably managed estates where the slaves' tasks 'are made to harmonise so as to assure rapidity and constant working', planters virtually doubled their production of sugar.[37] In the wake of the Civil War, Louisiana's regimented plantation order received further attention when Andrew McCollam joined fellow sugar master James L. Bowman on a tour of Brazilian sugar lands near Rio de Janeiro. Examining the lands and cane operations with the intention of commercially speculating in pro-slave Brazil, McCollam's shrewd business eye quickly focused on the deficiencies of Brazilian land and slave management. After a visit to Julian Rebeiro de Castro's plantation, McCollam noted in his travel diary that 'everything is going to decay', but significantly added that he could 'do more work with the same number of hands than was being done' on his Brazilian competitor's estate.[38]

Relying on methodical and structured order, the sugar masters enforced a work discipline and managerial style that visitors to the sugar country frequently described as militaristic in organization. Timothy Flint observed the imposition of formalized work rules, noting that 'there is in a large plantation as much precision in the rules, as much exactness in the times of going to labour, as in a garrison under military discipline or in a ship of war'. Extending his comment further, Flint recorded that systems dictated plantation management and that 'there is no pulling down to-day the scheme of yesterday, and the whole amount of force is directed by the teaching of experience to the best result'.[39] Moses Liddell mirrored these observations when he counselled his son that sugar planting requires 'energy, activity, and ingeniousness'. Success, Liddell continued, rests on 'strength and capital [combined] with remarkable energy and unbounded perseverance to succeed well'. Such qualities Liddell's son-in-law, John Hampden Randolph, surely possessed in great quantities, but even the master of the giant Nottoway Plantation realized that the true key to prosperity in the sugar bowl lay with 'perseverance' and above all 'good management'.[40] Former slave Charles Stewart mused on the African-American position when he recalled that his master 'wouldn't stand for no foolin' neither... it was jes' stiddy management'.[41]

Combining elements of factory and farm on one agro-industrial site, the sugar masters methodically routinized labour and transformed the organizational structure of the plantation to optimize productivity, economies of scale and team interdependence. During the grinding season, the exigencies of sugar production further impelled managerial reform as planters instituted drilled inter and intra-dependent gang work that supplied the voracious demand of the mechanized sugar mill from morning to night. Consolidating and synchronizing diverse plantation functions, estate managers reconfigured work patterns and managerial practices to weave unfree labour into a fabric of capitalist productivity. As Robert Fogel, Stanley Engerman and others have suggested, gang labour emerged as an unmerciful though efficient structure to provide the slaveholding elite with disciplined teams adept at intense work.[42] Through a stringent division of labour, planters could methodically routinize and specialize work while maintaining strict supervision of their slaves as they toiled beneath the overseer's eye in the open field. Louisiana's sugar masters adapted this model and created interdependent teams that would swiftly plant the crop in the new year and efficiently harvest the canes come November or December. The combination of these agricultural requirements and the pressures of mechanized sugar production necessitated a labour regime that would advance over the cane fields with military regulation and precision. During the frenetic harvest season, planters exploited potential economies of scale by relying on interdependent gang work and assembly line production techniques. As the lead hand in a gang of 50 to 100 slaves, Solomon Northup graphically described the interdependence of teamwork and the division of labour among the cane-cutters on Bayou Boeuf. Flanked on either side, the lead hand advanced slightly ahead of his compatriots, who formed the base of a triangle; all three worked wholly in unison and at the pace of their squad leader. Progressing with their razor-sharp knives, the lead hand sheared the cane from the ground, stripped the stalk of its flags, sliced off the top and placed it behind him. Slightly behind their pacesetter, the two other cane-cutters followed suit and laid their stripped canes upon the first, so that the young slave who followed the squad could gather up the bundle and place it in the cart that followed him. Once filled, the cart left for the sugarhouse, though it was quickly replaced by a second wagon, ensuring that the process of cutting, stripping, collecting and loading the cane rarely ceased or slowed.[43] Throughout the grinding season this brutal, yet efficient, field labour regime continued to supply the insatiable demand of the sugar mill from dawn to dusk.

Operating as the first stage in the assembly line production of sugar, the cane-cutters took their place in the vanguard of a plantation order characterized by labour-saving techniques and 'production-raising' methods. On leading estates, this included the replacement of mule trains by railroads and human brawn by steam power. At Madewood Plantation, Thomas Pugh brought the freshly-cut cane to the mill on a small iron railroad which arrived at sugarhouse door before dropping its load on to the cane carrier. Conveyor belts subsequently transported the cane shoots to the mill for grinding. Keen to utilize the crushed canes as a cheap and alternative fuel supply, Pugh collected the spent canes (or bagasse) as they fell from the mill. Once dry, the bagasse was recycled and used to fire the steam engines. The cane juice, editorialist Solon Robinson observed, 'runs to the vats . . . and thence to the kettles; thence to the coolers, and from there the sugar is carried upon railroad cars along lines of rails between the rows of hogsheads to the farther end of the building'.[44] Within the mill house and plantation complex, novel management practices additionally extended to sub-dividing production into distinct units while simultaneously integrating grinding operations through modern technology. Although the cane estates never evolved into complex modern multidepartment corporations that were both vertically and horizontally integrated, the presence of separate though interdependent branches of production suggests that the antebellum sugar mill stood within a transitional phase of industrial and organizational development that foreshadowed the corporate model of mass production.

While the introduction of advanced machinery imposed the regimented order of the industrial age, technology impelled the further sub-division of labour and established novel patterns of work organization. Compelling their labourers to toil at the methodical pace of the steam engine, sugar planters established that primitive assembly line management guaranteed optimal productivity and the exploitation of economies of speed in the mill house. Cognizant that speed defined the sugar harvest, planters categorized labour, allocated tasks, and defined work patterns to make sure that crew productivity eclipsed 'the sum of the marginal products' of the individual team members.[45] After a visit to the sugar country, New Orleans physician Dr Samuel Cartwright observed that 'all of the labourers . . . are divided into two portions – one to labour in the field and to supply the mill house with cane; the other to manufacture the juice . . . into molasses and sugar'.[46] On Robert Ruffin Barrow's Residence Plantation, overseer Ephraim Knowlton established a classification list that defined the occupational division of labour for the 1857 grinding season. Listing each slave's name below his or her expected task, Knowlton subdivided his labour force into a number of interdependent teams that worked on all tasks from cooking a communal meal to operating the diverse functions of the industrialized sugar mill.[47] Anxious to fit the pace of work to the unbending regimen of the steam age, planters established regular watches which guaranteed that comparatively fresh hands were readily available to staff the machines and to conduct the complex art of sugar making. Cycling slave workers through the cane shed at different points during the day and night, overseers ensured constant sugar production and resolved the imperative to maintain the mills turning. John Hampden Randolph of Nottoway Plantation employed these managerial strategies when he instituted a system of watches for the 1857 grinding season. Dividing his slave force according to task and to watch, Randolph established a revolving labour system where he divided the working day and night into three watches (approximately eight hours long), of which most slaves worked two. Big Alfred, for instance, began his working day as a cart loader who followed the cane cutters through the fields. Presumably, Big Alfred took a rest through the late afternoon and evening, until he entered the mill house in the early morning hours where he stood guard as the steam engine fireman on the second watch. Weary from his night's labour, where he controlled the fire beneath the sugar kettles, Big Alfred returned to the fields as a cart loader with the first morning light.[48] Brutally punishing for the bondsman, this labour regime hinged upon the imposition of a clock-ordered discipline where the working day was punctuated by formalized work rules and a labour regime that marched to the beat of the ticking clock.

Nineteenth-century industrialists shared a commitment to a clock-ordered labour regime where plant managers established iron-clad factory schedules that increasingly focused on optimizing work force productivity through the drill and punctuality of industrial capitalism. With machinery synchronized to operate as part of a larger calibrated system, the sugar masters punished tardiness and codified timed discipline at the work place. Imbibing the precepts of scientific management from a myriad of agricultural publications, planters seemingly fathomed the value of judicious slave management and the centrality of time-saving techniques. In a syndicated article, released at least six times between 1850 and 1855, one planter counselled fellow agrarians to employ a central slave cook to prepare all meals for the bondspeople. Prudent 'time-conscious' management of this sort would yield several hours of saved labour time that the planter could expropriate for fieldwork.[49] With broad dissemination, this advice appealed to the sugar masters who, on most plantations during the grinding season, selected one or two cooks to prepare meals for all. Estimating that each slave family probably required one hour to cook and eat their meal, planters realized that by pooling resources during the harvest, a significant saving in labour time might be achievable. On Oaklands Plantation, Samuel McCutchon delegated three rather elderly and sick women to cook for all hands in 1859. Noting that his cooks included Milly, a perennial rheumatic, 58-year-old physically handicapped Beersheba and asthma-suffering Betsey, McCutchon's kitchen staff prepared meals for 107 working adult hands on his Plaquemine Parish estate.[50] By organizing a refectory meal service, McCutchon expropriated the precious working time of healthy strong adults by centralizing food preparation. James P. Bowman similarly consolidated cooking operations prior to the rolling season at Frogmoor Plantation. After discharging his daily duties, Bowman's overseer, George Woodruff, wrote his plantation journal in a copy of Thomas Affleck's *Sugar Plantation Record and Account Book*. Published primarily for the improving planter, Affleck's register advised overseers to provide plenty of 'wholesome well cooked food... supplied at regular hours'. Evidently following this stricture, Woodruff commenced with centralized cooking on Monday 26 October 1857, exactly one day before the start of the grinding season.[51] Clearly understanding the potential gain in time by centralizing operations, Bowman underscored his commitment 'to learn as much of planting as possible... [so] that here after I may better understand management and all unnecessary mistakes'.[52] While thrifty time management cruelly optimized labour, sugar planters further sub-divided tasks and chimed timed and daily instructions to their slaves. On William Minor's plantations, overseers received strict orders to employ bells and established time signals in regimenting the slaves' day.[53] In exhorting plantation profitability, Minor counselled fellow land and labour elites that 'labour must be directed with an intelligent eye' and that agrarian success rested on 'the proper adaptation of the means to the end'.[54]

Although these managerial innovations paralleled those of the industrializing north, the sugar masters retained an ardent commitment to the omnipresent lash and archaic methods of antebellum labour discipline. Hunton Love, a former slave driver on Bayou Lafourche, revealed the axiomatic relationship between force, discipline and economic success when he recalled: 'I had to whip 'em, I had to show 'em I was boss, or the plantation would be wrecked'.[55] Upon visiting Andre Roman's sugar estate in Ascension Parish, William Howard Russell similarly underscored the symbiosis of force and proficient slave supervision when he remarked: 'the anxieties attending the cultivation of sugar are great and so much depends upon the judicious employment of labour, it is scarcely possible to exaggerate the importance of experience in directing it, and of the power to insist on its application'.[56] Thomas Hamilton expounded upon the prevalence of repression and intimidation in the slaveholders' armoury of control when he observed that during the grinding season 'the fatigue is so great that nothing but the severest application of the lash can stimulate the human frame to endure it'.[57] As a slave driver on Bayou Salle, Solomon Northup clarified the centrality of the lash and rigorous supervision in facilitating sugar production. Describing the frenetic pace of the harvest, Northup remembered 'the whip was given to me with directions to use it upon anyone who was caught standing idle. If I failed to the letter, there was another one for my own back.' In the hot and sticky conditions of the industrializing sugar mill, indolence and loafing evidently received swift punishment as Northup's duties extended beyond maintaining work discipline to additionally calling on and off 'the different gangs at the proper time'.[58] Confident that they possessed the ultimate inducement for hard work, planters and overseers consequently retained and frequently exercised the threat of physical coercion as a primitive, ancient and unmerciful means to compel break-neck speed in the fields and mill house. Ceceil George eloquently articulated the slaves' memory when she pointedly called south Louisiana 'de mos' wicked country God's son ever died for', while former bondsman Jacob Stroyer bitterly recalled that African-Americans considered the region 'a place of slaughter'.[59]

Spanning the gap between antiquated and modern, the late antebellum sugar estate exhibited an internal duality as entrepreneurial economic progress was tempered by a coerced labour system that evidently practised non-capitalist relations of production. Few planters, however, found this discrepancy insurmountable, and neither did they seriously question the intercompatibility of slavery, modernization, and labour stability. Indeed, by pursuing prudent slave management and a sagacious division of labour, planters confidently asserted that 'free labour cannot compete, in the manufacture of sugar, with better organised slave labour'.[60] These sentiments appear valid, as when alternative labourers entered the labour market, the sugar masters soon found them wanting for the specific crop and labour requirements of the sugar country. Recalling the story of one planter who dispensed with slave labour in favour of Irish and German emigrants, Sir Charles Lyell mused on the catastrophic labour crisis the planter faced when his workers struck for double pay in the midst of the harvest season. Gravely taking note, Lyell recorded that with neither additional labourers or slaves to hand, the planter lost his crop, valued at $10 000.[61] With high turnover costs and a thin labour market, sugar planters entrenched, calibrated the slave system to meet their needs, and rented additional workers to provide further stability during the grinding season.

   Despite decades of vigorous scholarship, the compatibility of slavery and modernization provokes constructive debate and prompts historiographic revision. The dominant Genovesean paradigm suggests that slaves rejected the bourgeois work ethic, and resisted the method and structure of the industrial revolution by clinging to a pre-modern work order where a traditional mentality prevailed.[62] More recently, Charles Dew highlighted the conservative effect of slavery on economic innovation in the Chesapeake iron industry, while Mark Smith analysed the linkages between pre-industrial slave culture and the introduction of clock-ordered discipline.[63] These fruitful approaches facilitate an examination on the interconnectivity of slave agency and the emergence of plantation capitalism in the sugar country. Theoretically, the exigencies of sugar cultivation in Louisiana placed the field hand and mill house operative in a potentially unparalleled position of power. As evidenced from Charles Lyell's account, planters could not afford labour instability, sabotage or production slow-downs during the grinding season. Indeed, by the 1840s many sugar planters had specifically introduced technical and managerial innovations to raise efficiency and increase production speed. The success of these programmes, however, rested on the compliance and complicity of the slave gangs who utilized their seminal position in sugar production to manipulate the master–slave relationship and generate further autonomy and signal prerogatives from the masters. Fully cognizant that the bondspeople represented the core of prosperity and wealth formation, the sugar masters acquiesced to slave demands but, in turn, they fashioned a mutual overwork system that proved financially profitable to both parties.[64] Reweaving the paternalist web, slaves and masters wrought a labour system that accommodated the bondspeoples' desires for greater autonomy while additionally providing the slaveholders with the labour stability they sought. Adopting novel modes of resistance in the new technologies of the modernizing sugar industry, Louisiana slaves adapted to mechanization: not because they had imbibed the Protestant work ethic and become 'metaphorical clock punchers' as Fogel suggests, but rather because the machine and steam age recast labour relations and provided the slaves with new avenues of economic and social space.[65]

Addressing the stark contradiction of the slaves' apparent willingness to work long hours in exhausting conditions, Frederick Law Olmsted proffered an explanation for this paradox when he observed that the slaves 'are better paid, they have better and more varied food and more stimulants than usual'.[66] While Olmsted misjudged the power of the whip, he accurately portrayed the central role of incentives in antebellum slave management. Beyond payment to skilled slaves, Christmas bonuses, rewards for rapid work, post- and pre-harvest celebrations, and improved accommodation, slaves and slaveholders established overwork systems whereby bondspeople received financial remuneration for chopping wood, growing corn, or trading moss, poultry and livestock.[67] As Dylan Penningroth, Roderick McDonald and others have shown, slaves eagerly embraced the overwork system and carved out a meaningful orbit of self- and communal identity through the trading of diverse goods. Through independent production, slaves found an avenue for autonomy through which the market emerged as an erratic and conflicted space where wage-earning slaves grasped the essence of liberty while, paradoxically, affirming the sordid economic logic of chattel bondage. In Louisiana's sugar country, slaves swiftly deemed it a customary right to receive payment for their wood and corn just prior to the grinding season, and on most plantations, the slaves entered harvest with their demand for disbursable income at least partially satiated and their fragmentary vision of independence tantalizingly affirmed through the sale of their labour for pecuniary advantage.[68]

Although overwork meshed planter and slave into a grid of mutual duties and obligations, these market relations proved mutually advantageous, for while slaves could sell the product of their labour and materially enrich their lives with goods purchased from the plantation commissary, the slaves' internal economy also fortified the institution of slavery. Not only did overwork seemingly hasten labour stability, but it ensured that the slaves produced key plantation commodities in their own time beyond the margins of the working day. By commodifying labour and purchasing wood or diverse commodities that bondspeople cut or cultivated during the night and on Sundays, planters could wring out the entire 'surplus-value' or profit from the slave.[69] A fine line evidently existed in encouraging slaves' market activities, but by exchanging commodities for credit at the plantation store, slaveholders circumscribed the availability of specie, minimized the potential for interaction with free labour and made sure that the fruit of the slaves' overwork seldom exited the confines of the plantation world.

The swift rise of steam power as the primary energy source for the sugar country guaranteed that each estate required at least three to four cords of wood to produce one hogshead of steam milled sugar. Conscious of the time- and labour-consuming nature of timber collection and the voracious appetite of the steam engine for fuel, the sugar masters increasingly relied on the slaves to cut and haul cordage from the backswamp at the cessation of the regular working day. Paying slaves 50 cents a cord to conduct this laborious work in their own time and not in his, a planter could assuage the slaves' pressure for remuneration while simultaneously saving hundreds of hours for alternative duties.[70]

Standing on the hurricane deck of a Mississippi steam-boat as it passed through the heart of the sugar country in 1838, Harriet Martineau observed that groups of slaves continued to chop wood under moonlight and 'toil along the shore line' even after dusk had turned to nightfall.[71] On the left bank of the river, as Martineau steamed downstream, lay Samuel Fagot's Constancia Plantation, an estate where both master and slave took full advantage of overwork. In preparation for the 1859 harvest, slaves collected and chopped 2018 cords of wood in their own time, for which they earned $1077. Aware that he could rely on his slaves' wood to grind the 435 hogsheads that the estate yielded in 1859, Fagot's 130 slaves proved capable woodsmen who produced not only fire wood but additionally over 1300 hewn boards that Fagot hoped to use as sheeting material. Crediting his slaves at the plantation commissary, Fagot sufficed his cordage requirements for the grinding season while forging an economic link that bound the slave's material wellbeing to the insatiable demand of the mechanized sugar mill.[72] The same calculating regard for time and profit shaped overwork payments for corn where planters such as Benjamin Tureaud paid his bondspeople to cultivate enough grain in the evenings to meet the plantation's annual dietary requirements. In 1858 alone, Tureaud expended over $1500 in remunerating slaves for a cereal crop that guaranteed plantation self-sufficiency and secured additional labour time for other tasks.[73] Further, by crediting his slaves just days prior to the rolling season,

Tureaud seemingly placated his bondspeople as they entered the most exacting period of the year.

Perennially calculating, John Hampden Randolph additionally fused plantation performance with Christmas bonuses to encourage maximum slave productivity. At Forest Home, Randolph paid the slaves 40 cents a hogshead or $175 as a Christmas bonus in December 1851. One year later, he increased his bonus by $25 and in January 1854, Randolph rewarded his slaves with $300, a significant increase to mark the signal success of the new vacuum pans that produced 680 hogsheads at Forest Home.[74] Randolph's slaves, who controlled the expensive and complex pans with considerable aplomb, found mechanization financially advantageous as each adult slave increased his annual bonus and gained approximately $5 by accepting the new machinery. By scaling the size of the Christmas rewards to the volume of the crop, Randolph quite probably triggered communal pressure in the slave quarters against those who loitered in the sugarhouse. Through overwork and bonuses, the slaveholders surely conceded to their bondsmen's desires for disbursable income, yet by shaping the system to maximize productivity, the slaveholders subtly turned the dynamics of the master–slave relationship to their own profit. Ghastly though it was, slavery had been effectively grafted on to plantation capitalism in the sugar country.

Residing on rich sugar land, William Hamilton wrote to his father expressing the quintessential values of the antebellum sugar master. 'I am a lover of order and system', Hamilton declared, 'to have a certain way of doing everything and a regular time for doing everything'.[75] Like Hamilton, those who controlled the sugar plantations of south Louisiana valued industry, discipline and diligence in the management of their estates. Finding little incongruity between their pre-capitalist labour system and the pressures of a capitalist economy, the sugar masters modernized their immense agricultural enterprises while simultaneously embracing both the modern and pre-modern impulses of southern society. In the cultivation and marketing of sugar on an agro-industrial scale, the sugar masters stood at the vanguard of a booming industry where the dynamics of economic growth lay in the synchronization of agriculture, industry and entrepreneurialism, but above all with the institution of racial slavery.

* The author and editors wish to thank Frank Cass for their permission to publish this essay, an earlier, slightly modified version of which was published as "Slavery and Plantation Capitalism in Louisiana's Sugar Country," in *American Nineteenth Century History* 1:3. (Autumn 2000), 1–27.

Notes

1   W. H. Russell, *My Diary North and South* (New York, 1954), p. 147.
2   J. Robertson, *A Few Months in America* (London, 1855), 90; *De Bow's Review* 15 (December 1853), p. 648.
3   F. L. Olmsted, *Journey in the Seaboard Slave States* (New York, 1904), p. 320.
4   *De Bow's Review* 15 (December 1853), pp. 647–8.
5   M. M. Smith, *Debating Slavery: Economy and Society in the Antebellum South* (Cambridge, 1998), p. 93.
6   E. D. Genovese, *The Slaveholder's Dilemma: Freedom and Progress in Southern Conservative Thought, 1820–1860* (Columbia, SC, 1992); J. Oakes, *Slavery and Freedom: An Interpretation of the Old South* (New York, 1990).
7   *De Bow's Review* 1 (February 1846), p. 166.
8   *Planter's Banner* (Franklin), 16 March 1848.
9   B. Duvallon, *Travels in Louisiana* (New York, 1806), p. 129.
10 *De Bow's Review* 1 (January 1846), pp. 55–6.
11 P. A. Champomier, *Statement of the Sugar Crop made in Louisiana in 1845–1846* (New Orleans, LA, 1846), p. 35; *Statement in 1849–1850*, p. 51; *Statement in 1859–1860*, p. 39.
12 R. Follett, 'The Sugar Masters: slavery, economic development, and modernization on Louisiana sugar plantations, 1820–1860', PhD dissertation, Louisiana State University, 1997, pp. 264–314.
13 J. Stirling, *Letters from the Slave States* (London, 1857), p. 124; T. Nutall, *A Journey of Travels into the Arkansa Territory* (Philadelphia, PA, 1821), p. 239.
14 R. A. McDonald, *The Economy and Material Culture of Slaves: Goods and Chattels on the Sugar Plantations of Jamaica and Louisiana* (Baton Rouge, LA, 1992), p. 3.
15 L. C. Gray, *History of Agriculture in the Southern United States to 1860*, 2 vols (Washington, DC, 1933), II: pp. 750–1; Follett, 'Sugar Masters', p. 222.
16 J. S. Johnston, *Letter of Mr. Johnston of Louisiana* (Washington, DC, 1831), p. 8.
17 *De Bow's Review* 4 (November 1847), pp. 385–6; E. J. Forstall, *Agricultural Productions of Louisiana* (New Orleans, LA, 1845), p. 6.
18 F. B. Kniffen, *Louisiana: its Land and People* (Baton Rouge, 1968), p. 21; W. J. Evans, *The Sugar Planter's Manual* (Philadelphia, PA, 1848).
19 Of 725 sugar estates in 1830, 100 possessed steam engines. By 1841, steam powered 361of 668 plantations and by 1850, steam engines operated in over 900 plantations. Johnston, *Letter*, p. 9; Forstall, *Agricultural Productions*, p. 4; Champomier, *Statement in 1850–51*, p. 43; Champomier, *Statement in 1860–61*, p. 39.
20 P. A. Coclanis, *The Shadow of a Dream: Economic Life and Death in the South Carolina Low Country, 1670–1920* (New York, 1989), ch. 3.
21 R. A. Margo, 'Wages and prices during the antebellum period', in R. E. Gallman and J. J. Wallis (eds), *American Economic Growth and Standards of Living before the Civil War,* (Chicago, IL, 1992), pp. 173–210; Follett, 'Sugar Masters,' pp. 133–5; A.H Cole, *Wholesale Commodity Prices in the United States, 1700–1861* (Cambridge, MA, 1938), pp. 192–357.

22 *Hunt's Merchant Magazine* 27 (December 1852), p. 681; US Patent Office, *Annual Report of the Commissioner of Patents for the Year 1858* (Washington, DC, 1859), p. 233.

23 *Hunt's Merchant Magazine* 39 (November 1858), p. 550; *Farmer's Cabinet and American Herd Book* 2 (October 1837), p. 78; *Journal of Agriculture* 1 (December 1845), p. 281.

24 *De Bow's Review* 22 (April 1857), p. 435.

25 W. Dusinberre, *Them Dark Days: Slavery in the American Rice Swamps* (New York, 1996); C. Earle, 'The Price of Precocity: Technical Choice and Ecological Constraints in the Cotton South, 1840–1890', *Agricultural History* 66 (Summer 1988), pp. 25–60; S. D. Bowman, *Masters and Lords: Mid-19th-Century U. S. Planters and Prussian Junkers* (New York, 1993).

26 Genovese, *Slaveholder's Dilemma*, especially pp. 1–45.

27 Follett, 'Sugar Masters', ch. 4.

28 C. L. Fleischmann, 'Report on the sugar cane and its culture', US Patent Office, *Annual Report of the Commissioner of Patents for the Year 1848* (Washington, DC, 1849), p. 275.

29 *De Bow's Review* 15 (December 1853), p. 648; *De Bow's Review* 1 (February 1846), p. 166.

30 *Baton Rouge Gazette*, 2 December 1843.

31 J. D. B. De Bow, *The Industrial Resources of the Southern and Western Estates*, 3 vols (New Orleans, LA, 1853), II: p. 206.

32 M. Schmitz, 'The economic analysis of antebellum sugar plantations in Louisiana', PhD dissertation, University of North Carolina, 1974, p. 35; *De Bow's Review* 5 (March 1848), p. 286; 29th Congress, 2nd Session – Senate Doc. No. 209, 'Investigations in Relation to Cane Sugar' (Washington, DC, 1847), p. 121.

33 Olmsted, *Journey in the Seaboard Slave States*, pp. 671–2.

34 Follett, 'Sugar Masters', pp. 90–109.

35 T. Veblen, *The Instinct of Workmanship* (New York, 1914), pp. 306–7.

36 *Planter's Banner* (Franklin), 5 January 1854.

37 Forstall, *Agricultural Productions*, p. 21.

38 Vol. 1, Brazilian Diary of Andrew McCollam, 1866–1867, 13 July 1866, Andrew McCollam Papers, Southern Historical Collection, University of North Carolina Libraries, Chapel Hill, North Carolina (hereafter cited as UNC).

39 T. Flint, *The History and Geography of the Mississippi Valley*, 2 vols (Cincinnati, 1832), I: pp. 244–5.

40 Moses Liddell to John R. Liddell, 28 July 1845; Moses Liddell to John R. Liddell, 25 August 1845; John H. Randolph to John R. Liddell, 22 March 1846, Liddell (Moses, St. John R., and Family) Papers, Louisiana and Lower Mississippi Valley Collections, LSU Libraries, Louisiana State University, Baton Rouge, LA (herafter LLMVC).

41 C. Stewart, 'My Life as a Slave', *Harper's New Monthly Magazine* 69 (October 1884), p. 738.

42 R. W. Fogel, *Without Consent or Contract: The Rise and Fall of American Slavery* (New York, 1991), pp. 74–9.

43 S. Northup, *Twelve Years a Slave*, edited by S. Eakin and J. Logsdon (Baton Rouge, LA, 1968), pp. 160, 162.

44 H. A. Kellar (ed.), *Solon Robinson: Pioneer and Agriculturist* (Indianapolis, IN, 1936), p. 200.
45 J. Metzer, 'Rational management, modern business practices, and economies of scale in ante-bellum southern plantations', *Explorations in Economic History* 12 (April 1975), p. 134.
46 *De Bow's Review* 13 (December 1852), p. 598.
47 Residence Journal of R. R. Barrow, Thursday, December 3, 1857, Robert Ruffin Barrow Papers, UNC.
48 Slave List, 1857, Randolph (John H.) Papers, LLMVC.
49 'The Management of Negroes', in *Southern Cultivator* 8 (November 1850), pp. 162–4; *Southern Planter* 2 (February 1851), pp. 39–43; *De Bow's Review* 10 (March 1851), pp. 326–8; De Bow, *The Industrial Resources*, II: pp. 333–6; *De Bow's Review* 19 (September 1855), pp. 358–63; *Southern Cultivator* 13 (June 1855), pp. 171–4.
50 Oaklands Plantation Document 1859, McCutchon (Samuel D.) Papers, LLMVC.
51 Frogmoor Plantation Diary 1857, Turnbull–Bowman–Lyons Family Papers, LLMVC.
52 J. P. Bowman to Sarah Turnbull, 29 June 1856, Turnbull–Bowman–Lyons Family Papers, LLMVC.
53 'Rules and Regulations on Governing Southdown and Hollywood Plantations', Vol. 34 of 'Plantation Diary, 1861–1868', Minor (William J.) and Family Papers, LLMVC.
54 *Southern Planter* 12 (June 1852), p. 163.
55 Interview with Hunton Love (Date unknown), Works Project Administration (WPA) Ex-Slave Narratives, LLMVC.
56 Russell, *Diary*, p. 180.
57 J. S. Kendall, 'New Orleans' Peculiar Institution', *Louisiana Historical Quarterly* 23 (July 1940), p. 87.
58 Northup, *Twelve Years a Slave*, p. 148.
59 Interview with Ceceil George (15 February 1940), WPA Ex-Slave Narratives, LLMVC; J. Stroyer, *My Life in the South* (Salem, MA, 1885), pp. 42–3.
60 R. Russell, *North America its Agriculture and Climate* (Edinburgh, 1857), p. 249.
61 C. Lyell, *A Second Visit to the United States of North America*, 2 vols (New York, 1849), I: p. 127.
62 Genovese, *Roll, Jordan, Roll: The World the Slaves Made* (New York, 1974) pp. 286, 309, 312.
63 C. Dew, *Bond of Iron: Master and Slave at Buffalo Forge* (New York, 1994), p. 333; M. M. Smith, *Mastered by the Clock: Time, Slavery, and Freedom in the American South* (Chapel Hill, NC, 1997), ch. 5.
64 Nutall, *Journey of Travels*, p. 239.
65 Fogel, *Without Consent*, p. 162.
66 Olmsted, *Journey in the Seaboard Slave States*, p. 327.
67 Follett, 'Sugar Masters', pp. 391–439.
68 D. Penningroth, 'Slavery, freedom, and social claims to property among African-Americans in Liberty County, Georgia, 1850–1880', *Journal of American History* 84 (June 1997), pp. 405–35; McDonald, *Economy and Material Culture*, ch. 2.

69   Marx quoted in R. Ransom and R. Sutch, 'Capitalists without capital: the burden of slavery and the impact of emancipation', *Agricultural History* 62 (Summer 1988), p. 133.
70   Residence Journal of R. R. Barrow, Tuesday 15 September 1857; Sunday, 18 October 1857, Robert Ruffin Barrow Papers, UNC.
71   H. Martineau, *Retrospect of Western Travel*, 3 vols (London, 1838), II: p. 166.
72   Vol. 28, Plantation Journal, 1859–1872, Uncle Sam Plantation Papers, LLMVC.
73   Vol. 46, Plantation Ledger, 1858–1872, Tureaud (Benjamin) Papers, LLMVC.
74   Vol. 5, Expense Book, 1847–1853; Volume 6, Expense Book, 1853–1863, Randolph (John H.) Papers, LLMVC.
75   William B. Hamilton to William S. Hamilton, 27 September 1858, Hamilton (William S.) Papers, LLMVC.

5
Land-Based Modernization and the Culture of Landed Elites in the Nineteenth-Century Mezzogiorno

Marta Petrusewicz

Among the many stereotypes associated with Italy's Mezzogiorno is the eternally conservative character of its landed elites. The Southern land-owners are represented as absentee *latifondisti*, devoted to conspicuous consumption at the expense of productive investment, culturally hostile to associationism and other manifestations of civil society, selfish, feudal in their mentality, lifestyle and economic behaviour, ignorant of or indifferent to applied economic and agronomic sciences, and generally opposed to any change or improvement. In the best of cases, the Southern landowner is like Giuseppe Tomasi di Lampedusa's *The Leopard* (refined and sophisticated, but economically and entrepreneurially inept); in the worst, he is like Giovanni Verga's Mastro Don Gesualdo: greedy, exploitative and ignorant.

In this chapter I propose to argue, to the contrary, that in the first half of the nineteenth century the Neapolitan landed elites showed a great cultural and entrepreneurial liveliness, and an eagerness to respond to and to promote 'modernization'. They became concerned with their country's backwardness, and active in a search for possible remedies in a creative and essentially autonomous way.[1]

Europe's modernizing elites

Such a hypothesis will no longer surprise scholars of early nineteenth-century Europe. As many national and regional studies demonstrated, the period from the Congress of Vienna to the 1848 revolutions witnessed a formidable explosion of interest in the modernization of agriculture among the European landed elites. This interest was widespread, from Ireland to Russia, from the Balkans to Norway, and so intense as to verge on maniacal; in fact, historian Jerome Blum termed it 'agromania'.[2] Improving landowners competed to increase their outputs and worked to adopt new products and new technologies, to develop rural industries, to improve animal breeds, to introduce new crop rotations, and to seek credit to finance all these operations. They saw agriculture not only as fashionable, but as a moral and true basis of 'private and public happiness'. To modernize and rationalize it was a new social *raison d'être* of the landed elites.

In a way, it was a 'natural' choice for the landed classes. On the one hand, there were profits to be made from agriculture in post-Napoleonic Europe; rising population, advancing urbanization and industrialization, and improving means of transportation acted as stimuli to agricultural production. On the other hand, the post-Vienna climate was generally favourable to landed elites, who enjoyed political and social security they had not known for decades.

Something did change, however. The Congress of Vienna did not restore the landed elites' traditional political and judicial roles, making it more difficult for them to hide behind the barriers of legal privilege and cast exclusivism. If they wanted to take advantage of the opportunities opened and claim (or reclaim) a leading role in society, they had to do it in a 'modern' way, in a regime of free competition, and justify their domination with the possession of necessary qualifications such as economic competence, energy, entrepreneurial spirit, learning and mental openness. Throughout Europe, even the traditional landed elites took up the challenge and turned out to be rather well prepared for, and eager to undertake, the task of 'self-modernization'. In fact, much of recent historiography explains this intellectual and social preparedness as a 'continuation' of the eighteenth-century reform movement, generally favoured by landowners, which involved such fundamental questions as transformation of land tenure, peasant emancipation and the curtailing of feudal and church privileges.[3]

Landed elites in the Kingdom of the Two Sicilies

In the Kingdom of Two Sicilies, too, landed elites supported the reforms attempted in the late eighteenth century by the 'enlightened' Bourbons in finance and taxation, justice and the prison system, and relations with the Church. Many of them also favoured the operations of the Cassa Sacra, created after the 1783 earthquake in Calabria with the aim of carrying out a form of land reform that involved expropriating and redistributing the Church's wealth and curtailing the baronial privileges. There was, of course, a tension within the landed class itself between the old *feudatari* (fendal lords), and the new *galantuomini* of landed but not feudal origins. The main interest of the *galantuomini*, as Augusto Placanica had pointed out, was to acquire land, more land, and land free from feudal restrictions; one could say that feudalism was for them no more than an obstacle to the privatization and the accumulation of land.[4] But it was not all simply about economics. The landed class as a whole had undergone, during the Enlightenment, a cultural evolution that led it to move beyond the caste particularism and assume initiative and responsibility on a more general, national level. Writing in 1791, Eleonora Fonseca Pimentel equated this cultural development to the virtual emergence of a new nation (*quasi una nuova nazione*).

The decade of the French rule, 1806–15, brought to the fore the tensions between the old feudal aristocracy, who followed the royal family into the Sicilian exile, and the *galantuomini* who acquired new wealth in the form of disentailed and ecclesiastical land. But those tensions should not be overestimated; many old aristocrats made their peace with Joachim Murat's government, and many others protected their landed interest through intermediaries. With the 1815 Restoration, landed elites re-appeared as a more or less homogeneous class. Their economic confidence was strengthened by the experience of venturing into experimental and import-substituting cultures, which they had acquired during the Continental Blockade and continued in the postbellum price slump. On the other hand, their ideal commitment to the modernization of agriculture acquired further justification as the means leading to 'public happiness', almost a panacea, which would eradicate old pernicious diseases (especially malaria), transform the life of the peasantry, promote the 'growth of civility' and increase the global wealth of the nation.

Like those of other agrarian peripheries, the landed elite of the Kingdom of Two Sicilies was *the* elite, in terms of wealth, social influence, and cultural domination. It was not the noble origin that defined social hierarchies and the dominant system of values – in fact, the Napoleonic period brought into landownership a vast urban patriciate and *galantuomini* – but simply the centrality of land. As Paolo Macry has shown, even as late as the end of the nineteenth century, the dominant values remained those associated traditionally with land and landed elites.[5] The sporadic character, imprecision, and unreliability of statistics and of the cadastres (both the Bourbon and the Murattian) do not allow a numerical estimate of this class or its wealth. But the Kingdom was a rural country, and its economic and social universe was agricultural and agrarian. In 1861, when the first census of united Italy was compiled, more than 60 per cent of the Mezzogiorno's active population was employed directly in agriculture and in the production of raw materials, and a further 12 per cent, or almost a million people, worked in agriculture-related or processing industries. A vast majority of this rural universe comprised the peasants. But the peasant masses were not yet seen as possessing any culture at all: they were a *plebe*, 'just beginning their transformation into a *popolo*', and were, for the time being, desperately poor, illiterate, unhealthy and superstitious. Although there actually existed a core of shared agrarian values between the peasantry and the landowners, to which we shall return later, popular culture was not seen as a possible competitor to the hegemonic position of the elite.

What there was of the bourgeoisie of land and professions, on the other hand, deferred to the landed interest: in fact, as prosopographic research has shown, it belonged there, as the professions (especially the large number of lawyers) and the clergy recruited their members almost exclusively from the agrarian classes. The non-agricultural industrial and commercial sectors – of possibly less agrarian outlook – were very small and accounted, in 1861, for no more than 3 per cent of the active population of the former kingdom.

Even the cities were 'rural'. Among the population of the capital city of Naples, one of the largest in Europe, the landowning and leisure classes were overwhelming; their rural and urban real estate (in equal parts) accounted for almost 70 per cent of the city's wealth. The pattern of settlement, prevailing throughout the country, further favoured the hegemony of the landed elites. As Jane Schneider has shown, the Southerners did not live in small villages, like their contemporaries in Northern Italy, but in rural towns.[6] In 1861, only six *comuni* on the mainland counted less than 500 inhabitants (compared to almost 500 in the smaller Kingdom of Sardegna), while more than half of all the *comuni* (971 out of 1840) were rural towns with populations between 2000 and 8000 and a further 128 had populations between 8000 and 20 000. This peculiar rural–urban setting facilitated the consolidation of the landed class's domination: on the main streets and in the squares of these towns, they displayed the signs, and enforced the superiority, of their life-style, value system, social distinctions and attitudes. The rural town also offered endless occasions for the exercise of favouritism and patronage.

Finally, the levels and social distribution of literacy confirm the hegemonic cultural role of the landed elites. Seventy-nine per cent of the

1846 class of Southern military recruits were totally illiterate (83 per cent in Sicily), and a further 4 per cent could read but not write (of the same class in Piedmont 58 per cent could read and write). Elementary schools were scarce in the Kingdom of Two Sicilies, and their pupils relatively even scarcer; decrees mandating some elementary education had always remained a dead letter. But the picture changes when we get to the high school and university levels: *licei* and *ginnasi* were as widespread in the Southern large and medium-sized cities as they were in the North, and the number of students was comparable. In other words, Southern elites were as educated as their Northern correspondents, but, in their country, they were the only ones to be so.

Thus, the culture of the elites was *the* culture of the country, at least until 1848; that is, as long as the landed elites had no competitors for cultural hegemony either from the weak and subaltern bourgeoisie or from the illiterate *popolo*. Although not in power, landed elites were then the only social actors who could construct a global societal project and envision the means of implementation. Furthermore, not unlike their contemporaries in the rest of rural Europe, they strongly desired to do just that. Borrowing a term for a contemporary and similar phenomenon in Russia, we can consider this a class of *landed intelligentsia*.

Elites' cultural 'openings'

The culture of the landed intelligentsia under Restoration had a double foundation, Enlightenment and anti-Enlightenment. The former was common to all the European elites and stemmed from the intellectual ferment of the late 1700s and from their cooperation with the reforming court. Like many other absolute rulers, Ferdinand IV had sought the opinion and approval of intellectuals and tolerated critical writings, as long as they did not question the institution of dynastic monarchy. The ailing University of Naples was revamped, where the first chair of political economy in Europe was established in 1754 for the noted economist, Antonio Genovesi. It was a period of intellectual giants, such as Genovesi, Galante, Broggia, Galiani and Palmieri, whose writings made the Neapolitan Enlightenment famous. Naples, though still surrounded by a countryside of exotic *barbarie*, became one of the cultural capitals of Europe. The splendid San Carlo theatre was built, intellectual salons, art and music flourished, the archaeological excavations at Herculaneum began and the discovery of Paestum took place. Intellectual debates flourished, many of them centring on the backwardness of the Kingdom and on social and institutional 'evils' that were hampering the country's progress. If there was a certain vagueness to the conclusions reached, the same was to be found among the enlightened reformers throughout Europe, as they all relied upon the same pool of reference. The main product of all the debates was a strong anti-feudal reaction: Feudalism was the main structural obstacle to Progress and Feudalism had to be abolished.

The second foundation of the Neapolitan culture of the Restoration was the country's experience, the traumatic and formidable vicissitudes of the period 1799–1815 – a revolution, a civil war, a foreign rule and more than one defeat – which drastically separated the younger generation from its enlightened *maîtres à penser* (mentors). Many of the students, readers and followers of the great masters, themselves offspring of landed families, fostered and joined the revolution in 1799, served the short-lived unhappy Partenopean Republic, and became victims of both the mob's rage and Ferdinand's vicious vengeance. In 1806 they joined the French kings, Joseph and then Murat, installed in Naples by Napoleon's troops, supporting them in their modernizing effort. In 1815, at the end of what Benedetto Croce called the 'happy decade', they found themselves with the restored Bourbons once again.

This experience left a deep scar on a generation that had been decimated, wounded and humiliated, and which also felt that it bore the responsibility of having surrendered Neapolitan sovereignty to the generals of foreign armies. It rendered the revolution 'passive', as Vincenzo Cuoco put it.[7] At the same time, the experience changed the way of thinking of the country's elites. While they did not reject the *problematique* of their enlightened masters, they began challenging many of their founding ideas, methods and political choices. Their main foe was the universalism of the Enlightenment, which resulted in the blind application of foreign recipes for economic and political development, contempt for native customs and institutions, and remoteness from the popular sentiment. The new generation, influenced by romanticism, searched for local traditions and 'spirits' of the local territory, *genii loci*. Rediscovering their own national past, they found inspiration in their Neapolitan forebear Giambattista Vico's teaching that different societies should be taken on their own terms, rather than in terms of some universal categories. The new romantic generation initiated programmes of local action, making use of new regional forms of sociability and communication (such as associations and journals). Their emphasis on 'localism' made them influential in the provinces and helped to form an 'opinion' increasingly focused on organizing and inhabiting what might be called a 'civic' space.

The culture of the Restoration

The Restoration regime also had a character of its own, distinct from the *ancien régime*. Bound by international treaties and advised by common sense, the king – who returned in 1815 as Ferdinand I – did not restore feudalism. Instead, he maintained much of the administrative and institutional structure and he continued the appointments of the 'decade'. The absolutism of the years 1815–48 was generally mild. Freedom of the press and of expression was relatively broad, although punctuated by periods of aggressive censorship. The King was reactionary, but not a fanatic; more like Louis XVIII than Charles X, he favoured at least some economic and institutional (but not political) modernization. The main bone of contention between the throne and the enlightened elites was the question of constitution. Between 1815 and 1848 there unfolded a succession of promises and negotiations, concessions, abrogations, repression and forgiveness. A constitution was granted in 1820 as a result of another revolution but was abrogated a year later. Ferdinand II, who ascended to the throne in 1830, promised no representative government, but a good government and a serious modernization of the state and the society. Although he was no friend to the intellectuals, he did grant amnesty, brought the exiles back, and carried out an 'administrative revolution'. He encouraged the development of industry and banking by initiating railway construction and other public works projects.

The cultural climate of the period was lively. Naples swarmed with students, artists, visitors and distinguished foreigners. The world of fine arts had been revamped by state and private patronage and was blooming. The domination of the classicist Academy of Fine Arts was challenged successfully by the new schools and by the 'revolutionary' romantics. The Court actively patronized artists through exhibitions and royal commissions, most of them in the annual *salon* that was started in 1825 on the French model by Francesco I. Private patronage followed the royal example, with purchases, commissions and fellowships for the art students, who were arriving truly *en masse*. There was much theatre in all the larger cities of the kingdom, with a long opera season, a shorter drama season and performances in the private *cenacoli*. There were many salons, whose activity was important in liberal circles, and where the landed elites' patronage was at its best. These salons in patrician houses, all wealthy landowners, were known as *case*, held by families rather than specifically by the women, and many of them counted scholars and authors among the family members, such as *casa* De Thomasis, *casa* Poerio, *casa* Ricciardi, *casa* Guacci-Nobile, *casa* Troya.

One of the most significant innovations of the period was the educational movement, which still awaits an in-depth study. The sheer proliferation and liveliness of the movement were extraordinary even if limited in social reach. While the prestige of the University was declining, a multitude of new public and private schools, institutes and academies, some of them started during Murat's time, mushroomed and thrived. Students came to Naples from all parts of the country, to study at private schools. Many of these schools were directed by the illustrious members of the Neapolitan intelligentsia, including the literary scholar Francesco De Sanctis, the economist Antonio Scialoia, the historian Francesco Trinchera and the jurist Pasquale Stanislao Mancini. Years later, in *La giovinezza*, De Sanctis painted an extraordinary portrait of private education in Naples in that period as being free, liberal and original. His own school was self-governed in the spirit of Proudhon-like anarchy, a 'small self-contained society, without rules, without discipline, without any authority of command, moved by sentiments of duty, value, and reciprocal respect'.[8] All those institutes actively sought out talented provincial youth and attracted them with fellowships, free admissions and competitive incentive awards. While upper-class provincial youth had always gone to Naples to study, now, in Pasquale Villari's words, 'students were flowing in thousands', many of them offspring of provincial gentry, lawyers, and even, occasionally, artisans.[9] One of the most influential of these institutions, the school founded and run by the Marquis Basilio Puoti, was free and open to all young men of talent regardless of their economic means or social class. Puoti taught 'pure' Italian language and literature, rejecting (knowingly, though) all the novelties, but other schools added (to the traditional disciplines of law, medicine, military arts and philosophy), new popular curricula in Italian, political economy, history, engineering and architecture. Schools also flourished in the provinces, from boarding schools and *collegi*, which were part of the university system, to private schools of law. Historian Alfredo Zazo counted some 800 disseminated throughout the cities of the kingdom, even in the smaller towns.[10] Sons of well-to-do landed families would still study at home with a tutor, often a local priest, but as teenagers they would be sent to schools or to the university, to board either at school or (more likely) with a relative, or with other students.

As a finishing touch of the education of a young member of the landed elite, there was also travel. Young Italians seem to have travelled less than their contemporaries from other parts of Europe, but they did travel, both in Italy and in Europe. In 1827 Giuseppe Ricciardi, aged 19, went with his family on a year-long *bildung tour*, during which he met everybody who was anybody in the world of intellect and art: Manzoni, Rosmini, Grossi, Monti, the group of *Antologia* including Nicolini and Capponi, Leopardi, even Lamartine, then secretary of the French mission in Turin. At Vieusseux he met Neapolitan exiles: Gabriele Pepe, Giuseppe Poerio, Matteo Imbriani and Pietro Colletta.[11]

Secret societies and masonry

These were years of strong politicization, with politics often mediated by culture. The *case* were generically liberal, the artists were liberal but obliged to the regime for its favours, and the students were more radical, often associated with the *Carboneria* and with conspiracies. Political passion would come into the open in 1848, when students on the streets manned the barricades and the *case* intellectuals appeared as members of parliaments and government. Luigi Settembrini, who came to study in Naples in 1828, thus remembered his fellow students: 'the young... are all good, with open hearts, prone to every beautiful and generous action... and all liberals'.[12]

No discussion of the sentimental and political education of the elites is complete without mentioning the role of free-masonry and secret societies, especially the *Carboneria*. The *vendite* (gathering places) of the *Carboneria* multiplied during Murat's reign, continued during the Restoration, and pervaded the climate of provincial towns. Luigi Settembrini recalls being offered a tricolor cockade in 1820, on his way to church: 'at the age of seven I was a Carbonaro'. General Guglielmo Pepe recounts in his *Memorie* how in 1820, working through the networks of the *Carboneria*, he managed to put together a large army in just a few weeks.[13] The *Carbonari* – radical, anti-clerical, anti-Bourbon – were the heroes of the provincial youth. The four brothers Palizzi, future eminent painters and participants in the 1848 revolution, grew up in the town of Vasto in the Abruzzi. The local hero and the model of all virtues was the *Carbonaro*, Gabriele Rossetti, poet, patriot and exile, whose sacred poem *Iddio e l'uomo* was on the Pope's *Index* of forbidden books. He was also the future father of the writer Christina and the painter Dante Gabriel. The poet's elder brother Antonio was Vasto's barber, conversationalist and poet, author of popular couplets that mocked the government's fiscal pressure. As all the autobiographies of the period witness, the young, especially in the provinces, were always involved in one or another conspiracy or secret society (in 1834, the 'Young Italy' was founded simultaneously in many towns). This underground activity often led to arrests, trials, prison sentences and even executions. The infamous Vallone di Rovito near Cosenza was the site of executions by beheading or shooting of young followers of De Matteis in 1821, of De Liguoro in 1837, of the Cosenza democrats in 1843, and of the Bandiera brothers in 1844. But prison, exile, flights or death added romantic flair to conspiracies.

The 'sons': romantic spirit

The romantic spirit was ever present. Students and young people in general, women included, were engrossed in stories, novellas and novels, fantastic and sentimental, and were attentive to all 'rumours' from Lombardia. With or without the encouragement of their teachers, they devoured French literature: Madame de Stäel, *La Nouvelle Heloise* by Rousseau, Chateaubriand's *Martyrs*, all the novels by D'Alincourt, *Matilde* by Cottin, Victor Hugo, Lamartine; they also read Walter Scott and Alessandro Manzoni, the tragedies of Alfieri and those of Shakespeare, the Daute and Hegel. They wrote profusely and published their own poems, ballads, tragedies and novellas in a growing number of reviews, in Naples as well as in the provincial cities. The new interests included also history, folklore, popular traditions, romantic novels, archaeology, philosophy and psychology. The vibrant mouthpiece of Calabrian romanticism, *Il Calabrese*, included the contributions of the best young writers, poets and journalists, such as Francesco Saverio Salfi, Pietro Giannone, Vincenzo Padula, Domenico Mauro and Giuseppe Campagna. Their poems, ballads, tragedies and novellas were intensely romantic, with titles such as *L'Esule*, *L'Abate Gioacchino* and *Cinque Novelle Calabresi*. An anecdote illustrates the diffusion of romantic references. During a criminal trial in Catanzaro, the prosecutor accused the defendant of being bolder than Manzoni's *Innominato*. The year was 1835. *The Betrothed* had just been published!

Repression, however romantic, was neither continuous nor universal. In 'normal' times there was room to express ideas and opinions. The local press flourished, and also non-Neapolitan journals and reviews circulated widely. Legal journals promoted the new juridical culture; literary reviews mushroomed. All the associations and professional organizations, as well as all the political and literary movements, published some kind of periodical literature. Upon his return from the *bildung tour*, Giuseppe Ricciardi founded in 1832 and edited for a few years (until his arrest for conspiracy) the journal *Il Progresso delle scienze, delle lettere, delle arti.* Liberal and pluralistic, it favoured a diversity of approaches and accommodated four political generations and political views that ranged from the radical republicanism of Ricciardi to the conservative municipalism of Luigi Blanch. There were also several left-wing journals, republican, radical, democratic, anticapitalist. *Le Charivari des deux Siciles* was a moderate republican paper close to the French *Le National*; *Caffè' di Buono*, named after the meeting place of the out-of-town students in Naples, was radical and democratic; *Mondo vecchio Mondo nuovo* was a good example of the newly emerging critique of capitalism; *Inferno* advocated a Constituent Assembly and universal male suffrage. Girolamo de Rada's *La bandiera albanese* (which in 1848 would be renamed *L'Albanese d'Italia*), promoted Italian–Albanian popular culture, and advocated its cause as well as instigated the 1837 rising.

The 'fathers': economistic mood

Although informed and influenced by the romantic mood of the 'sons', the opinion prevalent among the landed 'fathers' was not radical; but it was not conservative either. The best characterization remains the one used by Raffaele Ciasca, 'liberal conservative'.[14] The landed elites were not democratic by any stretch of imagination. Their attitudes towards popular classes oscillated between patronizing (*popolo*) and contemptuous (*plebe*). But they were sincerely interested in modernizing the economy and also improving the lot of the peasantry. They also desired political modernization, which they identified with constitutional monarchy. But above all, they were vastly interested in all the things related to land and agriculture. The proliferation of specialized presses and publications, an extraordinary growth of associationism, and the growing participation in meetings, conferences and scientific congresses, were all indicators of the landed elites forging a modern civil society.

The interest in things economic was generally broad. Economic and political debates of those years found their way into all the journals, national and local, with literary reviews publishing long articles on political economy and statistics. The questions passionately debated revolved mostly around the problems of development and backwardness: how does one measure progress? How does the Kingdom compare with France and England, or with Ireland and Poland? What role should government play in promoting industrial development? What rapidity of industrialization is desirable for a late-comer? Is centralized control comparatively more advantageous to economic development than municipal autonomy? What is the utility and impact of public works? How does free trade affect a backward country? Should there be, in an agrarian country, any control of land ownership and usage? The USA, another country with a natural agricultural calling, was often held as a model. Economist Carmine Antonio Lippi quoted a remark of President James Monroe that 'a nation... that is not able to satisfy autonomously its needs, does not deserve to exist', to remind the Neapolitans of the sinful backwardness of their agrarian system, which held back the whole economy.[15]

Many debates focused on education and good government, universally considered the most important pillars of a healthy development. In fact, a reform of education engaged the best intellects of the period, from Cuoco to De Sanctis, and the 'administrative revolution' of the 1830s occupied the best legal scholars such as Pasquale Stanislao Mancini, Matteo De Augustinis, and Giuseppe De Thomasis; this last was the leader of the new *amministrativisti* who advocated local autonomy and communal self-administration.

The readership of even specialized agrarian and economic journals was surprisingly broad. In addition to the popular journals, the Tuscan *Giornale Agrario* and the Milanese *Annali Universali di Statistica*, journals published in the Kingdom circulated widely. Among these were *Il Gran Sasso d'Italia*, founded and directed by Ignazio Rozzi, agronomist and professor of agriculture, dedicated mostly to social and economic problems, *Annali della Calabria Citeriore*, founded and directed in by Luigi Maria Greco, a lucid conservative social critic, and *Giornale di Statistica*, founded in 1835 in Palermo by two young brilliant liberal economists, Francesco Ferrara and Emerico Amari. Institutional or establishment-sponsored publications were used in a creative way, often in tension with the sponsoring institutions. It happened occasionally even with the government organ, *Giornale del Regno delle Due Sicilie*. The most influential of these institutional publications was the government-funded *Annali civili del Regno delle Due Sicilie*, founded in 1833 by a group of young journalists close to the established reformist circles. The *Annali* counted among its collaborators some of the best and most influential writers, civil servants and administrators of the period and it coordinated efforts of various economic and cultural associations. Locally, diverse journals were published by the Economic Societies (see below). Even the clergy partook in the general agromania. Many provincial priests became active members of the Economic Societies, contributors to economic journals, teachers in agrarian academies and schools, and active promoters of innovation and agrarian improvement. Some seminaries even established chairs of agriculture and schools of practical agronomy, and many cases were cited approvingly of parish confessors imposing tree planting as penance for sins.

Civil society: associationism

Much of the economic and reforming discourse described above became articulated in the works of a variety of associations. The Neapolitan associationism, traditionally dismissed because of its government-promoted origins,[16] is only now beginning to attract historians' interest. Recent studies have focused on Neapolitan associations as *loci* of the constituent civil society and have shown how they forged reform-oriented opinion and the landed elite's self-consciousness.[17] Among associations operating in the Kingdom, Economic Societies were especially active. Camillo Cavour's *Società Agraria Subalpina*, although founded later, has received much scholarly attention, but the history of the Neapolitan associations has yet to be written. In reality, what began there as instruments of government later developed into autonomous *loci* of projects and critical discourse. The Economic Societies were instituted by Murat in 1810 and were re-established by Ferdinando I in 1817. They flourished in the 1830s and 1840s; with 14 Societies on the Continent and some in Sicily, they constituted the largest network of their kind on the Italian Peninsula. They gathered and disseminated information and statistics, promoted mechanization and experimentation; they stimulated innovation and rationalization with exhibits, fairs, competitions and awards. Most important, by setting up agricultural schools at various levels, chairs of agriculture, model teaching farms and experimental gardens, and by establishing scholarships for poor students, they promoted vocational and general education at different social levels, from peasant sons to the gentry offspring. The network involved many people: each Society counted approximately 200 members, ordinary, honorary and corresponding, but their plenary meetings were attended by the whole local elite, delegates from other associations, and visiting scholars and celebrities. Moreover, in *comizi* or smaller town meetings, the Societies brought together the small-town middle class – professionals, entrepreneurial farmers, artisans – with landowners, judges, civil servants, and university professors. Economic Societies thus facilitated a mixing of classes which would have been unthinkable in a salon, while at the same time constituting a vehicle for the dissemination of the elite's ideas. In this sense, they were the best instrument of the re-forging of the landed elite's hegemonic role in modern terms.

Economic Societies reached even farther through their periodical publications. According to their foundation bill in 1817 each Society was supposed to publish its 'Proceedings', but by the early 1840s, the reality surpassed all expectations. More than 20 journals were published by the Societies, some annual, some bi-annual, some quarterly, some bimonthly. They covered agricultural, economic and literary-agrarian topics. These journals proudly modelled themselves on the well-read Italian or foreign journals, such as *Giornale Agrario Toscano* or *Annali Universali di Agricoltura*, and they in turn served as a model for the smaller provincial ones. The proceedings of the Economic Societies and the contents of their local journals were informally coordinated and disseminated by the metropolitan elite journal, *Annali Civili del Regno delle Due Sicilie*, which quickly became the most serious theoretical and practical reference for the improving elite. From 1839, the *Annali* ran a regular section devoted to the 'Proceedings of the Economic Societies of the Provinces of the Kingdom'. While praise by this authoritative organ was much sought, so also was reproach feared for lack of activism.

Finally, in addition to the 'Proceedings' and other journals, the Economic Societies published and sponsored a growing popular literature, from manuals and textbooks, to almanacs, calendars and 'agrarian catechisms'. The targets included barely literate peasants, small property owners, and medium-sized landowners engaged in specialized production.

A civilizing project?

All these debates and practices amount to a sort of 'civilizing project', a modernizing discourse of a liberal-conservative political orientation. In general lines, it could be summarized as follows. On the one hand, it was logically derived from the eighteenth-century philosophy of progress, but on the other, it took into account the concrete opportunities and feasibility of economic modernization. Its theoretical underpinnings, derived from the physiocrats, from the so-called Italian eclectic school of political economy, and from the 'second' de Sismondi, were simple. At the root, there were land, agriculture and the landowning class. Land was seen as the only and the truest source of both material wealth and moral *virtu'*; as a consequence, agriculture was also both the means of making that wealth yield and also an art and wisdom, the closest to the true (that is, moral) wisdom. The wealth of the nation as a whole thus depended on well managed agriculture. The key to the good management of agriculture, in turn, was the clearly defined land property, a sort of a central organ within the whole social body that was thought to give a vital impulse to all industry. Accordingly, landowners had a central role in making the whole society function and in improving its fate; all the good of the country depended on them, and any true patriot had to be a lover of agriculture. In addition, landowners were the only social group that combined in itself the tradition and the modernity, the spirit and the science, the private and the public interest (we could add, the romantic and the proto-positivist). Finally, only they knew the land (also in the sense of the country as a whole) well enough to understand its local ('natural' or 'proper') economic vocation. This unique combination made the landed elite the only social group both deserving and capable of leading the country towards modernization, and to give the modernizing effort the right direction, equated with the public good.

What underlies this vision is, of course, the assumption that the Neapolitan Kingdom was, as these modernizers loved to repeat, *una nazione agricola* with the natural vocation for producing foodstuffs. Modern techniques, instruments and methods were welcome and encouraged as long as they were conscientiously chosen and applied to the particular conditions of the land and to the agrarian character of its people. That vision did not exclude industry and manufacturing, but it abhorred what was called 'industrial civilization', made up of large industry, city-monsters, class antagonism, atomization, breaking-up of families, misery, and so on. Large industry was also suspicious on another account: protected by the government, it was seen as a hotbed of corruption, monopoly and inefficiency. The 'agrarian' project, in contrast, envisioned a harmonious and gradual development of manufacturing and commerce (hence, the frequent reference to Adam Smith's 'natural order of things'), which would follow and surround the modernized and rationalized agriculture. A small and medium-sized manufacture would gradually grow, preferably processing local agricultural products; commerce would follow, the freest possible, gradually extending its reach into the markets. This gradual, natural and 'harmonious' model of development would lead, in this elite's view, to a growth of a modern conservative society, based on rural harmony, and implicitly, on the preservation of the old hierarchical order. The dominant landed class would gradually become an open elite and include all modern landowners. One day, through education and gradual acquisition of civilization, the subaltern classes would also become capable of modern landowning and thus of joining the elite.

It is beyond the scope of this chapter, and not possible at the present state of research, to discuss the actual efforts to implement this 'agrarian project' and the general feasibility of an alternative to 'industrial civilization'. The landed elite's identity and identity management needs to be seen in relation to other social groups. On the one hand, we need to explore more closely their everyday management of social distance in relation to the urban bourgeoisie. On the other, most importantly, we must understand the nature of their relationship with the peasantry in the social interaction in rural towns and in the labour interaction on the estates. Even the presumed 'paternalism' of this relationship needs to be analysed in the terms and in the context in which it was proposed and practised. For example, a number of everyday transactions and negotiations in the *latifondo* system seem to point to the existence of some kind of complicity between 'paternalism' and the peasant patriarchy. The system of guarantees effectively assisted the male head of the peasant household in perpetuating his role of bread-provider, his children's (especially the sons') master, and intermediary with the public sphere (often represented by the landowner himself); all the while land was being further privatized and concentrated in the hands of landowners. Was this simply a functional *quid pro quo*, an exchange of reciprocal advantages between the landowner and the land-worker? Or can it be seen as part of the 'project' of preservation of the existing hierarchies? The question of possible complicity between paternalism and patriarchy leads necessarily to one of gender roles, values and attitudes. The harmonious agrarian project was clearly a gendered one; it was led by men, even in an interclass gender complicity. On the other hand, land-based civilization was represented as a more gentle and more feminine than the industrial one. *Madame la Terre*, in the nineteenth-century agronomic debates, was notoriously played against *Monsieur le Capital*.

Many other questions must be addressed before we can positively identify the nineteenth-century Neapolitan landed elite with an agrarian civilization project. All this chapter has tried to accomplish is to show the determined cultural activization of this class and its conscious involvement in the effort to modernize.

Notes

1   This work is part of a more general revisionist scholarship that recently has challenged established interpretations of, and has set out to re-formulate and re-address, the central themes in the historical development of the South. Numerous studies have debunked the frozen image of the Mezzogiorno by showing that there was not one South, or even two, as in Manlio Rossi Doria's famous '*l'osso e la polpa*', but many; that *latifondismo* was neither absentee nor

immobile, that the Mezzogiorno's various socioeconomic structures were rational responses to human and climatic factors rather than immobile relics of the past, and, finally, that its landed elites were far from hostile to things modern. For the overviews of this new agenda in the English language, see: A. Lyttelton, 'A new past for the *Mezzogiorno*', *Times Literary Supplement*, 4 October 1991, pp. 14–16; J. Davis, 'Remapping Italy's path to the twentieth century', *Journal of Modern History* 66 (1994) pp. 291–320; R. Lumley and J. Morris (eds.), *The New History of the Italian South: The Mezzogiorno Revisited* (Exeter, 1997); J. Schneider (ed.), *Italy's 'Southern Question': Orientalism in One Country* (Oxford and New York, 1998), especially J. Davis's chapter 'Casting off the "Southern Problem": Or the Peculiarities of the South Reconsidered', pp. 205–24.

2   J. Blum, *Noble Landowners and Agriculture in Austria, 1815–1848; A Study in the Origins of the Peasant Emancipation of 1848* (Baltimore, MD, 1948).

3   See, for example, F. Furet, 'The Revolutionary Catechism' and 'De Tocqueville and the Problem of the French Revolution', in *Interpreting the French Revolution* (Cambridge and New York, 1981); T. C. W. Blanning, *The French Revolution in Germany* (Oxford, 1994); M. Raeff, *Understanding Imperial Russia* (New York, 1984); L. Colley, *Britons: Forging the Nation, 1707–1837*; A. Sked, *The Decline and Fall of the Habsburg Empire, 1815–1918* (London, 1989).

4   A. Placanica, *Alle origini dell'egemonia borghese in Calabria* (Catanzaro, 1979).

5   P. Macry, *Ottocento: Famiglia, élites e patrimoni a Napoli* (Turin, 1988).

6   J. Schneider, 'Of vigilance and virgins', *Ethnology* 9:1 (1971).

7   V. Cuoco, *Saggio storico sulla rivoluzione napoletana del 1799* (Bari, 1913; orig. pub. 1800).

8   F. De Sanctis, *La giovinezza; memorie postume seguite da testimonianze biografiche di amici e discepoli* (Turin, 1961; orig. pub. 1888), p. 293.

9   P. Villari, *La giovinezza di Francesco de Sanctis, frammento autobiografico* (Naples, 1919; orig. pub. 1888), p. 336.

10 A. Zazo, *L'istruzione pubblica e privata nel Napoletano (1767–1860)* (Città di Castello, 1927), pp. 202 ff.

11 G. Ricciardi, *The Autobiography of an Italian Rebel* (London, 1860).

12 L. Settembrini, *Ricordanze della mia vita* (Bari, 1934; orig. pub. 1893).

13 G. Pepe, *Memorie della giovanezza* (Paris, 1846).

14 R. Ciasca, *L'origine del programma per 'l'opinione nazionale italiana' del 1847–1848* (Milan, 1955).

15 C. A. Lippi, *Prime idee concernenti il miglioramento delle nostre istituzioni* (Naples, 1820), p. 84.

16 D. L. Caglioti, 'Circoli, società e accademie nella Napoli postunitaria', *Meridiana* 22–3 (1995), pp. 19–38; and D. L. Caglioti, *Associazionismo e sociabilita' d'elite a Napoli nel XIX secolo* (Naples, 1996).

17 R. De Lorenzo, *Istituzioni e territorio nell'Ottocento borbonico: la Reale Società Economica di Principato Ultra* (Avellino, 1987); R. De Lorenzo, 'Gruppi dirigenti e associazionismo borbonico: le Società economiche', in G. M. Galanti (ed.), *Dal comunitarismo pastorale all'individualismo agrario* (Salerno, 1991); M. Petrusewicz, 'Agromania: innovatori agrari nelle periferie europee dell'Ottocento', in P. Bevilacqua (ed.), *Storia dell'agricoltura italiana in età contemporanea*, Vol. III: *Mercati e Istituzioni* (Venice, 1991), pp. 295–343.

6

The Politics of Black Rural Labourers in the Postemancipation South

Steven Hahn

It does not take very long for a historian of rural societies and labour systems to wonder about how fruitful a comparative treatment of the American South and the Italian Mezzogiorno might be. On the surface, of course, such an undertaking should appear promising since both regions seemed to share important common features (at least in the nineteenth and early twentieth centuries): they were dominated by large landed estates, ruled by a relatively small number of substantial property owners, involved in staple-crop agriculture, marked by great disparities of wealth and power, and increasingly integrated into emerging nation-states. But the scale of the estates, the size, composition and organization of the work forces, and the relationship between political unification and social transformation differed (in most regards) so dramatically that we could quickly conclude that these were, in truth, cases of apples and oranges (or better, cotton and olives).[1]

Yet, this judgement may perhaps be too hasty. The considerable variations to be identified within the Italian *latifundia* system, not simply between Sicily and the mainland but also within the mainland itself, should remind historians of the American South of the considerable variations to be identified within the plantation system, not simply between the cotton, sugar, tobacco and wheat sectors, but also within the sectors themselves; all of which complicate efforts to construct regional models or ideal types and compel close attention to relations, institutions and practices as they developed in particular contexts and over time. Furthermore, the benefits of comparative perspective do not come only from an assortment of direct comparisons and contrasts, and surely not only from an array of similarities that can be uncovered; they come, too, from the questions and insights that may be raised about either one of the cases owing to what we may have learned and thought about the other.

Thus, as I was reading Marta Petrusewicz's stimulating discussion of the social peace that prevailed on the Barracco estate during much of the nineteenth century, I could not help but reflect on the very different conditions to be found in the rural South of the post-war era, and especially on the intense social and political struggles that erupted both before and after the extension of the elective franchise to freed black men. To be sure, these struggles were framed by a process of emancipation and Reconstruction that set the American South apart from virtually all servile societies in Europe and the western hemisphere, but this does not explain how freedpeople so widely rejected and contested the authority of their former owners in the face of formidable obstacles. Southern planters may well have suffered military defeat and serious economic debilitation as a result of the Civil War, but for the most part they did retain control of their estates and, therefore, wielded significant leverage over the newly liberated black labour force. The federal Freedmen's Bureau, together with an army of occupation, may well have supervised the transition to free labour and bolstered the freedpeople's bargaining power, but the federal presence was relatively small in scale and brief in duration.

Indeed, even as they enacted the Military Reconstruction Acts of 1867, enfranchising black men in the former Confederate states, more than a few Radical Republicans worried that their erstwhile enemies might end up as the real beneficiaries. Most prospective black voters did still depend on white landowners for their livelihoods. Would they not then be vulnerable to a host of coercive tactics designed to control their political activities or render them inert? Would they not quickly succumb to the direct power and influence of ex-slaveholders and Democratic bosses, with national as well as local consequences now that the federal ratio had been abolished? Charles Sumner, the Republican senator from Massachusetts who championed 'political equality without distinction of color', could therefore greet the passage of the Reconstruction Acts by demanding 'further guarantees', chief among them being tougher 'precautions... against Rebel agency', 'public schools... for the equal good of all', and homesteads for the freedpeople 'so that at least every head of a family may have a piece of land'.[2]

Although the Congress would never provide these 'further guarantees', the freedpeople responded to the Reconstruction Acts in a manner that generally confounded Republican fears. They registered to vote in great numbers, aligned overwhelmingly with the Republican Party, widely resisted the overtures and threats of white Democrats, marched to the polls in legions, and helped to write new state constitutions that reconstructed the body politic of what had been a slave society. Simultaneously, they began to build – with an assortment of tensions and conflicts – new political relations, institutions and aspirations within their own communities. How former slaves accomplished these tasks not only sheds light on the political world of slavery but also suggests something of a *latifundist* politics of freedom.

When Congress passed the Military Reconstruction Acts, David Medlock was one of the well-established leaders of African-Americans in Limestone County, Texas. A former slave, then over 40 years of age, Medlock had been in the county since at least the 1840s when he was brought from Georgia by his master and set to work on what would become one of several large plantations along the banks of the Navasota River. Owning little or no property and soon to be called a 'labourer' by the federal census-taker, he nonetheless appears to have acquired the rudiments of literacy and preached the gospel, skills and activities that no doubt contributed to his local influence and prestige. His political independence and concern for the welfare of the county's freedpeople were surely critical, too, for although his former owner had been an ardent secessionist and supporter of the Confederate cause and may well have remained his employer, Medlock helped to organize a chapter of the Union League and played a leading role in the establishment of the local Republican Party.

Medlock worked to mobilize a community that was already multi-generational and bound together by extended ties of kinship and personal acquaintance. Joining Medlock in the Union League were his brothers John and Nacy as well as Dick Johnson, who grew up on an adjacent plantation and was probably related to the Medlock clan. Indeed, Medlocks headed numerous black households in postemancipation Limestone County, forming part of a family base of support that eventually catapulted David Medlock to a seat in the Texas State House of Representatives.[3]

Medlock was one of the very few African-Americans during the postbellum era who won election to state or county office from a white majority district. In his, whites outnumbered blacks by nearly 2:1.[4] But in other respects his example offers an important perspective on the dimensions of grassroots politicization in many parts of the rural postemancipation South. For freed African-Americans built their political communities – as enslaved African-Americans had done – from many of the basic materials of everyday life: from the ties and obligations of kinship, from the experiences and struggles of labour, from the traditions and skills of leadership, and from the spiritual energies and resources of religion.[5]

They began by attempting to assemble their immediate families and close kin, to lend those relations civil legitimacy, and to find circumstances in which those relations could find meaningful and useful foundations. Where slaves had lived on large and relatively stable plantations and where, upon emancipation, agents of the Freedmen's Bureau were readily accessible, these efforts could proceed quite expeditiously. Elsewhere, freedpeople faced the formidable task (whether over longer or shorter distances) of joining husbands and wives, registering marriages, collecting children and other dependent kin, finding suitable arrangements for life and labour, and fending off the many coercive interventions of landowners and employers. Insofar as slaves had been chained to their owners as individuals and denied official recognition of their marriages and families, these may be regarded as among the first political acts that simultaneously rejected the legacy of enslavement and celebrated the vitals of freedom.[6]

Collections of reconstituted freed families and their extended kinship networks played crucial parts in the early quests for landed independence, both helping to defend claims to property that had been abandoned or confiscated during the Civil War and attempting to generate the resources necessary to lease or purchase substantial-sized tracts.[7] But far more commonly, they struggled on white-owned plantations and farms to form a bedrock of social experience that undergirded what were otherwise a great variety of settings and crop cultures. The nearly 60 freedpeople who contracted to work W. R. Capehart's large estate in Edenton, North Carolina, in 1867 thus included Gabriel Capehart and his wife, Jackson Capehart, his wife Adeline and five of their children, Edmund Capehart, his wife and one child, Bristow Capehart and his wife, Isaac Capehart and his wife, Edward Williams, his wife and five children, Miles Williams and his wife, Jim Bolin, his wife and five children, and Andrew Bolin and Anthony Bolin, both single and in their twenties. In Russell County, Alabama, the planter Edgar Dawson employed almost 50 freedpeople in 1870, among whom were six families of Dawsons and three families of Terrells.[8] In the tobacco growing areas of southside Virginia, a Freedmen's Bureau agent, commenting in early 1866 on the 'mania for renting', added significantly that 'when one rents a place, he gets all of his "kinfolks" to join him that he possibly can'. Even where freedpeople found themselves in the decided minority and where plantation agriculture had established only a limited foothold, a similar process and pattern could be detected. Contemporary observers who failed or refused to recognize the centrality of kinship to the aspirations of the freedpeople therefore mistook the geographical mobility that attended emancipation or the completion of a crop year for mere wanderlust. J. C. Caruthers, who managed a plantation in Yazoo County, Mississippi, offered another explanation. 'Freedmen through the country have been unusually quiet the past week though a great many of them were changing homes', he told his uncle in January 1866; 'Wyatt and family including Manda and Ed left in my absence and went to Vaughns, Nath and his were already there. John married one of Dick Swayzes women and settled at Bells...The others are contracting to stay with me.'[9]

In reconstituting their kinship networks on a more proximate and stable basis, freedpeople not only tried to provide loved ones with protection and subsistence but also acknowledged the fundamental threads of economic and political solidarity that they had woven and learned to rely upon as slaves. For whether they had lived on plantations or farms, whether in cotton, tobacco, rice, sugar, or general farming districts, the kin (and fictive-kin) relations and groups they painstakingly constructed and reconstructed had come to serve as the central weapons in their struggles to limit utter dependence and exploitation. And so, amidst the myriad contracts and other labour agreements to be found in the immediate postemancipation South – involving share wages, cash wages, tenancy, and leases of many varieties – black families seemed to represent a foundational link. In them, freedpeople saw the best opportunity to guarantee that freedom would build upon their prior achievements and expectations.

The relation between kinship and labour was by no means uniform. Most often (owing in part to the role of the Freedmen's Bureau and other northern officials) it involved agreements between landowners and black nuclear families, the latter usually represented by the male head. But there were arrangements, too, with collections of black families, with groups of family heads representing other family members, and with 'headmen' representing family-based work groups. And these hardly exhausted the possibilities.[10] Equally important, kinship may have infused the contest over the reorganization of agricultural labour far more widely and quickly than has generally been assumed. This can be observed most clearly in the appearance of work groups referred to variously as 'companies', 'clubs', and (even more likely) as 'squads', that accompanied the efforts of landowners to maintain antebellum patterns of control under the new conditions of emancipation. Some historians have, in fact, come to speak of a 'squad system' comprising an intermediate stage on the road from gang labour to family-based tenancy and sharecropping, but it appears to have been less a 'system' than a loose set of arrangements connecting the struggles that flared during slavery with the more decentralized land tenure forms common to the 1870s and 1880s. Numbering somewhere between two and ten, and usually embracing, in the words of a leading authority on the subject, 'members of the same kinship network and friends', squads and companies were probably integral to postbellum gang labour structures from the first; then, where possible, they may have taken on an increasingly 'self-regulating' character, replete with their own leaders and forms of discipline, due in part to the prevalence and complexities of share wage payments.[11]

It appears that squads consisted chiefly of men, and while this may further substantiate the ties between 'gangs' and 'squads', it points also to the recrafting of social relations and gender roles within black households. The earliest indications of the phenomenon come from the reports of southern landowners and federal officials, who were alike dismayed. They complained frequently that black women (and married black women in particular) refused to work, were lazy and troublesome, wished to live off their husbands and employers as non-producers, and seemed more interested in 'playing the lady' much in the manner of their former white mistresses. Together, they described a virtual 'withdrawal' of freedwomen and children from field labour. What they failed or refused to see was a process of reorganization and renegotiation designed to limit the discretionary power of employers, better protect vulnerable family members, and redeploy the labour force to the advantage of freed households, a process initiated by emancipation in most every former slave society of the western hemisphere.[12]

The specific objectives and arrangements varied widely as to crop cultures and customary practices. In the rice-growing districts of South Carolina, for example, where task labour and petty provisioning had become deeply entrenched, the post-war period saw the rapid emergence of a system (bearing some resemblance to forms of labour organization in the postemancipation Caribbean) under which freedpeople exchanged two or three days of plantation work each week for small plots of land they could cultivate independently. Much of the responsibility for tending to rice and other subsistence crops on these plots fell, in turn, to freedwomen and children while freedmen chiefly performed the plantation tasks and then, for the remainder of the week, sought out wage-paying jobs in the rural or urban vicinity. Freed families in the cotton belt usually had less leverage in formally marking distinctions between the time and work owed to their employers and that reserved to themselves, but they too quickly pressed to associate those distinctions with gender-based norms and divisions of labour. A Burke County, Georgia, planter could therefore gripe in January 1866 that his 'old or former slaves' refused a contract offering full-time hands $7 per month and only agreed 'to stay with me ... upon the condition that I feed and clothe them and the non-workers on my place, and give them the privilege to continue to raise their hogs and poultry' and 'to work their *own* crops on my place with my stock'. Where labour requirements and rhythms were more seasonal and urban settings close by, as they were in some mixed farming sections of the Upper South, the logistics of household, gender and labour could become quite complex. A Freedmen's Bureau agent in Lexington, Virginia, consequently found that black men 'in many cases' had gone to work in the country while renting 'rooms in town for their wives and children', the women hating 'the restraint that a life of service in the country imposes'.[13]

It may be tempting, and perhaps not wholly inaccurate, to see in these developments the construction of patriarchal relations of power and gendered 'spheres' of activity in which black women as well as black men had a genuine investment. There were, after all, a good many anticipatory customs and practices to be discerned well before emancipation. Yet it would be mistaken then to imagine that rural black gender roles and norms took shape speedily, fell into neat categories, and gained wide and easy acceptance. The picture is rather one of shifting boundaries, of overlapping zones of identity and responsibility, and of official representation and posturing coupled with community-sanctioned ambiguities; and also of potentially explosive tensions and conflicts. In reports of 'domestic quarrels', of 'complaints that the freedmen do not exercise proper control over their families', and of freedwomen being 'seized with the idea of living indolently and independent of the authority of their liege lords', we very much sense the strains and discontents.[14]

It should not be surprising, therefore, that many of the earliest collective activities and formal organizations to be undertaken by the freedpeople – those evident well in advance of the franchise – were held together by sinews of kinship, concerned with issues bearing directly on labour and households, and marked by ambiguity as to gender distinctions. The most conspicuous and dramatic examples could be seen in those areas of the former Confederate South that had fallen under federal occupation sometime before the war's end and witnessed the eruption of intense social struggles owing to disputes over land claims and labour obligations: most notably along the south Atlantic coast, but also where black troops and returning black veterans helped to inspire local confidence and spark a rapid mobilization. These ranged from the colonies of freed families established in early 1865 on Sapelo and St Catherine's Islands under the leadership of northern free black Tunis G. Campbell, which quickly framed a government, founded a militia, and opened schools, to the 'committees' formed by freed communities on Edisto Island, South Carolina, or at Trent River Settlement in North Carolina in an effort to resist the effects of land restoration, to the prospective freeholders on several of the Sea Islands who battled former slave and plantation owners as well as federal troops seeking to dispossess them. Even more widely in evidence were 'associations' and 'companies' of black labourers who met, marched and drilled in pursuit of their aspirations.[15]

It has been easy to dismiss or ignore these associations in part because of the extravagant charges made by local whites and in part because the charges usually turned out to be groundless,[16] but a report by a US army officer regarding alleged disturbances in the District of Charleston offers a more intriguing perspective. 'The rumor of intended risings among the freedmen and of their banding together and organizing military companies proves upon investigation to be without foundation', he could write in January 1867, while at the same time conceding 'that they have been and are holding meetings at various points for the purpose of consulting together on their condition and arranging their plans and terms for labour during the year'. In the Abbeville District to the northwest, planters fretted about 300 'armed' freedmen who had met every other week since 1 September 1867 at Morrow's Old Field 'for the purpose of drilling and . . . preparing to fight for land', and, as a consequence, 'absent[ed] themselves from their farms and farm work'. They had, it seems, selected their own officers, taken to wearing old army uniforms, 'and usually spen[t] the entire day drilling, firing &c'. Closer scrutiny confirmed that 300 regularly assembled and about 75 drilled under the command of Captain Edward Brown and Lieutenant Aaron Johnson, both former slaves, but added that the 'company' had 'sticks in place of guns' and organized 'for no other purpose than to establish among them a uniform rate of prices for next year' and to 'arrest and punish . . . all that let themselves to planters for less'.[17]

Observers often 'supposed' that the drilling and 'military evolutions' were 'directed by some who have served in the federal army', and it appears almost certain that the mobilization of freed labourers took on military features in areas closely in contact with federal (and especially with black) troops, perhaps as early as the autumn of 1865 when harvest settlements, preparations for a new crop year, and rumours of federal land redistribution combined to inspire collective discussions and activities.[18] Yet these were hardly exercises in simple mimicry, for the quasi-militarization of organizational and work life had both practical and symbolic importance. Most obviously, it simultaneously acknowledged and responded to the dangers of collective action in a world in which social relations had always been based on the use and threat of personal violence and in which any challenge to white authority could be treated summarily. By drilling, marching and posting sentinels freedpeople reminded each other of the risks they faced while offering protections of various sorts. Equally significant, they helped forge solidarities across plantations and farms that necessarily transcended ties of kinship while investing the process with special political meaning and helping to establish and enforce internal discipline.[19]

That the drilling companies appear to have been composed chiefly, if not exclusively, of black males should not at all suggest that the early collective actions of freed labourers were directed and carried out only by men. Indeed, precisely because the issues involved normally bore immediately upon the welfare of families, households, kin networks and emerging communities, the boundaries of participation were by no means tightly drawn. Black women could be found at meetings where the 'plans and terms for labour during the year' were being discussed, including those at which drills were conducted, and by many accounts they quickly earned reputations for truculence and militancy, often in the very areas where drilling associations were also prevalent. What seems instead to have been the case was that communities as a whole were being mobilized, while collective action and militancy took a variety of forms, some of it gender-specific. Hence, whereas black men increasingly used the institutional expressions of 'organized' politics to demonstrate their unity and resolve and to maintain discipline, black women were more likely to rely on verbal abuse and defiant language, physical confrontations and attacks, and quasi-ritualized shaming and harassment which had long been embedded in their resistance to enslavement, not only in the USA but elsewhere in the hemisphere.[20]

By the summer of 1867, complaints of 'armed organizations among the freedmen', of late-hour drilling and of threatening 'assemblages' had grown both in volume and geographical scope. The entire plantation South, it appeared, pulsed with militant and quasi-military activity. But now, in the months after the passage of the Reconstruction Acts, investigation revealed a more formal process of politicization, and one tied directly to the extension of the elective franchise and the organizational initiatives of the Republican Party. From Virginia to Georgia, from the Carolinas to the Mississippi Valley and Texas, the freedpeople showed 'a remarkable interest in all political information', were fast becoming thoroughly informed about their civil and political rights, and, most consequentially, were avidly 'organizing clubs and leagues throughout the counties'. Of these, none was more important to the former slaves or more emblematic of the developing character of local politics in the postemancipation South than the Union League.[21]

The Union League spread rapidly through the southern plantation belt because of its association with the Republican Party, the military defeat of the Confederacy, the abolition of slavery, and the expansion of civil and political rights for African-Americans. But the League could also build upon the organizational struggles and structures that freed communities had already established or accommodate the less formal networks and practices that had deeper roots in slavery. Institutionally hierarchical, with national and state councils, the League was at the same time intensely local in its composition and orientation. And although its mobilization strategies embraced the basic unit of official political life (election precincts), it proved quite adaptable to the basic units of black social and cultural life: church congregations, labourers' associations, drilling companies, fraternal lodges and mutual aid societies. The Reverend Henry McNeal Turner, American Methodist Episcopal Church (AME) minister and Republican Party leader in Georgia, acknowledged as much when, in the summer of 1867, he and a group of black activists representing 40 counties in the state determined to educate 'in our country churches, societies, leagues, clubs, balls, picnics, and other gatherings'.[22]

Most important, the unit of local League organization comfortably meshed with the perimeters of reconstituted kinship groups that could span a number of plantations and farms. Indeed, in the black belt, the proliferation of League councils may have been defined more by the geography of black kinship clans than by the official boundaries of state and county politics. Consider the Leasburg League in tobacco-growing Caswell County, North Carolina, where blacks comprised about 70 per cent of the population. Sometime in 1868, the League had 29 members, all of whom were formerly enslaved and all but four of whom lived in Leasburg Township. At the centre of activity was the Yancey family. Frank Yancey, a blacksmith in his mid-to-late forties, served as the president and Felix Yancey, a house servant about 20 years of age, served as the marshal. Felix, in turn, lived in the household of yet another League member, Daniel Yancey, a blacksmith around 80 years of age, who may well have been Frank's father, as did William Yancey, a 20-year-old farm labourer, who also belonged to the League. Frank's household included League member Watt Johnson, a 60-odd year old blacksmith who probably worked with Frank and was probably related to two other League members: David Johnson, the assistant secretary, and Armistead Johnson, aged 36 and 54 respectively and both employed in a tobacco factory. Two Cunninghams, two Numans, two Curries and three Leas filled out most of the remaining membership. In Limestone County, Texas, where fewer than one inhabitant in five was black, at least three League councils could be found in operation. One was the bailiwick of David Medlock and his clan; one was located in the black Methodist community of Springfield; and the third, based in the small county seat of Groesbuck, appears to have been dominated by the Trammels, another large and influential black family in the county.[23]

Not surprisingly, therefore, the Union League's goal of mobilizing black support for the national government and the Republican Party simultaneously fed upon and nourished the sensibilities and customs that organizers found in many African-American communities. League councils served as crucial political schools, educating newly enfranchised blacks in the ways of the official political culture. Members were not only instructed in the League's history, in the 'duties of American citizenship' and in the role of the Republican Party in advancing their freedom, but also learned about 'parliamentary law and debating', about courts, juries and militia service, about the conduct of elections and various political offices, and about important events near and far. With meetings often devoted in part to the reading aloud of newspapers, pamphlets and government decrees, freedmen gained a growing political literacy even if most could neither read nor write. Yet the League was by no means simply pedantic and hierarchical in its function and culture. Rural blacks could certainly appreciate the organization's secrecy, acquainted as some already were with 'secret societies' and as all undoubtedly were with the temper of their former owners. And they surely did not have to be reminded about the importance of solidarity and mutual loyalty, at least in the face of their likely enemies. 'No earthly motive will ever induce them to betray one another', the northern planter Charles Stearns observed of the Georgia freedpeople he had come to know, comparing them to 'free-masons'. 'They *dare* not tell of each other, even if so disposed.' The League's initiation ritual, in which inductees took a sacred pledge while forming a circle 'with clasped and uplifted hands', in fact bore some resemblance to the ring shout and other forms of spiritual communion in their religious worship.[24]

Even the most didactic of League exercises could be assimilated to the cultural and spiritual styles of rural black audiences. The 'dialogue' was thus regarded as a central educational device for League and party organizers alike, and it was said to have been in the 'hands of every Radical who could read'. Presented as a conversation between 'a white Republican and a colored citizen', it was a series of pat questions and answers designed to acquaint the 'new-made voter' with 'his political duties' and cement his allegiance to the Republican Party. Critics derisively referred to the 'dialogue' as the 'League Catechism' because blacks apparently 'were drilled in its principles' and subjected to an almost religious indoctrination. But blacks themselves infused it with a different sort of community and spiritual vibrancy, reminiscent instead of the 'call and response' rhythms that traditionally went into the making of spirituals, sermons, prayer and the general celebration of religious faith. When, for example, the Reverend Henry M. Turner prepared local black leaders for their work, he and fellow organizer Tunis G. Campbell faced each other across the room and 'read over the dialogues', Turner acting 'as the freedman and Mr. Campbell as the true Republican, I asking and he answering in a suitable voice'. The 'effect' was electric. 'When Campbell would read some of those pointed replies', Turner marvelled, 'the whole house would ring with shouts, and shake with spasmodic motions and peculiar gestures of the audience'. A white South Carolinian, commenting on the 'disorder' that could prevail at League meetings, noted a similar phenomenon: 'At their gatherings all have something to say, and all are up at once. They have a free flow of language, and their older men exhibit a practical, get-at-the-facts disposition... While they are speaking, their orators are subjected to all kinds of interruptions – questions, impertinences, points of order, etc.'[25]

League councils sought to tie their own official objectives to the political practices and concerns of rural black communities in other ways. Reflecting the provisions of the elective franchise and the gender conventions of mainstream political culture, formal membership in the Union League was restricted to males, 21 years of age and older, and the available records and minutes of local councils reveal no exceptions. To this extent, the League also seems to have been in tune with the social division of politics detected among rural African-Americans. But the record suggests, too, that 'membership' did not fully define the range of participation, and that the League depended on a much wider level of mobilization and involvement. In many locales, women and children, as well as men, took part in League processions, in organizing assemblages, in League-sponsored public meetings and speakings, and even in the business of the councils. There is, in fact, scattered evidence of black women engaged in the selection of officers, the drafting of by-laws, and the give-and-take of council discussion and debate; in some cases, they may have gone so far as forming auxiliaries. At all events, they had a genuine visibility designed to symbolize the nature and depth of League support and to bring sanction against those who resisted the call, violated the pledge, or strayed from the fold.[26]

Indeed, League councils quickly constituted themselves as vehicles, not only of Republican electoral mobilization, but also of community development, defence, and self-determination. In Harnett County, North Carolina, they formed a procession 'with fife and drum and flag and banner' and demanded the return of 'any children in the county bound to white men', singling out a Dr McNeil for special scrutiny. In Oktibbeha County, Mississippi, they organized a cooperative store, accepting 'corn and other products...in lieu of money', and, when a local black man suffered arrest, 'the whole League...armed themselves and marched' to the county seat. In Twiggs County, Georgia, they raised funds to pay the legal fees for black defendants charged with theft and other misdemeanours. In Randolph County, Alabama, and San Jacinto County, Texas, they worked to establish local schools so that, as one activist put it, 'every colored man [now] beleaves in the Leage'. In Lincolnton, North Carolina, they invited a northern Methodist minister 'to hold meetings at certain designated places and pledg[ed] themselves to provide accommodations and...protection', helping him bring out 'large crowds'. In the Fairfield District of South Carolina, they gathered on land some freedmen had leased, 'establish[ed] a court of their own ...and advise[d]...the freedpeople to carry their complaints' there rather than to 'the District Court of Fairfield'. And, in the neighbourhood of Perote, in Bullock County, Alabama, they similarly 'resisted the processes of civil law', and instead formed a code of laws, opened a court, and selected a sheriff and deputy to govern their community, provoking charges of 'insurrection' and the eventual arrest of their leader.[27]

However, the League may well have had its widest early impact on labour relations, building as it often did on previous struggles and less formal associations. '[T]he is a grate menny Womens and Childrens and boys going about working for people and dont know how to make a Bargain and they is not theyr Rights by a grate dail', a council leader in

Lincoln County, North Carolina, told Governor William Holden, 'and we want to know if Some of the Best men of our Ligue Could Stand as garddeans for all such people in our Reach not let them make a Bargain them selfs but some of us go and make it for them and see that they git the money &c'. Here and elsewhere in the plantation South, League councils enabled and encouraged freedpeople to negotiate better contracts, contest the abuses of their employers, engage in strikes and boycotts, claim their just wages and shares of the crop, and generally alter the balance of power on the land. How much League activities contributed to the overall transition from gang labour to tenancy and sharecropping is a matter of some conjecture, but there can be little doubt that the League helped rural labourers achieve greater bargaining leverage, improved terms and more independence. Small wonder that League organizers were commonly accused of 'promising the freedmen a division of stock land & money of the country' and of promoting rebellion.[28]

When the US Congress investigated the Ku Klux Klan in the early 1870s, more than a few of the reputed Klan leaders testified that their organization was merely a response to the frightening activities and tactics of the Union League: to the secret oaths, clandestine meetings, accumulation of arms, nocturnal drilling, threatening mobilizations, and general flouting of civilities thought to be in evidence among former slaves across the plantation South. Later scholarly apologists for slavery and white supremacy effectively adopted this view in demonizing Radical Reconstruction and justifying the white vigilantism that paved the road to 'Redemption'. For these reasons alone we should probably pay it no heed, and since the 1960s this is pretty well the stance that serious historians have taken.[29]

Yet I would suggest that we give this view another and deeper look, not because the Klan and its supporters deserve a further hearing but rather because, ironically, it may contribute to a greater appreciation of black political agency in the nineteenth-century South and to a far fuller understanding of the fields of southern politics. For if we are to bring enslaved and freed African-Americans (and especially rural African-Americans) out of the political shadows and on to the main political stage – where they belong – we must recognize that electoral politics was only one arena of political struggle, and that political violence and paramilitary organization were not aberrations occasioned by emancipation and racial panics but instead were fundamentals of the political order. Antebellum politics, contrary to the way it is customarily treated, was not simply about the parameters and mechanisms of the franchise;

it was also about the exclusion and subjection of the disfranchised: about petty sovereignties and personal domination, about militias and slave patrols, about patrons and clients; about patriarchs and dependents; about rumour and other forms of subterranean discourse; and about deadly confrontations of several sorts.

The Union League and other lesser known, though similarly constituted, associations showed appropriate cognizance of this political world, and must not therefore be seen only as 'precursors' of the Republican Party and electoral politics. They must be seen as an essential core of effective political practice that included electoral politics and without which electoral activity would have been (and eventually was) undermined. Community-wide (and often) paramilitary mobilizations enabled African–American men to register to vote in stunning numbers and then to resist the early efforts of white Democrats to control their ballots. They helped rally the faithful and prod the timid, offer some protection to leaders and the rank-and-file, and punish the apathetic or disloyal. As a consequence, during most of the Reconstruction period, black Democrats were few in number and tended to fit a particular social profile: they were generally to be found in cities and smaller towns, physically cut off from the mass of freedpeople, and engaged in occupations wholly reliant on white patrons.[30]

Loosely organized though it was, the Ku Klux Klan spread across much of the South in 1867 and especially 1868. It was not so much a response to black enfranchisement as it was to the mass political mobilization of freedmen by the Republican Party and the failure of the Democrats to attract or compel meaningful black support. Building upon its own networks of kinship and political patronage, as well as on the generational legacies of military defeat, the Klan did set as perhaps its chief goal the destruction of the Union League. Klansmen raided League meetings, burned black churches and schools where League councils gathered, harassed white landowners who welcomed or tolerated League activities, and intimidated and assassinated the League's local leadership. In some states and counties, these Klan forays quickly doomed the prospects for black and Republican political power; elsewhere, African-Americans managed to dig in until the defection of white allies and the political violence carried out by later paramilitary outfits steadily dislodged them.

It is in this sense – of political struggles being waged by private armies attached variously to the Democratic Party, to local bosses, and to estate-owning families against emerging communities of African-Americans who were themselves linked by kinship and semi-secret associations –

that we may think of a *latifundist* politics in the postemancipation South. 'I imagine [in] this state of things there is something similar to Mexico. [In] A Mexican state of society', an observer in Amite County, Mississippi could testify, 'anyone who can get fifteen or twenty desperate fellows at his heels can do as he pleases'.[31] And it is in this sense that we may have more than a little to learn from the experiences and political dynamics of other societies dominated by large landed estates, the Italian Mezzogiorno representing one important example.

Notes

1 There appears to be very little on the social history or political economy of the Mezzogiorno during this period in English, but for what little I have been able to learn I have relied on M. Petrusewicz, *Latifundium: Moral Economy and Material Life in a European Periphery* (Ann Arbor, MI, 1996); F. M. Snowden, *Violence and the Great Estates in the South of Italy: Apulia, 1900–1922* (Cambridge, 1986); J. A. Davis, 'Changing Perspectives on Italy's "Southern Problem"', in C. Levy (ed.), *Italian Regionalism: History, Identity, and Politics* (Oxford, 1996), pp. 53–68; A. Lyttelton, 'A New Past for the *Mezzogiorno*', *Times Literary Supplement*, 4 October 1991, pp. 14–15.

2 C. Sumner, *His Complete Works* (Boston, MA, 1874), XIII, pp. 282–3; XIV, pp. 304–5, 314–15. We may contrast the economic position of the freedpeople with that of farmhands on the Barracco estate, who were small, poor peasants and whose work on the estate supplemented their self-produced subsistence, as well as with the *giornatari* in Apulia, who were fully divorced from the land but also lived in the region's large agro-cities and were hired by the day. See Petrusewicz, *Latifundium*, pp. 156–7; Snowden, *Violence and Great Estates*, pp. 20–3.

3 David Medlock to James P. Newcomb, 29 May 1872, James P. Newcomb Papers, Barker Texas History Collection, Austin, Texas, box 2F106, folder 3; Federal Manuscript Census, Limestone County, Texas, Schedule of Population, 1870, National Archives, Washington, DC (hereinafter NA); W. F. Cotton, *History of Negroes in Limestone County, from 1860 to 1939* (Mexia, TX, 1939), pp. 2–10; D. Hollis Pemberton, *Juneteenth at Comanche Crossing* (Austin, TX, 1983), pp. 2–3, 47–52, 56–7; M. Pitre, *Through many Dangers, Toils and Snares: The Black Leadership of Texas, 1868–1900* (Austin, TX, 1985), pp. 24, 28, 205.

4 Medlock represented Texas's Nineteenth Legislative District in 1870–71. The district included Limestone, Falls, and McLennan Counties, where blacks together comprised about 35 per cent of the population. In Limestone County blacks comprised just under 20 per cent. See Pitre, *Through many Dangers*, p. 205; Dept of the Interior, *Statistics of the Population of the United States at the Tenth Census* (Washington, DC, 1873), pp. 409–10.

5 My emphasis in this chapter will be on kinship and labour struggles, but there is a much wider-ranging discussion in my book, *To Build a New Jerusalem: The African-American Political Experience in the Rural South, 1860–1900* (Cambridge, MA, in progress), chps IV–V.

6   This point is made with particular clarity in L. F. Edwards, *'Gendered Strife and Confusion': The Political Culture of Reconstruction* (Urbana, IL, 1997), ch. I. But also see L. F. Litwack, *Been in the Storm So Long: The Aftermath of Slavery* (New York, 1979); H. G. Gutman, *The Black Family in Slavery and Freedom, 1750–1925* (New York, 1976); J. Saville, *The Work of Reconstruction: From Slave to Wage Labourer in South Carolina, 1860–1870* (Cambridge, 1994), pp. 105–6; S. E. O'Donovan, 'Transforming Work: Slavery, Free Labour, and the Household in Southwest Georgia, 1850–1880', PhD dissertation, University of California, San Diego, 1997, ch. III; I. Berlin *et al.* (eds), 'Afro-American Families in the Transition from Slavery to Freedom', *Radical History Review* 42 (1988), pp. 92–7.

7   See, for example, E. Magdol, *A Right to the Land: Essays on the Freedmen's Community* (Westport, CT, 1977), pp. 181–6; Brig. Gen. Davis Tillson to Major Hastings, 15 Nov. 1865, Bureau of Refugees, Freedmen, and Abandoned Lands (hereinafter BRFAL), RG 105, GA Asst. Comr., Ser. 625, Letters Sent, Vol. 11, NA (A-5196; designates file number at the Freedmen and Southern Society Project, University of Maryland); P. A. Cimbala, 'A Black Colony in Dougherty County: The Freedmen's Bureau and the Failure of Reconstruction in Southwest Georgia', *Journal of Southwest Georgia History* 4 (1986), pp. 72–89; James Davison to Gen. Tillson, 6 Dec. 1866, BRFAL, RG 105, GA Asst. Comr., Ser. 632, Unreg. Letters Rec'd (A-217).

8   Labour Contract: W. R. Capehart and Freedpeople, 29 Dec. 1866, BRFAL, RG 105, NC Asst. Comr., Letters Rec'd, Reel 10; Labour Contract: Edgar G. Dawson and Freedmen and Women, 1870, Edgar Dawson Labour Contracts, Barker Texas History Center.

9   Lt Lewis W. Stevenson, quoted in L. Morgan, *Emancipation in Virginia's Tobacco Belt, 1850–1870* (Athens, GA, 1992), p. 192; Johnson County Tax Digest, 1874, Georgia Department of Archives and History, Atlanta; J. C. Caruthers to Robert L. Caruthers, 2 Jan. 1866, Robert L. Caruthers Papers, folder 48, Southern Historical Collection, Chapel Hill, NC.

10 See, for example, Lt Albert Metzner to Lt J. T. Kirkman, 31 Jan. 1867, BRFAL, TX Asst. Comr., Reg. Repts on Operations, Reel 20; H. C. Smart to Lt L. Baker, 18 July 1866, Dept of the South, RG 393, Pt 1, Ser. 4112, Letters and Repts Rec'd, Box 1, NA; F. B. Leigh, *Ten Years on a Georgia Plantation since the War* (London, 1883), pp. 87–8, 139; O. V. Burton, *In my Father's House are Many Mansions: Family and Community in Edgefield, South Carolina* (Chapel Hill, NC, 1985), pp. 230–2.

11 Some of the earliest research on squads was done by R. Shlomowitz, 'The Squad System on Postbellum Cotton Plantations', in O. V. Burton and R. C. McMath, Jr (eds), *Toward a New South? Studies in Post-Civil War Southern Communities* (Westport, CT, 1982), pp. 265–80; R. Shlomowitz, 'The Transition From Slave to Freedmen Labour Arrangements in Southern Agriculture, 1865–1870', PhD dissertation, University of Chicago, 1978. But see also C. M. Thompson, *Reconstruction in Georgia* (Gloucester, MA, 1968; orig. pub. 1915), p. 294; P. Kolchin, *First Freedom: The Response of Alabama Blacks to Emancipation and Reconstruction* (Westport, CT, 1972), pp. 45–7; C. Orser, *The Material Basis of the Postbellum Tenant Plantation* (Athens, GA, 1988), pp. 54–5; Saville, *Work of Reconstruction*, pp. 109–10; and especially the penetrating and challenging treatment in G. D. Jaynes, *Branches Without Roots: Genesis of the Black*

Working Class in the American South, 1862–1882 (New York, 1986), pp. 158–90. I discuss kinship based labour struggles under slavery in *To Build a New Jerusalem*, ch. I. For the relation of kinship and work gangs on *latifundia* in the Mezzogiorno see Petrusewicz, *Latifundium*, pp. 157–60.

12 See, for example, P. F. Duggan to Lt J. T. Kirkman, 1 Aug. 1867, BRFAL, TX Asst. Comr., Reg. Repts of Operations and Conditions, Reel 21; Capt. Samuel W. Carpenter to Bvt. Maj. W. R. Morse, 28 Feb. 1867, ibid., VA Asst. Comr., Monthly Repts, Reel 46; Lt A. S. Bennett to Maj. George Shockley, 31 Mar. 1868, ibid., AL Asst. Comr., Reel 18; T. Glymph, ' "I'se Mrs. Tatom Now": Freedom and Black Women's Reconstruction', paper presented to the Annual Convention of the Southern Historical Association, 1992; T. C. Holt, *The Problem of Freedom: Race, Labour, and Politics in Jamaica and Britain, 1832–1938* (Baltimore, MD, 1992), pp. 151–2; W. Rodney, *A History of the Guyanese Working People, 1881–1905* (Baltimore, MD, 1981), pp. 31–5.

13 L. Schwalm, 'The Meaning of Freedom: African-American Women and their Transition from Slavery to Freedom in Lowcountry South Carolina', PhD dissertation, University of Wisconsin, 1991, pp. 312–17; J. S. Strickland, 'Traditional Culture and Moral Economy: Social and Economic Change in the South Carolina Low Country, 1865–1910', in S. Hahn and J. Prude (eds), *The Countryside in the Age of Capitalist Transformation: Essays in the Social History of Rural America* (Chapel Hill, NC, 1985), pp. 153–62; Saville, *Work of Reconstruction*, pp. 130–5; W. W. Lawson to Capt. Ed. N. Ketchum, 1 Jan. 1866, BRFAL, Waynesboro GA Agt., Ser. 1055, Letters Rec'd (A-5064);——— to Bvt. Brig. Gen. Orlando Brown, 28 Feb. 1867, ibid., VA Asst. Comr., Monthly Repts, Reel 46.

14 W. E. Connelly to Col. O. D. Kinsman, 1 Aug. 1867, BRFAL, AL Asst. Comr., Reel 18; Bvt. Lt Col. Jno. W. Jordan to Maj. J. R. Stone, 28 Feb. 1867, *ibid.*, VA Asst. Comr., Monthly Repts., Reel 46; Joel Mathews to Brig. Gen. Davis Tillson, 6 Dec. 1865, *ibid.*, GA Asst. Comr., Ser. 632, Unreg. Letters Rec'd (A-5247); S. A. Mann, 'Slavery, Sharecropping, and Sexual Inequality', in D. C. Hine (ed.), *'We Specialize in the Wholly Impossible': A Reader in Black Women's History* (New York, 1995), pp. 281–96; Edwards, *'Gendered Strife and Confusion'*, chs. I–II, IV.

15 R. Duncan, *Freedom's Shore: Tunis Campbell and the Georgia Freedmen* (Athens, GA, 1986); M. Ames, *From a New England Woman's Diary in Dixie in 1865* (New York, 1969; orig. pub. 1906), pp. 99–103; Henry W. Anderson *et al.*, To———, enclosed in Stephen Moore to Bvt. Lt Col. J. F. Chur, 2 Feb. 1868, BRFAL, NC Asst. Comr., Letters Rec'd, Reel 13; Bvt. Maj. Gen. Tillson to Gen. O. O. Howard, 1 Nov. 1866, ibid., Wash. Hdqrs, Ser. 32, Annual Repts. (A-5001–8); M. Gottlieb, 'The Land Question in Georgia During Reconstruction', *Science and Society* 3 (1939), pp. 364–75.

16 See, for example, Charles E. Chovin to Maj. Gen. Canby, 3 Dec. 1867, Second Military District, RG 393, Pt 1, Ser. 4111, Letters Rec'd, C-122, box 6; *Christian Recorder*, 25 May 1867; H. H. Means *et al.* to Col. O. D. Greene, 2 Dec. 1867, Fourth Military District, RG 393, Pt 1, Ser. 385, Letters Rec'd, A-173, box 1; Gov. Jonathan Worth to Col. Bernford, ? Dec. 1866, BRFAL, NC Asst. Comr., Letters Rec'd, Reel 13.

17 Bvt. Maj. Gen. R. K. Scott to Maj. Gen. O. O. Howard, 23 Jan. 1867, Dept of the South, RG 393, Pt 1, Ser. 4112, Letters and Repts. Rec'd, box 1; James

L. Orr to Gen. E. R. S. Canby, 31 Oct. 1867, Second Military Dist., RG 393, Pt 1, Ser. 4111, Letters Rec'd, S-25, Box 12; Bvt. Maj. Gen. Canby to Gov. James Orr, 25 Nov. 1867, Gov. Orr Papers, box 11, folder 6, South Carolina Dept of Archives and History, Columbia, South Carolina.

18 Worth to Bernford, ? Dec. 1866; S. Hahn, ' "Extravagant Expectations" of Freedom: Rumor, Political Struggle, and the Christmas Insurrection Scare of 1865 in the American South', *Past and Present* 157:4 (1997), pp. 122–58.

19 For the best treatment of these quasi-military associations during the early postemancipation period see Saville, *Work of Reconstruction*, pp. 147–51. On the slaves' familiarity with the militia and their appropriation of military titles during community festivities such as corn-shuckings, see R. D. Abrahams, *Singing the Master: The Emergence of African-American Culture in the Plantation South* (New York, 1992), pp. 10–11, 107–30.

20 See, for example, Schwalm, 'Meaning of Freedom', 252; Saville, *Work of Reconstruction*, pp. 99–100; L. N. Powell, *New Masters: Northern Planters during the Civil War and Reconstruction* (New Haven, CT, 1980), pp. 108–9; Holt, *Problem of Freedom*, pp. 64–5; B. Bush, *Slave Women in Caribbean Society, 1650–1838* (Bloomington, IN, 1990), pp. 79–82.

21 Capt. D. J. Connolly to Bvt. Maj. G. Mallory, 31 Aug. 1867, BRFAL, VA Asst. Comr., Monthly Repts, Reel 47; Lt R. G. Rutherford to Bvt. Capt. W. A. Coulter, 30 June 1868, ibid., Reel 49; David Schenck Diary, 26 May 1867, 17 June 1867, Southern Historical Collection; Jno. R. Cook to Lt Louis V. Caziarc, 27 Sept. 1867, Second Military District, RG 393, Pt 1, Ser. 4111, Letters Rec'd, R-20, Box 9; Bvt. Maj. Geo. W. Smith to Lt J. T. Kirkman, 31 May 1867, TX Asst. Comr., Ser. 3624, Repts. (A-3094). On the rise of the Union League see A. Nevins, *The War for the Union: The Organized War, 1863–1864* (New York, 1971), pp. 161–7; M. Fitzgerald, *The Union League Movement in the Deep South: Politics and Agricultural Change during Reconstruction* (Baton Rouge, 1989), pp. 2–22; W. L. Fleming (ed.), *Documents Relating to Reconstruction: Union League Documents* (Morgantown, WV, 1904); and E. Foner, *Reconstruction: America's Unfinished Revolution, 1863–1877* (New York, 1988).

22 Rev. Henry M. Turner to Dear Sir, 8 July 1867, in R. Abbott (ed.), 'Black Ministers and the Organization of the Republican Party in the South in 1867: Letters From the Field', *Hayes Historical Journal* 6 (1986), p. 33.

23 Frank Yancey *et al.* to Gov. William Holden, n.d., Governors' Papers, GP 226, North Carolina Dept of Archives and History, Raleigh; Federal Manuscript Census, Caswell County, NC, Schedule of Population, 1870; W. M. Waddell to James P. Newcomb, 28 Sept. 1870, Newcomb Papers, box 2F105, folder 2a; Election of Officers for Union League of Groesbuck, Limestone County, 7 June 1871, ibid., box 2F108; Cotton, *Negroes of Limestone County*, pp. 9–12; Pemberton, *Juneteenth*, pp. 62–83.

24 Capt. Wm P. Austin to Capt. G. Mallory, 31 July 1867, BRFAL, VA Asst. Comr., Monthly Repts, Reel 47; Lt Jno. W. Jordan to Maj. J. R. Stone, 30 April 1867, ibid.; South Carolinian, 'Political Conditions of South Carolina', *Atlantic Monthly* (Feb. 1877), pp. 192–3; C. Stearns, *The Black Man of the South and the Rebels* (New York, 1969; orig. pub. 1872), 343; 'Ritual of the Union League', in Fleming (ed.), *Union League Documents*, pp. 17–23; Fitzgerald, *Union League Movement*, p. 61.

25 'Loyal League Catechism', in Fleming (ed.), *Union League Documents*, pp. 28–33; Turner to Dear Sir, 8 July 1867, in Abbott, 'Black Ministers', p. 33; O'Donovan, 'Transforming Work', ch. VI; South Carolinian, 'Political Condition of South Carolina', pp. 192–3.

26 Cook to Hosmer, Third Military District, RG 393, Pt 1 Letters Rec'd; Morris to Newcomb, 30 Oct. 1870, Newcomb Papers, box 2F105, folder 2a; Turner to Dear Sir, in Abbott, 'Negro Ministers', p. 33; R. Hinton, 'Cotton Culture on the Tar River: The Politics of Agricultural Labour in the Coastal Plain of North Carolina, 1862–1902', PhD dissertation, Yale University, 1993, p. 102; J. P. Reidy, *From Slavery to Agrarian Capitalism in the Cotton Plantation South: Central Georgia, 1800–1880* (Chapel Hill, NC, 1992), pp. 178–9.

27 J. R. Grady to ?, 27 Aug. 1867, BRFAL, NC Asst. Comr., Letters Rec'd, Reel 10; F. Z. Browne, 'Reconstruction in Oktibbeha County', *Publications of the Mississippi Historical Society* 13 (1913), pp. 77–8, 282–6; W. E. Connolly to Maj. Gen. Swayne, 15 April 1867, Wager Swayne Papers, Alabama Dept of Archives and History, Montgomery; William Strander to James P. Newcomb, 24 Jan. 1871, Newcomb Papers, box 2F105, folder 3; R. F. Cason, 'The Loyal League in Georgia', *Georgia Historical Quarterly* 20 (1936), p. 140; William George Matton Memoirs, 1867, Duke University Archives, Durham; Cook to Caziarc, 27 Sept. 1867; *Richmond Enquirer*, 5 Dec. 1867.

28 Rev. Samuel Lewis to Gov. W. W. Holden, 4 Jan. 1869, Gov. Papers, Box 215; W. E. Wiggins to Lt Geo. Wagner, 11 June 1867, BRFAL, LaGrange GA Agt., Ser. 924, Letters Rec'd (A-5615); Susan E. O'Donovan, 'Philip Joiner: Southwest Georgia Black Republican', *Journal of Southwest Georgia History* 4 (1986), pp. 58–9; Fitzgerald, *Union League Movement*, pp. 136–76; Foner, *Reconstruction*, p. 285. Fitzgerald makes the strongest case for the Union League's role in the shift from gang labour to tenancy and cropping.

29 See, for example, John W. Kyle, 'Reconstruction in Panola County', *Publications of the Mississippi Historical Society*, 13 (1913), pp. 51–2; Thompson, *Reconstruction in Georgia*, pp. 386–93.

30 These developments are treated at considerable length in my book, *To Build a New Jerusalem*, chs IV–V.

31 US Senate, *Report of the Select Committee to Inquire into the Mississippi Election of 1875*, Senate Rept. No. 527, 44th Cong., 1st Sess. (Washington, DC, 1876), p. 102.

7

'Ill-Contrived, Badly Executed [and] ... of no Avail'? Reform and its Impact in the Sicilian *Latifondo* (c.1770–1910)

Lucy Riall

Perceptions of southern Italy's economic 'backwardness' have long been associated with the problem of land. The survival of the *latifondo* (extensive grain estates), the restriction of landownership to a privileged few and the 'idle', 'parasitical'[1] behaviour of the landowners themselves are mirrored in the Italian South's failure to shed the burdens of feudalism, in its inability to embrace the benefits of economic modernization and in its seemingly endemic social conflict. Without a commercially-minded middle class or any kind of landowners with medium-sized holdings, southern rural society appeared divided into those who had no land and those who owned it all: into desperately poor peasants and all-powerful, absentee noblemen. In the absence of commercial pressures, agriculture remained based on a rigidly unprofitable, grain mono-culture. And the landowners lived on the income from rent; they let and sub-let their land on short-term contracts, a system which offered little return on investment and encouraged a short-term approach which exhausted the land. All the ills of the South could be identified with this system of agriculture, and through the poverty of the countryside a whole social class stood indicted.[2]

The system of landownership in the southern *latifondo* is also a central issue in debates about the so-called 'peculiarities' of Italy's road to modernity.[3] The absence of a landowning peasantry in the South and the resulting subordination of the southern peasant economy to that of the rapidly industrializing North has been linked to the emergence of an economic 'divide' between northern Italy and the South after national unification in 1860.[4] In this way, the *latifondo* also became a symbol of Italy's 'Southern Question'. Historians may disagree – and disagree strongly – about the role which southern backwardness played in the development of the North[5] but, ultimately, the identification of the *latifondo* with all that was wrong with the South has never really been called into question. Infested 'by malaria and by the arrogance of the barons and the knights',[6] resistant to social change and commercialization, the vast, empty spaces of the *latifondo* epitomized the abandonment of the land by landowners and the government alike.

The recent challenge mounted by historians of the Italian South, both to explanations of southern backwardness and to the categories on which such explanations are based, offers us an alternative view of southern economic development in the nineteenth century. It is not, it now seems, that the South invariably lagged so far behind the North but that historians have posited a too simple opposition between progress and backwardness, and a too rigid sense of 'difference' from the North. Assuming the existence of a single, homogeneous South, they have ignored areas of intense commercial farming (in, for example, parts of Apulia and the Sicilian coastal regions) and, notably, the emergence there of an active, entrepreneurial middle class.[7] Others have challenged the categories on which explanations of backwardness are based, tracing the origins of what Jane Schneider calls the 'tenacious catalogue of stereotypes'[8] associated with Southern difference both to problems of Italian unification and to subsequent inquiries into the 'Southern Question'.[9] This new approach to the Italian South is reflected in Marta Petrusewicz's detailed reconstruction of the economic and social history of the Calabrian *latifondo*, which points to the emergence of a new economic system based in part on the market economy. She also emphasizes that the *latifondo* – or at least the Barracco estate in Calabria – was a postfeudal creation which grew in size and importance until the agrarian crises of the 1880s.[10]

Petrusewicz's work is controversial and by no means universally accepted.[11] The established image of the *latifondo* remains one of backwardness, immobility and feudal oppression, 'crystallized', in the words of one historian, 'within the conditions of preceding centuries'.[12] Yet this image partly derives from the *latifondo's* capacity for survival; indeed, from what Petrusewicz identifies as a 'formidable project of land concentration' which took place in the early nineteenth century.[13] It is this aspect of the *latifondo* which I propose to investigate in the present study. I focus in particular on landownership in the Sicilian *latifondo*, an area at the centre of one of the first, and arguably most celebrated, inquiries into conditions in the South: the 1876 study by two Tuscan reformers, Leopoldo Franchetti and Sidney Sonnino.[14] The *latifondo* as a term is difficult to define; and in Sicily, the *latifondo* was perhaps rather different from the Calabrian estate described by Petruse-wicz (the largest in Southern Italy). The Sicilian *latifondo* was character-ized first and foremost by its size, but the term also refers to a form of land tenure and a system of agriculture. Large (over 200 hectares or 500 acres) estates, given over mostly to grain-cultivation and to pasture, dominated the high plateau (what Sonnino called the 'internal uplands') of the Sicilian interior.[15] Although smaller, market-gardening farms were to be found in many coastal regions, grain fields and pasture still accounted for around 75–80 per cent of Sicily's total agricultural land.[16] Thus, to the traveller crossing rural Sicily, it would have seemed – as the agricultural reformer Paolo Balsamo remarked in 1792 – that 'you go from one fief (*feudo*) to another, that is, from the land of one large landowner to that of another'.[17]

Another striking feature of the Sicilian *latifondo* was its social structure and pattern of settlement. During the fifteenth and sixteenth centuries, and responding to rapid price rises, the local nobility had 'colonized' the interior and transformed the landscape for the purposes of grain culti-vation. They also established new, often substantial, rural communities (*paesi* or 'agro-towns')[18], into which labourers crowded in great numbers, living with their animals in one-room houses without windows, built one on top of the other.[19] The *paese* became the centre of life in the Sicilian *latifondo*, but it was an isolated, introverted and rigidly hierarchical life. The feudal landowners had been largely absen-tee, leaving the *paese* divided between a small elite (*civili*) of gentry, professionals and clergy and an uneducated, malnourished peasantry. And the roadless, treeless countryside which surrounded these commu-nities served to emphasize their congested, urban character. Peasants had migrated there (some came from as far away as Albania), attracted by the promise of cheap land on long leases and by numerous customary rights (*usi civici*) or easements, such as the right to graze cattle, cut or gather wood and/or sow crops on the feudal estates.[20] But until the reforms of the nineteenth century, landownership was confined to the nobility and the clergy; although, where the community enjoyed inde-pendent feudal status, it often owned a diminishing amount of common land on a collective basis.[21] Thus, notwithstanding the impres-sion of space created by the empty grain-fields, land-hunger was an acute problem in the *latifondo*. This problem grew worse as declining fertility and yields increased the pressure on available land.

In 1847, the economist Francesco Ferrara described 'three fourths' of the Sicilian peasantry 'up country' as 'sallow, sickly and deformed...

[b]orn to no other ends but to moisten the clods with the sweat of their brows, they feed upon herbs, clothe themselves in rags, and sleep huddled up together in smoky huts, amidst the stench of a dunghill'.[22] The poverty of Sicilian peasants reflected the nature of work in the *latifondo*. This required a large labour force, but only at certain times of the year (sowing and harvest time). As a result, a variety of strategies had emerged to ensure that enough men would be desperate enough to offer their labour on a seasonal basis.[23]

Generally, the land possessed by the peasants was the least fertile and divided into tiny smallholdings immediately adjacent to the *paese*. Thus, even peasants with landholdings would supplement their incomes by working, or by migrating to work, as day-labourers (*braccianti*); descending at dawn with their tools into the town square, and walking – if they were hired – many miles across country to do their job.[24] Even then, wages could not guarantee their livelihood: Balsamo estimated, at the end of the eighteenth century, that labour in Sicily was between 40 and 100 times cheaper than in England.[25] The bulk of the work done by the peasants on the *latifondo* was done as share-croppers. Peasants would rent land on short (3–6 year) leases, usually on the basis of verbal contracts and in return for rent in kind or a portion of the produce. They farmed the land on a rotating basis (typically wheat, fava beans; pasture), but neither knew, nor could afford, enough to let the land lie fallow, so that the land was quickly exhausted. An agent or *gabellotto* (rent-collector) acted as a middleman, leasing land from the absentee landowner and sub-dividing it among the local peasantry.

The *gabellotto* was the linchpin of *latifondo* life. By dealing with both the nobleman in Palermo and the local peasant, he acquired a considerable amount of power over both, often by judicious loans and debt management. To the peasant, in particular, he advanced seed for grain and often an 'assistance' (*soccorso*) to keep the family going until the harvest. These were, in practice, high-interest anticipatory loans, easy money for the *gabellotto*, acquired at the expense of the peasant.[26]

'Usury', Sidney Sonnino wrote in 1876, made it 'impossible' for the 'industrious' Sicilian peasant 'to save anything, to improve his lot in any way; and what is worse, by keeping him in a permanent state of legal enslavement and moral depression [it] deprives him of every liberty, of any sense of self-respect'.[27] Eighty years earlier Balsamo had argued that sharecroppers and tenants were 'the most hard-working of citizens' in Sicily but also the 'most oppressed and tyrannized by the main leaseholders'. Land was rented to them on terms 'so exorbitant' that they could never make money. Harvest-time was not a time for rejoicing for the sharecropper but a time of loss, 'desolation' and 'ruin' as the *gabellotto* called in his debt, sometimes using force to extract the surplus.[28] Grain-merchants, profiting from the isolation of rural communities, also imposed their harsh terms.[29] 'Write down that, above all, we are all crazy to cultivate land in the certainty of losing not earning' a Sicilian peasant told Balsamo in the course of his inquiries, but 'we neither can nor know how to do anything else, and it's better to live a miserable life than to die of hunger'.[30]

Only some areas of eastern Sicily appeared to be untouched by this exploitative system. There a system of peasant smallholdings had developed, however unevenly, and peasant farmers were to be found farming their own land on perpetual leases (*enfiteusi*).[31] It was this ideal of the independent peasant farmer, who could co-exist with large-scale commercial enterprise, which was to inspire successive generations of reformers in Sicily. Yet here too, there is evidence that peasants had mortgaged their leases, and were burdened by increasing debts.[32]

Franchetti and Sonnino were by no means the first to condemn the Sicilian *latifondo*. Almost a century before they identified the problem of land with the 'Southern Question', Sicilian reformers had pointed to the *latifondo* and its structure of landownership as an obstacle both to social progress and to economic development. The proposals of men such as Baron Tomaso Natale and, later, the economists Paolo Balsamo and Nicolò Palmieri reflect the influence of agricultural reformers in Britain and France; Balsamo was a particular admirer of the famous British agronomist, Arthur Young.[33] Not surprisingly, given this background, there was broad agreement among them that the *latifondo* needed modernizing. The landholdings were too large and too dominated by grain, there was 'hardly one of our large landowners who is a farmer',[34] the *gabellotti* exploited the peasants and the peasants were both too ignorant and too poor to be capable of improving the land. Short leases discouraged farmers from practising proper crop-rotation or using fertilizer; the persistence of customary rights undermined other forms of investment.[35] This, Balsamo concluded, was why the productivity of Sicilian agriculture was low relative to northern Italy and northern Europe. The only way to improve the state of agriculture was for the government to ensure that the landowner was 'secure in the ownership of his capital and possessions, free in his speculations and in the exercise of his industry, free in the use and in the sale of his products'; in short, that he farmed his own land and was motivated by profit.[36]

The first attack on the *latifondo* was made on the immense landholdings of the Catholic Church. After the expulsion of the Jesuits from the

kingdom in 1767, a plan was drawn up to divide their property among
the peasantry; this was followed by a series of decrees restricting and
confiscating Church property.[37] Property rights in general were drastically altered in 1812, when the Sicilian noble parliament declared feudalism to be officially abolished. Henceforth, feudal tenures – with their
attendant obligations and privileges – were converted into 'unfettered
private property'.[38] Further reforms after the Bourbon government's
restoration to Naples in 1814–15 confirmed the change in legal status.
In 1816, the enclosure and division of common land (land held collect-
ively by local communities) into private hands was ordered. Through a
complex web of legislation between 1817 and 1841, the government
also confirmed the abolition of customary rights belonging to the peasants. Norms and procedures to compensate the peasants for these various losses were also established. At the other end of the social spectrum,
the government also used land reform to undermine the power of the
Sicilian nobility.[39] The system of primogeniture was abandoned in 1818,
forcing the nobility to divide their estates equally among their male
offspring. And, in 1824, the government ordered the sale of encumbered
estates, which forced noblemen to redeem their (often, considerable)
debts by selling landed property.[40]

With the exception of the 1812 law abolishing feudalism, passed
during the British occupation of Sicily, all of these reforms were introduced by the conservative Bourbon monarchy. Land reform was even
more of a concern among liberal opposition groups. The Cordova
reform, drawn up during the 1848 revolution in Sicily (but never
enacted), aimed to redistribute confiscated Church property among
the rural poor.[41] After the overthrow of Bourbon government by Giuseppe Garibaldi's 'Thousand' volunteers in 1860, an equally ambitious
programme of reform was introduced. Immediately on arrival in Sicily,
Garibaldi promised a quota of common land to every peasant who
joined his army; this was backed up in a later decree (2 June) announ-
cing the division of common land among the peasantry. In October
1860, Garibaldi's pro-dictator, Antonio Mordini, brought in a more
sweeping measure of land reform, ordering that some 230 000 hectares
of Church and common land be transferred into perpetual leases for
smallholders.[42] And, although Mordini's reform was suspended by his
Piedmontese successors, the new Italian government introduced a similar, if more restricted, measure of land reform (the Corleo law) in 1862.[43]
Between 1862 and the outbreak of the First World War, the government
undertook a series of inquiries into the land-tenure system in Sicily
and the problem of Sicilian agriculture (the most notable ones were

published in 1876, 1885 and in 1910).[44] New proposals for land reform were also made in the 1880s.

Sadly, and besides the manifest need for a measure of land reform, what these repeated efforts reveal most of all is a catalogue of defeat. Of the official aims behind these reforms – to reduce the overall size of landholdings, to create medium-sized, commercial farms, to assist the rural poor and to undermine the power of the nobility – only the last one was effectively achieved. After 1812, the size of the average landholding in Sicily did not significantly diminish; in 1876, according to Sonnino, landed estates averaged around 1000–2000 hectares, and some were larger than 6000.[45] The *latifondo* also continued to dominate the countryside; for example, in 1910 the 19 *latifondi* of the community of Contessa Entellina still made up more than 50 per cent of the entire territory.[46] Peasant landholdings, where they existed, remained minuscule, at around 1–5 hectares.[47] Even the minister of agriculture, Grimaldi, remarked in 1884, that 'in 78 years, this huge division of land has not even been half completed and has left behind it no visible trace of agrarian and social improvement'.[48]

What did change, however, was the nature of elite power in the countryside. In the course of the eighteenth century, many of Palermo's most celebrated noble families (for example, the princes of Trabia, Palagonia and Paternò) had heavily mortgaged their estates to raise cash; after the 1824 legislation forcing the redemption of mortgages through land sales, they lost control of a great deal of property.[49] As the *grande nobiltà* began to disappear from the countryside, their ex-fiefs were snapped up by an agrarian middle class. Subsequent reforms accentuated the struggle between the old nobility and this new class, who were often *gabellotti* grown rich on the lucrative market in leasing and sub-leasing land.[50] As we shall see below, in many communities they were also able to profit from administrative reforms to gain control of local government. What characterized them all was a veritable will for power. In Biancavilla, an ambitious group of *civili* concentrated their 'career ambitions and anxiety for wealth' on a 'ferocious exploitation of the town's resources'.[51] They owned, rented and 'usurped' (illegally enclosed) land, they took control of tax collection, they obtained public works contracts and they loaned money at usurious rates.[52] Most notably, monopolization of communal offices gave these new landowners control over the allocation of common land.

Yet this new class, about whom so much has been and continues to be written, proved a disappointment to both conservative and liberal reformers. They never became the standard-bearers of agricultural innovation and improvement which the middle class was perceived to be elsewhere. Quickly, they became associated with the very worst kind of backward-looking indolence and corruption. According to Rosario Romeo, the Sicilian *gabellotto* was a parasite, not an entrepreneur. Apparently lacking in either a 'capitalist spirit' or the paternalistic culture of the old nobility, the *gabellotti* were no more motivated by market forces and no more prone to making investments or adding value than their predecessors had been.[53] They spent their wealth on conspicuous consumption in the community, on what Sonnino calls 'a mania, a fury of luxury spending',[54] on building grand houses and local theatres, rather than on improving the land. Rental income remained the basis of every *gabellotto's* livelihood. Thus, notwithstanding Petrusewicz's rehabilitation of the Barracco family in Calabria, the consensus for Sicily is that these were the 'wrong' people, people who, far from improving Sicilian agriculture, did nothing but 'emphasize the ills and increase the burdens of the old system'.[55]

Government efforts to assist the Sicilian peasantry were equally counter-productive. The effect of 'freeing' land from feudal burdens was to deprive peasants of an important source of their livelihood. By abolishing grazing, wood and water rights, the government destroyed an important component of the peasant subsistence economy. Plans to compensate them were ultimately unhelpful. The division of common land never benefited the peasantry; instead it intensified a process of legal enclosure and illegal encroachment by the existing landowners, which had already been under way for some time.[56] Thus, two-thirds of the Church land sold at auction in Contessa Entellina during the 1860s was acquired by one man, 'a nouveau riche merchant from a neighbouring town'.[57] In the mining town of Lercara, the Nicolosi family took advantage of the same legislation to establish a sulphur mine (with presumably devastating consequences to the environment) on common land.[58] In Bronte, the land claimed as common was divided up by the local elite amongst themselves, and only then sub-let to poor sharecroppers. A petition signed by some 80 *Brontesi* and sent to the *intendente* of Catania in 1850 claimed that the land had been divided in such a way that they ('the poor farmers') received the worst land and at the highest rent. The commune was also quick to abolish all the free grazing and wood rights which peasants had enjoyed on common lands and rent these out to shepherds from adjacent communities.[59] Elsewhere, peasants received uneconomic and 'tiny plots of barren land in the remote countryside', which they quickly abandoned or sold to pay their debts.[60]

'*Muore il feudo, resta il latifondo*' (feudalism dies, the *latifondo* remains).[61] All the evidence suggests, indeed, that land reform in Southern Italy enabled a few people to accumulate vast tracts of land. Why did this happen? One obvious reason is the misconceived nature of the land reforms themselves. The arguments of intellectuals and reformers notwithstanding, land reform in Sicily was essentially the expression of contradictory motives, short-term political goals and a fundamental misunderstanding of the nature of power in the *latifondo*. The legislation itself caused chaos. Particular problems were caused by the sale of common land and customary rights, and by attempts to compensate peasants for this loss. Not surprisingly perhaps, given their age, these rights were not always recorded, or recorded accurately, in official documents; peasants relied often on verbal concessions and/or traditional practice. Neither was the issue of common land any clearer; indeed, land boundaries had long been a source of contention between the commune and the feudal landowner.[62] Hence, the task of establishing rights and boundaries was immensely complicated, with both sides simply asserting possessions and/or usurpations. In communities where the struggle over land was particularly acute, such as Bronte, the commune looked to court rulings from the seventeenth century to prove its claims, which were entirely rejected by the ex-feudal landowner (the Duchy of Bronte).[63] The dispute about boundaries revolved around a description of the roads in Bronte as '*via a monte ed a pendino*'. An expert sent to adjudicate 'wandered (*peregrinò*) like Diogenes' gathering information throughout the territory, only to conclude that the phrase had different meanings in different places.[64] Thus, although appeals were made to history, archive searches often proved inconclusive. Even the opinions of experts were usually open to challenge.

Unfortunately, the vagueness of government legislation confused this confused situation still further. Between 1817 and 1841, the government tried repeatedly, and without success, to give instructions for compensation, to set up a system for judging disputes over compensation and to establish who was responsible for judging them. In 1825 and 1827, some procedures were drawn up but it was only in 1841, after the intervention of the king, that it was finally established that peasants would receive between one-fifth and two-thirds of the land, to be allocated in each community by the local administration. Again, only in 1841 was it confirmed that the provincial *intendenti* had the power to mediate disputes and order the allocation of lands.[65]

Although, according to a contemporary British observer in Palermo, the policy to abolish customary rights was 'well-intended', it was also:

ill-contrived, and being badly executed proved of no avail... Most of
the intendenti took part with the communes against the landlords
and admitted uses, the prevalence of which at any time since 1735
was simply asserted; so that an estate purchased a century ago free
from all uses, was liable to be dismembered [66]

The initial impact of this policy was a bitter struggle between, on the
one hand, the commune and the local elite and, on the other, the ex-
feudal landowners. Thus, far from making landowners 'secure in the
ownership of capital and possessions', as Balsamo had anticipated, the
attempt to convert feudal property to private property undermined
everybody's property rights, thereby encouraging precisely the short-
term 'parasitic' approach to agriculture which the land reform was
meant to curtail. Beginning in the 1820s, litigation over property rights
could delay the division of common land almost indefinitely. In Adernò
and Belpasso, disputes between the landlords and the commune over
territorial boundaries, the nature of customary rights, the extent of
illegal encroachment and the amount of compensation due dragged
on until the 1870s.[67] This was not an exception: the records for Catania
and Palermo suggest that settlements before the 1860 revolution were a
rarity. Similar disputes in Bronte ended up before 'a definitive and
unappealable arbitration' by a supreme court judge in Palermo, but
too late to prevent an explosion of peasant violence there in 1860.[68]
Even when settlements were reached, it took years before the division
of common land was carried out. According to the Lorenzoni inquiry
(1910), only half the ordered divisions had been carried out by 1884; a
commission nominated to report into the matter had also not done so
by 1910.[69] In Belpasso, the ordered division of land took 60 years;[70] in
Alessandria della Rocca, the order of division had still not been enacted
in 1910.[71] It was for this reason that powerful landowners were able
simply to seize and illegally enclose the land for their own use. Thus the
mechanisms introduced by the liberal government after 1860 were no
more (and perhaps less) effective than the Bourbon system. In an attempt to avoid the chaos of the old system (and certainly to raise money
for shrinking coffers), it was decided to sell confiscated church land at
public auctions. Peasants fared particularly badly with this system as
the whole process was open to intimidation. Moreover, the government removed barriers to monopoly purchase and failed to make any
credit available to peasants. This too favoured those with money and
power and excluded those with neither.[72] One report to the 1876 government inquiry spoke of a long tradition whereby 'as soon as the decree

[dividing land] was published, all of the land was seized by the commune'.[73] For all these reasons, it is hardly surprising that land reform in
Sicily represented little more than an opportunity for those with land to
acquire more.

'It is useless to think', a commentator ventured at the end of the
century, 'that the municipal authorities ... can or with the present laws
even want to ... distribute the land which they themselves have taken
illegally and enjoyed for the last 20 years'.[74] In a sense, the problems of
implementation described above reveal a far more fundamental problem with land reform, which is that it was simply not enough by itself.
What successive governments failed to address was the physical, political and social underpinnings of *latifondo* society. Without improved
communications and investment in education, for example, peasants
could do little with the land allocated them. Without credit and an
alteration of the leaseholding system on existing land, they would
remain in debt and dependent on the *gabellotti*. Land reform, in other
words, failed to alter the basic structure of power in the *latifondo*, which
was the power of the *gabellotto* over the peasant.

Politics largely reinforced this situation. In order to control the countryside, both the Bourbon monarchy and its liberal successor relied on
the support and compliance of local power-holders. Even among the
democrats in 1860, a genuine concern for the appalling situation of the
peasantry was tempered by the practical need to win the support of local
power-holders; and, to do this, they had no choice but to resist peasant
demands.[75] As a result, the chances of land reform succeeding in Sicily
depended on a group of men whose entire livelihood depended on the
reform failing. Agricultural diversification was entrusted to a class grown
rich on grain, who drew a substantial profit from rent and who would
perceive little material benefit from commercializing their crop. Men
whose wealth and security derived from 'the frenzied exploitation'[76] of a
debt-ridden labour force were expected to allocate land to the peasantry,
thus freeing them from exploitation. The disappointing, even disas-
trous, results of land reform in Sicily can largely be traced to this fundamental fallacy.

Hence, the success of the new agrarian middle class in Sicily lay
partly in its ability to control the political process. As we have seen,
the powers given to local government – public works contracts, tax
collection, allocation of common land – were used as a means of personal enrichment, of 'looting the public purse' for private gain.[77] Politics could equally be used to build or enhance a personal power base.
Control over local policing backed up the extensive use of private force.

Control over decision-making, public appointments and the 'public purse' could form the basis of a web of patronage, where clientelistic relations of reciprocal friendships and personal favours predominated. 'Participation in local government', Paolo Pezzino writes, also came to represent 'a confirmation of intrinsic status' and 'a means to revive old hegemonies and to boost the processes of elevation in social status'.[78] As a process, moreover, where power was exercised as much to exclude as include, politics also offered a means of maintaining a hold over peasants. In nineteenth-century Sicily, politics was king.

Before unification, the key to controlling the political process was the list of those eligible for public office (*la lista degli eleggibili*). This was a list of the local wealth and property-holders, and compiled by them, from which council members were chosen and from which the mayor and the first and second 'elect' were nominated by the provincial intendant. The list provided access to power and, initially at least, it tended to be dominated by a restricted number of influential families. Between the reforms of 1817 and 1848, for example, the names of a few rich families – Spitalieri, Meli, Sanfilippo and Minissale – recur repeatedly on the list of those eligible for office in Bronte. Moreover, the Spitalieri, Sanfilippo and Minissale were all related to each other by marriage.[79] These families aimed to share out positions in the Bronte council on a rotating basis, effectively excluding others from office. In 1818, the council, 'not being able to find more able people to fill these offices', asked the *intendente* to chose between Don Giaochino Spitalieri, his brother Don Luigi, and their 74 year-old father, Don Nicolò, as mayor. Two of the choices for both first and second 'elect' were also related.[80] 'Networks', according to Giarrizzo, 'of a more or less complex nature, tied … all the members of Biancavilla's ruling group (*ceto*) together' and they all, at one time or another, held political office:

> the Milone had married into the Uccellatore and Caselli family, and into the Castro and the Rizzo; the Motta, through the Castro, had married into the Sangiorgio, in their turn married into Don Angelo Biondi's family, who had relatives with the Reina; Don Filippo Reina was the nephew of Don Ferdinando Portale, of Don Luigi Verzì, of Don Emmanuele, and of Don Placido, the local doctor, whose son Don Francesco would become mayor; and so on and so on.[81]

To all appearances, the introduction of elections after unification did little to alter the ability of influential families to monopolize communal offices. Nicolò Nicolosi, whose family were former *gabellotti* for the

Prince of Palagonia, controlled local government in Lercara under the Bourbons. With Garibaldi's arrival in 1860, his four sons and their cousin seized power in the name of the revolution. The local council, National Guard, and responsibility for local taxation and finance came under the control of the Nicolosi family and their in-laws. Their power also survived well into the liberal period.[82] An 1862 report on Lercara argued that the town council's 'origins' lay in 'an irregular electoral list, in an assembly which violated all the best laws and in the *prepotenza* (power) and intrigues of the reactionary family by which it is dominated'.[83] Certainly, the introduction of a more centralized administration after 1860, with, for example, new police powers, new taxation and a system of conscription, made the spoils of local government more attractive than ever. This, in turn, reflected the weakness of central government. While the provincial *intendente* nominally controlled appointments, in practice, he could do little more than mediate disputes and/or approve the choices offered to him.[84]

Local power in nineteenth-century Sicily was thus based on a potent combination of land and politics, reinforced by a series of clientelistic relations. More striking still, perhaps, was the extent to which local power revolved around family and kinship structures. Marriage and inheritance was a means of acquiring and securing wealth, status and upward mobility; kinship ties gave the new elite stability and solidarity.[85] Of course, it is worth noting that there is nothing especially remarkable about the clientelistic basis of *latifondo* politics.[86] Clientelistic relations, as Briquet argues, should not be considered the 'prerogative' of any particular society; they are found in modern political institutions as often as in traditional ones.[87] What is, arguably, more unusual is the extent to which the oligarchic façade of local power in Sicily masked a much more unstable and contested reality. We have already seen the extent to which the acquisition of land – especially the struggle for titles to common land – involved the new elite in prolonged litigation with ex-feudal landowners. By and large, this was a process from which they emerged victorious. However, partly because the use of local government for private ends was so successful, a series of fresh challenges then began in an effort, to shake their grip on power.

One clear symptom was what Barone calls the 'irresistible expansion' of the 'list of eligibles', which in some communes almost tripled between 1818 and the mid-1840s (in Bronte, the numbers increased from 70 to 180).[88] Another indication was the intensification of factional struggle, both for control of local government and for the ownership of land. During the political upheavals of the 1840s and after, the fight for control of local government began to destabilize local politics. In Bronte, the elite split into rival factions: on one side, the traditionally influential families of Meli and Spitalieri hung grimly on to power while, on the other, a group of self-proclaimed radicals pursued power for themselves. In both Bronte and Biancavilla, this factionalism exploded into the terrible violence of 1860, which saw the effective 'disintegration' of the local elite over the question of jobs in local government.[89] Elsewhere, contemporary reports testify to intensifying power struggles among rival élites. Factional struggle in the provincial capital, Girgenti (Agrigento), was said in 1861 to be due to the 'perennial question of jobs and influence'.[90] Local elections, the prefect of Palermo complained a few years later, were not concerned with political principles but with private matters, 'and they all go back to the families who hold excessive power (*prepotenza*) or those who seek to hold it for themselves'.[91] All the evidence suggests, finally, that these conflicts could provoke a kind of 'forced' circulation of elites. A monopoly of power there may have been, but it could easily pass from one faction to another; appearances of feudal longevity notwithstanding, political fortunes could be made and lost with remarkable speed.[92]

Clientele networks, Briquet tells us, can serve as an instrument of social and political legitimization. They can work as a process of adaptation, to reconcile state power with that of the community, and as a process of integration, a means by which elites acquire and mobilize popular support.[93] It is interesting, therefore, to reflect on the extent to which the nineteenth-century elites of the Sicilian *latifondo* possessed this kind of mass appeal. Pezzino draws our attention to what he terms the 'weak social hegemony of the dominant classes in the South',[94] and argues that the economically and politically powerful families of the *latifondo* enjoyed little social legitimacy. While this may overstate the case, the monopolistic hold of the new elite on political power could create resentment, and the spectacle of factional rivalry provided little space for the construction of consent. In particular, the means by which these families had accumulated wealth caused huge popular resentment; and the upsurge of peasant unrest posed a major threat to their position. Peasant anger over the appropriation and 'usurpation' of common land expressed itself in the invasion of enclosed land and the destruction of fences and crops. In 1848, peasant agitation over their lack of land led to the 'devastation' of woods in Bronte and Biancavilla. In Ficuzza, Prizzi, Bivona, Sclafani and Ganci, woods were similarly laid waste by peasants desperate for arable land.[95] Anger over the enclosure of common land also played a central role in the violent attacks on landowners during 1860 in Bronte and Biancavilla, when a mob dragged members of local government, responsible for the partition of common land, from their beds and brutally murdered them.[96] A local expert in the province of Catania, interviewed for the 1876 government inquiry, attributed popular 'hatred for a certain class of person' and 'general grumbling' entirely to the commune's seizure of common land.[97] Property crimes also increased in the *latifondo*, reflecting a rise in the numbers of destitute: the British commentator John Goodwin estimated that 'out of every 100 robbers convicted in 1835, 88 were found utterly destitute, and the other 12 more or less needy'.[98] Indeed, the threat of crime and lawlessness in the *latifondo* made the new elites far more dependent on central government – or at least on its security forces – than they appeared to be, or would have ever cared to admit.[99]

Much recent debate about the Sicilian *latifondo* has focused on its economic survival until the late nineteenth century, and the causes of its rapid demise thereafter. There has been less debate about its changing social and political relations. We have seen that peasant poverty and land-hunger was necessary to the power and wealth of the new elite in the *latifondo*. Peasant anger over land was also initially encouraged by them, so as to intimidate and discourage the ex-feudal landowners from making claims on land. In some cases, perhaps most notably Bronte, peasant revolt was actively encouraged by the opposition as a weapon in the struggle to gain political power. Partly as a result, however, the issue of common land came to radicalize and, to an extent, galvanize the Sicilian peasantry against the *gabellotti* as never before. Jane and Peter Schneider have pointed to changes taking place on the *latifondo* during the 1890s, when the impact of emigration to the Americas led to economic improvement through remittances and the setting up of credit banks.[100] While this evidence is important, adding as it does another layer to our understanding of this complex society, it is also true that the process of litigation and agitation over common land lasted throughout the liberal period in Sicily and persisted, indeed, into the twentieth century. Attempts to 'vindicate' (*rivendicare*) peasant claims to common land lost in the 1820s were made as late as the 1890s, during the first organized popular movement against the *latifondo*, the peasant union struggles of the *fasci siciliani*.[101] And although the *fasci* were suppressed by the government, the issue re-emerged again during the Giolittian period immediately preceding the First World War. During the 1920s, land occupations became commonplace and a ferocious 'struggle for land' continued to divide many communities.[102]

The association of the *latifondo* with feudalism is a tenacious one. Vast grain-fields, a middle class uninterested in the benefits of commercialization and liberalism, and an apparently helpless rural poor may all seem like survivors from a feudal past. The reality is rather different. Despite appearances to the contrary, the nineteenth-century Sicilian *latifondo* was largely a nineteenth-century creation. However counter-productively, government reforms did affect the distribution of wealth within the Sicilian *latifondo*. However seemingly spurious, a process of reaction and adaptation to this did occur. And while these adaptations left the *latifondo* largely intact, they altered – in complex and important ways – the relations of power within this rural society.

The effect of land reform on the Sicilian *latifondo* was to create a powerful, new ruling elite. But because the members of this elite did not respond to the opportunities of land reform in a 'proper' capitalist manner, they have always been condemned as idle, backward and corrupt. The scale of their initial success has largely been ignored. They used their control over the rental market in land and, subsequently, over the political process, not only to frustrate the purpose of the reforms, but to manipulate its provisions so as to concentrate as much land as they could into as few hands as possible. Family and friendship became the means of consolidating their new position. And, as this chapter has sought to show, this strategy should be considered an entirely rational one. Their material well-being lay with the *latifondo* and the means for accumulating wealth lay largely in the political process. The skill of this new elite in perceiving and controlling this advantage meant that the grain estates survived repeated attempts to dismantle them.

However, an analysis of landownership in the Sicilian *latifondo* in the early to mid-nineteenth century suggests that the process of accumulation and concentration ultimately left rural elites in a curiously weak position. Quite understandably perhaps, the new families of the Sicilian *latifondo* achieved little economic stability and still less in the way of commercial success. Much of their status and power was dependent on state employment. They were increasingly threatened by peasant unrest, frightened by crime and undermined by the pressures of factional rivalry. Thus, the extraordinary combination of family-ties, landownership and political power may enable us to understand the power of this new elite and, with them, the *latifondo*'s grip on nineteenth-century rural society. Yet family, land and politics also laid the foundations for the *latifondo*'s perennial problems and, arguably, for its harsh treatment at the hands of historians.

Notes

1   R. Romeo, *Il Risorgimento in Sicilia* (Bari, 1950), p. 197.
2   The clearest statement of this position was made in successive private and public inquiries into conditions in the South between the 1870s and the First World War. See, in particular, S. Sonnino, 'I contadini in Sicilia', in L. Franchetti and S. Sonnino, *Inchiesta in Sicilia* (Florence, 1974; orig. pub. 1876), but also R. Bonfadini, *Relazione della giunta per l'inchiesta sulle condizione della Sicilia del 1876* (Rome, 1876), A. Damiani (ed.), *Atti della giunta per l'inchiesta agraria e sulle condizione della classe agricola*, Vol. xiii (Rome, 1885) and the Lorenzoni inquiry, *Inchiesta parlamentare dulle condizioni dei contadini nelle provincie meridionali e nella Sicilia*, Vol. vi (Rome, 1910). For a more recent discussion along these lines see D. Mack Smith, 'The *Latifundia* in Modern Sicilian History', *Proceedings of the British Academy* 4 (1965), 85–124.
3   On which see J. A. Davis, 'Remapping Italy's Path to the Twentieth Century', *Journal of Modern History* 66 (1994), pp. 291–320.
4   R. Romeo, *Risorgimento e capitalismo* (Bari/Rome, 1998; orig. pub. 1959); E. Sereni, *Il capitalismo nelle campagne (1860–1900)* (Turin, 1968); E. Sereni, *Capitalismo e mercato nazionale* (Rome, 1974).
5   For Rosario Romeo, the exploitation of the landless Southern peasantry was a necessary condition for the primitive accumulation of capital and, thus, for Northern industrialization, while Sereni argued that low levels of domestic consumption, a direct consequence of peasant poverty, actually retarded industrial development. For a summary of the debate, see Guido Pescosolido's *'premessa'* to the 1998 edition of Romeo's *Risorgimento e capitalismo*.
6   According to Gaetano Salvemini, quoted in M. Petrusewicz, *Latifundium. Moral Economy and Material Life in a European Periphery* (Ann Arbor, MI, 1996), p. 1.
7   For discussions in English of this new approach to the Italian South, see A. Lyttleton, 'A new past for the *Mezzogiorno*', *Times Literary Supplement* 4 Oct. 1991, pp. 14–15; J. Morris, 'Challenging *Meridionalismo*. Constructing a new history for Southern Italy', in J. Morris and R. Lumley (eds), *The New History of the Italian South* (Exeter, 1997), pp. 1–19 and J. A. Davis, 'Casting off the "Southern problem": Or the Peculiarities of the South Reconsidered', in J. Schneider, (ed.), *Italy's 'Southern Question'. Orientalism in One Country* (Oxford/New York, 1998), pp. 205–24.
8   J. Schneider, 'Introduction: The Dynamics of Neo-orientalism in Italy (1848–1995)', in J. Schneider, *Italy's 'Southern Question'*, p. 1.
9   See G. Giarrizzo, 'Per una storia della Sicilia', in *Mezzogiorno senza meridionalismo: la Sicilia, lo sviluppo, il potere* (Venice, 1992), pp. 3–46, and, in particular, John Dickie, 'Stereotypes of the Italian South', in Lumley and Morris, *The New History of the Italian South*, pp. 114–47 and *Darkest Italy: the Nation and Stereotypes of the Mezzogiorno, 1860–1900* (London, 1999); Nelson Moe, '"Altro che Italia." Il Sud dei Piemontesi (1860–61)', *Meridiana* 15 (1992), pp. 53–89; Nelson Moe, 'The emergence of the Southern Question in Villari, Franchetti, and Sonnino', in Schneider, *Italy's 'Southern Question'*, pp. 51–76; and Silvana Patriarca, 'How many Italies? Representing the South in official statistics', in Schneider, *Italy's 'Southern Question'*, pp. 77–97.

10 Petrusewicz, *Latifundium*, esp. pp. 7–21. For a more general discussion, see also P. Bevilacqua, *Breve storia dell'Italia meridionale dall'Ottocento a oggi* (Rome, 1992), esp. pp. 15–20.

11 See the debate in the *Times Literary Supplement*, between de Vivo, Davis and Bevilacqua, 8 Nov. 1991; 29 Nov. 1991; 6 Dec. 1991; 27 Dec. 1991; and the criticism of G. Montroni, *Gli uomini del Re. La nobiltà napoletana nell'Ottocento* (Catanzaro, 1996), p. ix. Petrusewicz replies in part to her critics in 'The demise of *latifondismo*', in Lumley and Morris, *The New History of the Italian South*, pp. 20–41.

12 A. Scifo, 'La proprietà della terra nella Sicilia preunitaria', *Nuovi Quaderni del Meridione* 54 (1976), p. 129.

13 Petrusewicz, *Latifundium*, p. 8.

14 L. Franchetti, 'Condizioni politiche e amministrative della Sicilia', and S. Sonnino, 'I contadini in Sicilia', both in Franchetti and Sonnino, *Inchiesta in Sicilia*.

15 Sonnino, 'I contadini in Sicilia', p. 10.

16 F. Renda, *Storia della Sicilia dal 1860 al 1970*, Vol. I: *I caratteri originari e gli anni dell'unificazione* (Palermo, 1984), p. 93.

17 P. Balsamo, *Memorie inedite di pubblica economia e agricoltura*, II (Palermo, 1845), p. 190.

18 A. Blok, 'South Italian Agro-Towns', *Comparative Studies in Society and History*, 11 (1969), 121–35.

19 Sonnino, 'I contadini in Sicilia', p. 53.

20 On the expansion of the *latifondo* see O. Cancila, *Baroni e popoli nella Sicilia del grano* (Palermo, 1983) and F. Benigno, 'Aspetti territoriali e ruralizzazione nella Sicilia del Seicento: note per una discussione', in *La popolazione delle campagne italiane in età moderna* (Bologna, 1993).

21 Sometimes common land was quite extensive (notably in Caltagirone, Piazza Armerina, Corleone), although equally often under threat from private encroachments. See O. Cancila, 'Dal feudo alla proprietà borghese: la distribuzione della terra', in O. Cancila, *L'Economia della Sicilia. Aspetti storici* (Palermo, 1992), p. 65.

22 Quoted in J. Goodwin, 'Sicily: Social and Political' (1848), British Library Ms. 42150, pp. 5–6.

23 M. Verga, 'Il "settecento del baronaggio": l'aristocrazia siciliana tra politica e cultura', in F. Benigno and C. Torrisi (eds), *Élites e potere in Sicilia dal medioevo ad oggi* (Catanzaro, 1995), pp. 93–4.

24 Sonnino, 'I contadini in Sicilia', pp. 49–50.

25 Balsamo, *Memorie inedite*, II, p. 193.

26 See the analysis of contracts in Sonnino, 'I contadini in Sicilia', pp. 18–29, 53–6, 130–1; Balsamo, *Memorie inedite*, II, pp. 191–3; G. Oddo, *Lo sviluppo incompiuto: Villafrati 1596–1960* (Palermo, 1986), pp. 58–61.

27 'I contadini in Sicilia', p. 107.

28 Balsamo, *Memorie inedite*, II, p. 191.

29 Sonnino, 'I contadini in Sicilia', p. 56; J. Schneider and P. Schneider, *Culture and Economy in Western Sicily* (New York, 1976), pp. 66–72; L. Riall, 'Nelson versus Bronte: Land, Litigation and Local Politics in Restoration Sicily', *European History Quarterly* 1 (1999).

30 Balsamo, *Memorie inedite*, p. 192.

31   Romeo, *Il Risorgimento in Sicilia*, pp. 124–5, L. Riall, *Sicily and the Unification of Italy: Liberal Policy and Local Power, 1859–66* (Oxford, 1998), p. 39.
32   G. Giarrizzo, *Un comune rurale nella Sicilia etnea. (Biancavilla 1810–1860)* (Catania, 1963), pp. 31–2.
33   Romeo, *Il Risorgimento in Sicilia*, pp. 117–21.
34   Balsamo, *Memorie inedite*, p. 190.
35   Mack Smith, 'The *Latifundia* in Modern Sicilian History', pp. 88–90; Cancila, 'Dal feudo alla proprietà borghese', p. 82.
36   N. Palmieri, 'Necrologia per Paolo Balsamo', in Balsamo, *Memorie inedite*, I, pp. vi–vii.
37   F. Renda, *Bernardo Tanucci e i beni dei Gesuiti in Sicilia* (Rome, 1974).
38   Mack Smith, 'The *Latifundia* in Modern Sicilian History', p. 93. For a discussion of the significance of the 1812 reform, see Romeo, *Il Risorgimento in Sicilia*, pp. 140–5.
39   Riall, *Sicily and the Unification of Italy*, pp. 33–4.
40   Cancila, 'Dal feudo alla proprietà borghese', pp. 108–22.
41   Romeo, *Il Risorgimento in Sicilia*, pp. 326–31.
42   Riall, *Sicily and the Unification of Italy*, pp. 71, 87.
43   Riall, *Sicily and the Unification of Italy*, pp. 134–5.
44   See note 2, above.
45   Sonnino, 'I contadini in Sicilia', p. 17.
46   'Genuardo' in Anton Blok's study, *The Mafia of a Sicilian Village, 1860–1960. A Study of Violent Peasant Entrepreneurs* (Oxford, 1974), p. 42.
47   J. Schneider and P. Schneider, *Festival of the Poor: Fertility Decline and the Ideology of Class in Sicily, 1860–1980* (Tucson, AZ, 1996), p. 67.
48   In Lorenzoni, *Inchiesta parlamentare*, p. 257.
49   Romeo, *Il Risorgimento in Sicilia*, pp. 112, 180–1; J. Goodwin, 'An Essay on Sicilian Industry' (1836), British Library, Ms. 42152, p. 13.
50   For a discussion, see Blok, *The Mafia of a Sicilian Village*, pp. 32–4, 38.
51   Giarrizzo, *Un comune rurale*, p. 106.
52   Giarrizzo, *Un comune rurale*, p. 109.
53   Romeo, *Il Risorgimento in Sicilia*, p. 29.
54   Sonnino, 'I contadini in Sicilia', p. 109.
55   Romeo, *Il Risorgimento in Sicilia*, p. 31.
56   Cancila, 'Dal feudo alla proprietà borghese', pp. 118–23.
57   Blok, *The Mafia of a Sicilian Village*, p. 41.
58   See the correspondence in Archivio di Stato di Palermo (ASP), Intendenza di Palermo, Scioglimento di promiscuità dei comuni della provincia di Palermo (1819–1860 e oltre), b. 30.
59   15 Sept. 1850, Archivio di Stato di Catania (ASC), Intendenza, cat.II, b.253.
60   Mack Smith, 'The *Latifundia* in Modern Sicilian History', p. 101.
61   Cancila, 'Dal feudo alla proprietà borghese', p. 107.
62   Ibid., pp. 72–84.
63   Court deliberations of 30 October 1957 in ASP, Fondo Nelson, f.2, b.209.
64   '*Difesa per la duchessa di Bronte contro la comune di Bronte scritta dell'avvocato Antonio Battaglia*' (1838), ibid., f.2, b.294.
65   Cancila, 'Dal feudo alla proprietà borghese', pp. 119–22; Scifo, 'La proprieta della terra', pp. 134–6. On government policy see also A. Scirocco, 'Ferdinando II e la Sicilia: gli anni della speranza e della delusione (1830–1837)',

in S. Russo, (ed.), *I moti del 1837 a Siracusa negli anni trenta* (Caltanissetta, 1987).

66 Goodwin, 'Sicily: Social and Political', pp. 38–9.

67 ASP, Intendenza di Catania, 'Atti relativi allo scioglimento dei diritti promiscui', b.2, ff.4, 39–40.

68 Riall, 'Nelson versus Bronte'.

69 Lorenzoni, *Inchiesta parlamentare*, pp. 266–7.

70 Romeo, *Il Risorgimento in Sicilia*, p. 186.

71 Lorenzoni, *Inchiesta parlamentare* p. 268. See also Mack Smith, 'The *Latifundia* in Modern Sicilian History', p. 97.

72 Ibid., pp. 101–3; G. Cerrito, 'La questione della liquidazione dell'asse ecclesiastico in Sicilia', *Rassegna Storica del Risorgimento* 43 (1956), pp. 270–83.

73 Sebastiano Carnazza, in Bonfadini, *Relazione*, p. 852.

74 Quoted in Mack Smith, 'The *Latifundia* in Modern Sicilian History', p. 101.

75 For a discussion, see Riall, *Sicily and the Unification of Italy*, esp. pp. 86–90, 225–30; on 1860, see F. Renda, 'Garibaldi e la questione contadina in Sicilia nel 1860', in G. Cingari, (ed.), *Garibaldi e il socialismo* (Rome/Bari, 1984), pp. 40–3.

76 Romeo, *Il Risorgimento in Sicilia*, p. 30.

77 G. Fiume, 'Introduzione', in G. Rampolla, *Suicidio per mafia* (Palermo, 1986), p. 17.

78 P. Pezzino, 'Local Power in Southern Italy', in Lumley and Morris, *The New History of the Italian South*, p. 50.

79 Riall, 'Nelson versus Bronte'.

80 ASC, *Intendenza*, cat.1, b.126.

81 Giarrizzo, *Un comune rurale*, p. 107.

82 Riall, *Sicily and the Unification of Italy*, pp. 99–100.

83 Riall, *Sicily and the Unification of Italy*, p. 141.

84 Riall, *Sicily and the Unification of Italy*, pp. 139–49.

85 G. Barone, 'Dai nobili ai notabili. Note sul sistema politico in Sicilia in età contemporanea', in Benigno and Torrisi, *Élites e potere in Sicilia*, pp. 168–70; Pezzino, 'Local power in Southern Italy', pp. 51–4.

86 See, however, the debate about Edward Banfield's concept of 'amoral familialism' as an explanation of Southern backwardness, in *The Moral Basis of a Backward Society* (New York, 1958); recently revived in a somewhat different guise in D. Putnam, *Making Democracy Work: Civic Traditions in Modern Italy* (Princeton, NJ, 1993), esp. pp. 121–62. For a discussion and critique, see G. Gribaudi, 'Images of the South: The *Mezzogiorno* Seen by Insiders and Outsiders' in Lumley and Morris, *The New History of the Italian South*, pp. 106–9.

87 J. L. Briquet, 'Premessa', in *Clientelismi*, special issue of *Quaderni Storici*, 97:1 (1998), p. 6.

88 Barone, 'Dai nobili ai notabili', p. 170.

89 On the events of 1860 in Biancavilla, see Giarrizzo, *Un comune rurale*, pp. 319–74. On the famous revolt in Bronte, the literature is huge but see, in particular, B. Radice, 'Nino Bixio a Bronte', *Archivio Storico per la Sicilia Orientale*, 7 (1910), pp. 252–94; D. Mack Smith, 'The Peasants' Revolt in Sicily, 1860', in *Victor Emmanuel, Cavour and the Risorgimento* (London, 1972), pp. 190–224; and my analysis in 'Nelson versus Bronte'.

90   Quoted in Riall, *Sicily and the Unification of Italy*, p. 143.
91   Riall, *Sicily and the Unification of Italy*, p. 195.
92   Riall, *Sicily and the Unification of Italy*, pp. 51–6.
93   J. L. Briquet, 'Clientelismi e processi politici', *Quaderni Storici*, 97:1 (1998), pp. 12–20.
94   Pezzino, 'Local Power in Southern Italy', p. 55.
95   G. Fiume, *La crisi sociale del 1848 in Sicilia* (Messina, 1982), esp. pp. 118–29.
96   See above, n.85.
97   Sebastiano Carnazza, in Bonfadini, *Relazione*, p. 854.
98   Goodwin, 'Sicily: Social and Political', p. 22.
99   Riall, *Sicily and the Unification of Italy*, pp. 227–9.
100 J. and P. Schneider, *Festival of the Poor*, pp. 123–31.
101 On the *fasci siciliani*, see S. F. Romano, *Storia dei fasci siciliani* (Bari, 1959); F. Renda, *I fasci siciliani 1892–94* (Turin, 1977); and the essays by Giarrizzo, Manacorda, Renda and Manganaro in *I fasci siciliani* (Bari, 1975).
102 S. Lupo, 'L'utopia totalitaria del fascismo (1918–1942)', in M. Aymard and G. Giarrizzo, (eds), *La Sicilia* (Turin, 1987), pp. 376–81.

Part III

Gender as a Category of Historical Comparison

8
Gender in the Recent Historiography of the US South and some Speculations on the Prospects for Comparative History

J. William Harris

The rise of 'gender' as a category of historical analysis is associated, quite correctly, with the explosion on women's history from the 1960s on, but it is worth keeping in mind that the concept, if not the term, was important in interpretations of southern history well before its increasing importance in historical writing after about 1980. In particular, Wilbur Cash's *Mind of the South*, one of the most famous interpretations of southern history and culture, was, in many respects, a gendered analysis. To Cash, the southern mind (more properly, temperament) was a product of 'the Man at the Center', himself a product of a frontier environment: simple, individualistic, hedonistic, often violent, a 'hell of a fellow'. A 'common brotherhood of white men' trumped class, according to Cash, binding planters, yeoman, and poor whites on the basis of shared ideals of masculinity. While much of Cash's analysis is obviously a product of its time, he anticipated many of the ways in which recent scholars have connected this white masculine ideal to both white supremacy and male domination. Whiteness (as we would now put it) elevated poor whites with its 'vastly ego-warming and ego-expanding distinction between the white man and the black'. Further, white men's guilt over sexual connections with slave women (which Cash did not recognize as exploitative), combined with an extreme version of Victorian sentimentality, led them to exalt the white woman, who, 'as perpetuator of white superiority in legitimate line, and as a creature absolutely inaccessible to the males of the inferior group', became the focus of what amounted to a 'downright gyneolatry'.[1]

In varying forms, more recent influential studies have made similar arguments without either adopting all of Cash's claims or beginning from explicit attention to the meanings of gender. A good deal of Bertram Wyatt-Brown's analysis in his justly celebrated *Southern Honor* can be understood as a scholarly and systematic extension of some of Cash's key arguments. For Wyatt-Brown, the 'keystone of the slaveholding South's morality' was 'honor', defined primarily in terms of ideals of masculinity and femininity. Honour accepted hierarchy but bound white men in a common ethic and standard of behaviour; it entailed a public defence of reputation (by violence, if necessary) and a patriarchal family system in which women were the repositories of virtue but faced severely circumscribed roles. Honour's ideals, according to Wyatt-Brown, decisively structured law, politics and popular mores.[2] Extending Cash in a quite different direction is Joel Williamson's *Crucible of Race*, in which the author argues that white violence against blacks in the late nineteenth century was rooted in white men's unconscious fear and guilt over their failed masculinity. Like Cash, Williamson argued that an extreme version of Victorian morality promoted the sentimental exaltation of white women. Because of an economic depression in the countryside, white men lost the ability to properly support their wives and daughters; this made them unusually vulnerable to the guilt that was promoted in any case by the severe sexual repression engendered by Victorian values. Projection of this unconscious guilt on to black men led to the racial violence characteristic of late nineteenth-century southern life.[3] Eugene Genovese's *Roll, Jordan, Roll*, perhaps the most influential single book in southern history among scholars today, also incorporates a gendered analysis. For Genovese, paternalism rather than honour is the keystone of southern ethics, but Genovese's explication of planter behaviour and values shares much with Wyatt-Brown's and Cash's in its details. For Genovese, slaveholders 'in essential respects ... grew to be a particular type of men and women'; slaveholding men were 'tough, proud, and arrogant; liberal-spirited in all that did not touch their honor; gracious and courteous; generous and kind; quick to anger and extraordinarily cruel; attentive to duty and careless of any time and effort that did not control their direct interests'.[4]

Concern with the nature of southern masculinity (and, to a lesser extent, southern femininity) was thus central in southern historiography well before the current wave of writings, with its more self-conscious consideration of gender as a category of analysis. Nevertheless, it makes sense to trace most of that current writing to the rise of women's history among professional historians. The key work was Anne Firor Scott's *The Southern Lady: From Pedestal to Politics* (1970). While a number of earlier studies of southern women appeared before Scott's book, they had been, like most such studies before the reinvigoration of feminism in the 1960s, marginalized in the academy. Scott took as her subject the elite women of the nineteenth-century South, primarily slaveholding mistresses and their post-Civil War descendants. In the first part of her book she outlined both the gender expectations for women – their 'pedestal' – and the ways in which their actual lives often belied the image of the 'lady'. The second half traces the eventual creation of the 'new women' in the South who launched the southern wing of the suffrage movement. Many of Scott's claims continue to inspire debate: for example, that many women of the planter class were covert abolitionists, that the Civil War experience liberated many women from traditional roles, and that participation in voluntary organizations such as missionary societies and the Women's Christian Temperance Union were key formative experiences for southern suffrage activists in the Progressive era.[5]

Much writing since *The Southern Lady* can be seen as a continuing confrontation with Scott's interpretations. Jacqueline Dowd Hall's biography of the anti-lynching activist, Jesse Daniel Ames, was one of the first to take up Scott's themes. Ames was a progressive era 'new woman': a Texas reformer and suffrage campaigner who, after the suffrage amendment was passed in 1920, moved into interracial work in the 1920s and later headed the Southern Association of Women for the Prevention of Lynching. Ames's anti-lynching work directly attacked white men's claims that lynching was necessary to 'protect' white women like herself, and Hall shows how her 'revolt against chivalry' was (within limits) a revolt against both racist and patriarchal practice.[6] Hall's work was, however, unusual in the initial burst of writing following Scott in its focus on the post-Civil War period; most of the books on southern women published in the 1980s focused on the antebellum era. Catherine Clinton's *The Plantation Mistress* (1982) was the first of these. Taking up many of Scott's themes and, like her, writing about elite women, Clinton stressed even more than Scott the ways in which antebellum patriarchal culture confined and oppressed southern women. She also emphasized women's work, particularly the work that devolved upon mistresses because of their responsibilities for their slaves ('slave of slaves,' as Clinton overstated the case in a provocative chapter title). Clinton, like Scott, thought that slavery produced powerful and conflicting emotions among mistresses; more than Scott, she emphasized the 'sexual dynamics of slavery', arguing that the sexual exploitation of slave women was both slavery's greatest curse and the most important source of white women's guilt over, and, sometimes, outright opposition to slavery.[7]

Clinton's study was the first of many that dealt with antebellum southern women. Several writers approached the study of gender roles through family life or specialized studies of women. Jan Lewis analysed emotional ties within elite Virginia families in the late eighteenth and early nineteenth centuries, and Jane Turner Censer the complex relationships between parents and children in North Carolina's antebellum planter families; both offered portraits of family behaviour and values that strongly resembled family life as described by historians of the North. Suzanne Lebsock imaginatively exploited property and court records in a study of white and free black women in Petersburg, Virginia, and concluded that the evidence demonstrated the existence of a female culture of 'personalism' that, to some extent, crossed both class and racial boundaries and implicitly challenged publicly dominant patriarchal values. Other studies took issue with Scott's and Clinton's claims that many southern women consciously resented their constraints and, unlike Lebsock, Lewis and Censer, stressed the differences between southern and northern women and families. In her broad study of the slaveholding elite, for example, Elizabeth Fox-Genovese argued that slaveholding women were, on the whole, well-satisfied with their high positions in the class and race hierarchy, and she dismissed most of the evidence pointing towards anti-slavery views as superficial. Jean Friedman's work on southern women's religion and kinship ties and Sally McMillen's on southern motherhood both agreed that southern women accepted, for the most part, limitations on their roles and power. Friedman also stressed the continuities in women's culture after the Civil War, implicitly challenging Scott's assertion that the war had 'functionally' destroyed patriarchy and brought a decisive break for southern women. However, Scott's view of the 'new woman' received reinforcement in the first full treatment of southern suffrage leaders. According to Marjorie Wheeler's *New Women of the New South*, these women presented a radical challenge to southern traditions.[8]

These studies all focused on elite, primarily slaveholding women, who are, of course, much more likely to leave the diaries, letters and other sources that make it easy to document everyday life and values, and more likely to own the property that leaves multiple traces in public records. Meanwhile, other scholars were turning to slave sources and census records to study women and families among slaves, free blacks and ordinary whites. Orville Vernon Burton's study of family life among both whites and blacks in Edgefield County, South Carolina, drew on a large quantitative data base as well as extensive manuscript collections. Norreece T. Jones paid close attention to family roles and values in his study of slave control and resistance in South Carolina. Jacqueline Jones's sweeping synthesis of African American women's history stressed black women's devotion to their children and husbands and pictured the slave family as primarily nuclear in structure, with strictly gendered domestic roles. All three argued that, in a broad sense, black and white family values and ideals were similar, even when the constraints of slavery prevented blacks from living up these ideals in practice. Deborah White, however, in the first book-length treatment of slave women, argued that slave families were matrifocal and organized primarily around the mother–child tie rather than the husband–wife tie that anchored nuclear families, and that slave women often had close ties to a wide variety of real and fictive kin.[9]

By the mid-1980s, many of these works were already using an explicit gender analysis to shape their approach to women's historical experience: an analysis, that is, which sees the biological differences between men and women as less important than the cultural and social construction of masculinity and femininity in shaping women's lives and in shaping the institutions and values that often bind them into limited roles with limited power. In Joan Scott's helpful definition, gender is 'a way of referring to the social organization of the relationship between the sexes'. As Scott noted in the 1986 essay in which this definition appeared, the concept of gender had, by then, become attractive to feminist historians who wanted to show that women's subordinate position throughout history was neither 'natural' nor permanent. Her essay proved to be particularly influential, serving simultaneously as a summing up and critique of earlier approaches and as a suggestive guide to future work.[10]

Far more than simply extending women's history, the concept of gender has spurred new subjects and new kinds of scholarship. Perhaps most obviously, it has prompted greater attention to men, attention that frequently returns to themes of earlier work by Cash, Wyatt-Brown and Williamson. Thus historians have investigated the nature of male culture and its creation, content and performance at various times and in various circumstances. A number of historians have written about culture of Civil War soldiers, exploring how southern (and northern) concepts of masculinity motivated soldiers to volunteer and fight, and how for black soldiers, perhaps even more than for white, the war was a proving ground for 'manhood'. Essays by Kenneth Greenberg explored the language and behaviour of 'manly honor' among slaveholders, as evidenced in their duels, sports and pro-slavery arguments. For the post-war period, Ted Ownby examined the male culture of hunting, drinking and gambling and the attempt of New South reformers to repress such forms of traditional masculinity in favour of a home-centred, evangelical culture.[11] Others explicitly compared women's and men's culture, psychology and behaviours. Joan Cashin's examination of planter families who moved to the antebellum south-west cotton frontier contrasted men's motives and responses with women's. She argued that men in migrating families were often motivated as much by a search for 'manly independence' as by the search for profits, while women dreaded the loss of the contact with family and friends that made up a major part of their worlds. Betty Wood found that work roles in slave families along the Georgia coast were heavily influenced by gender. Women, in particular, often became petty traders and merchants, so much so that they nearly monopolized the sale of some kinds of food markets in Savannah and other cities.[12]

In addition to work on masculinity and men's culture, gender analyses have pointed to the ways in which the concepts and language of gender often pervade public discourse and shape institutions. Here, Joan Scott's formulation of gender as 'a primary way of signifying relationships of power' pointed the way. Thus, a political institution may be supported (especially, but not solely, by men) to the degree that it is seen to embody a properly masculine set of values, or it may be undermined and pressed to reform (especially, but not solely, by women) who see it as failing to embody certain feminine values. The language of gender has also permeated popular discourse about race and class, so that in the South both claims to, and denials of, equality were often based in part on arguments about the 'manliness' or 'womanliness' of poor whites and African-Americans. Scott's formulation of the relationship between gender and the political also helped to break down the sharp distinction between a public (man's) sphere and a private (woman's) sphere, and to expose the ways in which the public and private intertwine.[13]

Such approaches have informed numerous reinterpretations of moments in southern history. In a sweeping interpretation of the development of colonial Virginia, Kathleen Brown argues that gender constructs and the conflicts they sometimes produced were central to the rise of racial slavery. Basing much of her analysis on surviving court records, Brown argues, for example, that demographic and economic conditions in Virginia, together with the European encounter with indigenous people having quite different ideas about the proper behaviour of men and women, threatened deeply-held beliefs of Englishmen about gender roles. The resulting conflicts helped to produce Bacon's Rebellion in 1676 and played a major role in the reconstruction of patriarchy in the colony along racial, rather than class, lines. In the seventeenth century, elite women were, in theory, separable from lower-class 'wenches' of any 'race', but, by the eighteenth, whites construed all African women as 'wenches' while all white women were eligible to become 'good wives'. The net result was a strengthened patriarchal slaveholding class that successfully protected its political authority, although this patriarchal power was softened somewhat by being clothed in the garments of paternalism.[14]

For the antebellum period, Stephanie McCurry argued that a shared sense of masculinity and patriarchal control over wives and other household dependants convinced the South's small farmers that they had a powerful stake in the slaveholding regime, even if most of them did not own slaves. For McCurry, the southern political world was white and masculine through and through, with white men monopolizing public discourse, and planters and yeomen coming together in public space as equally 'masters' of at least their 'small worlds'. Such patriarchal power, she further argues, was strongly reinforced by male-controlled evangelical churches and a heavily gendered ideology of republicanism. Peter Bardaglio examined southern law through the lens of gender, and sought to demonstrate that master–slave relations were typically seen by southerners as an aspect of more general household relationships. Both McCurry and Bardaglio contrast a southern patriarchal model of the family with a northern, bourgeois model, though Bardaglio, as he carries his account into the later nineteenth century, argues that the emancipation was a watershed in the reshaping of family.[15]

Other studies have taken on the Civil War and Reconstruction periods. In her local study of Augusta, Georgia, LeeAnn Whites portrays the Civil War as a 'crisis in gender' in the South. The war undermined men's patriarchal place and elevated the importance of women in both practical and symbolic ways. After the war, men's authority was further threatened by their inability to protect their women and families from Yankee power, and sometimes women literally provided family support by going to work outside the home. Over the post-war decades, however, the crisis for white men was resolved as their power and authority were rebuilt, ironically with the help of elite women who took charge of the first memorials to the Confederacy and, by anointing the war as the 'Lost Cause', helped to rehabilitate men by portraying their fight as a manly one against impossible odds. In another local study, this one of a North Carolina county, Laura Edwards made similarly broad claims that the success of southern whites in 'redeeming' the South from republican Reconstruction was based in large part on the ability of white men to rebuild patriarchy around new domestic ideals and then define politics as a world open only to the 'best' men. This legitimized the disfranchisement and degradation of African-Americans on the grounds that they were supposedly incapable of filling proper masculine and feminine roles in family life.[16]

Gender analysis has proved to be an important tool for understanding the rise of Jim Crow in the late nineteenth century as well. Glenda Gilmore's *Gender and Jim Crow* recounted North Carolina's political history from 1890 to 1920 from the viewpoint of well-educated African-American women. On the one hand, these women defied in their persons the white claim that black women were incapable of upholding truly 'civilized' (meaning Victorian) feminine values and behaviour; on the other, they differed from most white women in their determination to be 'useful', which meant both pursuing education equal to that of men and working outside the home. Gilmore (like Edwards) argues that the white seizure of political control in a violent coup in Wilmington, North Carolina, in 1898 was justified by whites, largely in gendered terms, as being necessary to protect white women from black men. Even after most blacks were disfranchised in North Carolina, however, black women were active as lobbyists, exploiting gender conventions of whites as they pressed white women for help with the needs of their own communities. Grace Elizabeth Hale explored the ways in which the white South's imposition of segregation at the turn of the century required the making of new cultural meanings for 'whiteness', meanings in which gender played a crucial role. White women, she argues, created the image of the antebellum black 'Mammy', an image that performed multiple functions. 'Mammy' was a comforting symbol of continuity between the domestic worlds of the Old and New Souths, and she was sufficiently domesticated that she did not have to be literally segregated to ensure the tranquillity of the domestic space. 'Mammy' thus gave white women a safe black presence against which they could define their own whiteness.[17]

Historians of the twentieth-century South also found gender useful in understanding social movements. In her study of the second Ku Klux Klan (KKK) in Athens, Georgia, Nancy MacLean argued that gender concerns – especially the felt need to control the behaviour of young women – were central to the rise of the Klan in the 1920s. The KKK in Athens devoted much of its attention to the policing of gender boundaries (for example, by punishing white men suspected of 'seducing' women or of abusing their wives). Charles Payne found that women's structural position in the black community, especially their 'pre-existing social networks of kinship and friendship,' on the one hand, and gendered patterns of religious belief, on the other, help to explain the greater willingness of middle-aged women than middle-aged men to take an active role in the Civil Rights Movement in Mississippi. Pushing Payne's argument even further, Belinda Robnett, a historically informed sociologist, argued that African-American women played a crucial role as intermediate-level 'bridge leaders' in the Civil Rights Movement, connecting the virtually all-male formal leadership with the grassroots supporters who made the movement possible.[18]

Although the movement to gender history encouraged to some extent a turn away from women's history, another effect was to bring to the study of women's history new questions and approaches that added still more depth and nuance to a well-established field. The clear connections and interpenetrations among the categories of race, class and gender in ideologies and institutions encouraged close attention to the ways in which gender conventions varied by race and class and over time, and the questioning of the public/private distinction suggested new interpretations of women's 'place'. Thus, in addition to promoting a specific interest in men and masculine culture, and to raising new questions about the relationships of culture and politics, the move to gender history gave still more vigour to the study of women and the family. (Indeed, several of the works mentioned above could be categorized under 'women's history'.)

Brenda Stevenson, in a broad-ranging study of both black and white families in Loudoun County, Virginia, amplified Deborah Gray White's argument that female slaves took on gender roles quite different from those of most white families. Stevenson agreed with Gray White that 'structural and functional matrifocality were extremely prominent in slave domestic life'. In her study of slave women in South Carolina's rice country, Leslie Schwalm agreed with this emphasis and endorsed White's claim that women's ties to real and fictive kin outside the conjugal family could be more important than ties within nuclear families. Marli Weiner, however, came to a somewhat different conclusion in her work on plantation mistresses and their domestic servants. Much of Weiner's evidence about white women's work confirmed the earlier studies of Anne Scott, Catherine Clinton and Elizabeth Fox-Genovese, but Weiner found considerably more evidence of sympathy and emotional ties between some mistresses and their slaves than did earlier authors. In addition she argued that, while slavery made it impossible for many female slaves to live up to their most cherished ideals, slave women shared with white mistresses 'deeply held fundamental assumptions about female behavior' rooted in the ideas of domesticity.[19]

The records left by white elite and middle-class women have continued to offer a rich trove of evidence for women's historians. Cynthia Kierner's study of white women in the colonial and early national South and Elizabeth Varon's study of antebellum Virginia women both challenged one of the most enduring ideas about southern women, that they were virtually excluded from the 'public sphere', and especially from the world of politics. Kierner, like others, questioned the usual definitions of the 'public sphere' as gender-bound and placing too much emphasis on formal political institutions and participation. Using a broader definition that included 'not only formal political participation but also informal civic and sociable life, the world of letters, certain business and market transactions, and religious and benevolent activities', Kierner found abundant evidence for women's participation in public life in early South, albeit in ways that did not openly challenge patriarchal values and that typically reinforced, rather than undermined, elite women's class privileges. Varon, taking up the story in the 1830s where Kierner left off, found even more surprising evidence for women's participation in public life. In Virginia, elite women established benevolent societies and lobbied for state support of them, contributed to the debates that raged over slavery and sectional conflict, and openly allied themselves with specific political parties and candidates.[20] Drew Faust examined in depth the experiences of elite white women in the Civil War in her *Mothers of Invention*. Many of the women she portrays were thrust into a situation of self-reliance and independence for which they were unprepared and which they did not welcome. The war, by emancipating slaves and demonstrating that white men could not always support and protect their women, destroyed much of the basis of antebellum patriarchy but, Faust argues, elite women were most reluctant to give up the privileges that had come with their high status. The war, Faust concluded, 'left them with profound doubts about what lay within their power to accomplish and thus with serious questions about the desirability of female independence or emancipation'. Faust thus qualifies Anne Scott's argument that the war was ultimately emancipating for southern white women; rather, the legacy of women's war experiences included a sense of women's limitations as much as women's possibilities, an ambivalence that helped to shackle southern feminism for decades after the war.[21]

Faust's argument is based partly on her acceptance of a commonly made argument about the south's female suffragists in the progressive era, that they backed their claim to the vote in large part on the argument that white women's votes would help to ensure the continuation of white supremacy. New work by Elna Green sharply challenges that understanding of southern suffragists. While some did make appeals to white supremacy a major part of their work, such arguments were much more likely to come from opponents (including female opponents) of women's suffrage. Green found that appeals to white supremacy played very little role in the pro-suffrage campaign in most southern states, and that when such arguments did appear they were mainly attempts, based on statistics, to deflect anti-suffragists' claims that votes for women would work to increase the number and proportion of African-American voters. Green's point receives strong support in Gilmore's study of North Carolina, Anastatia Sims's book on North Carolina women's organizations, and Judith McArthur's recent book on Texas women's progressives; indeed, both Gilmore and McArthur suggest that white suffragists, while they almost never challenged segregation itself, at times reached out in cooperative as well as paternalistic ways to black female progressives. At the same time, Sims's argument that female reformers saw their work in terms of the empowerment of femininity in some ways reinforces Faust's point about the limitations of southern feminism.[22]

Evelyn Brooks Higginbotham's work on women in the black Baptist Church in the Progressive era, like Gilmore's on black women in North Carolina, offered a new, gendered perspective, in this case on the much-studied black church. She placed women at the centre of the church's work and argued that 'women were crucial to broadening the public arm of the church and making it the most powerful institution of racial self-help in the African-American community'. Through the church, women contested racism and discrimination; within the church, they developed a 'feminist theology' and fought for greater equality for themselves. Like the educated women described by Gilmore, black Baptist women asserted a 'politics of respectability' and plunged into progressive reform activities. The black working-class women of Atlanta in this period, subjects of a study by Tera Hunter, by contrast often rejected the 'respectability' so prized by elite women. Militantly resisting white exploitation when possible, they were as likely to enjoy 'dancing and carousing the night away' as they were a Sunday sermon. Hunter has done much to uncover the lives of poor black urban women after the Civil War, and to show how their own views, and views of them held by others, were shaped by class as well as race.[23]

Like Hunter, other historians of women have expanded their research
beyond elite women (both black and white) and slaves to investigate
poor and working-class women. Victoria Bynum, in a local study of
antebellum and Civil War North Carolina, used court records to document the lives of antebellum poor white and black women, perhaps the
least visible of all antebellum southerners. Bynum's evidence suggested
that southern white gender ideals for women varied sharply by class,
with poor women both less idealized and less protected than those from
the upper and middle classes. Many poor women resisted male and
upper-class control of their families and sexual behaviour. Bynum also
found evidence for a considerably relaxed racial boundary among her
poor women, some of whom caroused, drank and gambled together,
part of a 'subculture of mostly poor people who did not abide by the
rules of polite society', regardless of race. Bynum's poor women clearly
rejected the gender conventions of elite southern society. Diane Somerville similarly found evidence that the rejection worked in both directions in her study of the trials of black men for rape of white women. In
the antebellum era, black men accused of rape sometimes received fair
trials and, even if convicted, sometimes escaped with relatively light
sentences or had harsher sentenced commuted. Elite men clearly differentiated among the victims of the alleged rapists, and poor women who
were not 'respectable' did not receive the protection promised by men to
other white women. In the twentieth century, 'disorderly' women,
through 'dress, language, and gesture', helped to initiate and fight
some of the major labour upheavals in southern industry, as Jacqueline
Dowd Hall found in her analysis of the 1929 textile strike in Elizabeth-
ton, Tennessee.[24]

Hall's article also exemplifies historians efforts to expand the geographical and ethnic boundaries of southern women's history. Louisiana's distinctive origins as a French and Spanish colony helped to create a
culture that was in many respects an anomaly in the South: predominantly Catholic, more accepting of miscegenation, home to a small group
of wealthy and highly educated women of colour, and, in consequence,
site of a more complex system of racial categorization and control than
in most of the South. Such differences could, in theory, offer an illuminating source of comparative analyses of gender and its operation. Some
of the possibilities are suggested in the recent work by Kimberly Hanger
and Virginia Gould on free black and slave women in colonial and
antebellum New Orleans. Francophone Louisiana is only the most obvious of many 'other' souths, however. A recent collection edited by
Christie Farnham suggests some of the other possibilities, with essays

on Jews and Moravians, Choctaws and Cherokees, Appalachian women, and lesbians in the South.[25]

What are the prospects for a comparative history of the 'two souths' in the realm of gender? One should note first, perhaps, that they depend partly on what version or versions of US southern history we mean to compare. It should be clear even from the necessarily cursory account above that, despite the high quality and growing volume of research on women and on gender in the South, it is by no means certain that historians are reaching final agreement on many of the larger issues. To take a very recent example, Stephanie McCurry's original (and multiple prize-winning) interpretation of the role of gender in creating cross-class solidarity between planters and yeomen has been sharply disputed by historians such as Elizabeth Varon, working on the same period and with many of the same sources.[26] In the larger sense, there is no clear agreement on the major question of whether the South should be seen as exceptional within the USA for its patterns of family and gender relationships, or rather as a variation on a theme common to both North and South. Moreover, it seems more than a little presumptuous for a specialist in only one of the souths to say much about how a comparison might proceed. However, in the spirit of the 'Two Souths' project and conference, let me put such concerns aside and, guided by the contribution in this volume by Giovanna Fiume, pose at least some tentative questions and approaches. In doing so, I find especially illuminating Peter Kolchin's comment in his keynote address to the conference that, in some cases, a comparison of historiographies may be at least as fruitful as comparisons of institutions, events, economies and so on.[27]

While both Italian and US women's history in recent decades grew out of feminist movements in the 1960s and share many fundamental concerns and approaches, and while in both cases a concern with women has evolved into a broader consideration of gender, the differences in the two historiographical traditions is also striking. In the Italian case, as Fiume outlines it, the historiographical context has been the 'southern question' and the large literature, often the work of anthropologists, attempting to explain southern 'backwardness' *vis-à-vis* the north. A central aspect of these explanations is a picture of a 'traditional' peasant woman. Excluded from work outside the home, segregated in the home and submissive to the authority of husbands and fathers, with an 'archaic, conservative and superstitious mentality, particularly resistant to innovations, totally indifferent to the interests that had nothing to do with one's own family and the tight circle of blood relatives', the 'backward' peasant woman was, in this interpretation, one of the major foundations on which rested the 'backwardness' of the Mezzogiorno as a whole. According to Fiume, much of the work of historians of women and gender has involved the questioning, complicating, and ultimately undermining of this image, and furthermore it has been a part of the larger project of freeing the history of the Mezzogiorno from the history of the southern question. Thus, for example, we have investigations of the 'invention of tradition' in the first place; careful studies of women's role in the transmission of property; comparative studies of communities within the South that found quite different patterns for female work and marriage, depending on the nature of the local economy; and serious examinations of urban women.

For the US South, while images of southern 'backwardness' certainly play a part in both the history and historiography of the region, the historiography of women and gender tends to be organized, not surprisingly, around the interrelated issues of slavery, white supremacy, the Civil War and southern exceptionalism; in other words, around the same broad questions that inform most of the historiography of the US South. The dominant popular female image of the southern female is not the peasant woman – indeed, the very notion of a southern peasantry rarely rears its head – but the southern 'belle' and plantation mistress. Much of the historiography of southern women and gender can be understood as a project to displace the 'belle' from her pedestal: to reinterpret her if not to banish her entirely from history, and to embrace in southern history black and poor women in all their complexity. While, in the most general way, this has led to similar kinds of inquiries as in the Italian case – investigations into the production and reproduction of the popular image itself and its production; of the role of women in holding and transmitting property; of women's activities outside the home, either in paid or unpaid work, and so on – the differences also seem fundamental, with one case starting from an image of a poor peasant woman and the other from an image of an elite mistress of slaves. To judge at least from Fiume's account, much writing about women in the Mezzogiorno has remained closely tied to the history of the family, where the 'backward' peasant woman allegedly did her damage, while historians of the US South have been especially concerned with elite white women's public roles at various times and in various places and with uncovering the worlds of poor whites and of slave and free African-American women.

If comparative historiography, then, may deserve first place on the agenda for a comparative history of gender in the 'two souths,' other specific projects also suggest themselves, based on work done thus far.

1   What is the relationship between women's place in the family and their roles in the transmission of property? In both souths, historians have uncovered ways in which women sometimes controlled important property interests. Did such property regimes arise because of similar family strategies or demographic patterns? For example, Fiume cites studies showing that women's role in property transmission was greater in places with high male mortality and instability of family life, a situation that seems to resemble the early colonial Virginia as analysed by Kathleen Brown.

2   As Fiume points out, the attack on the image of the backward peasant woman began with 'the rediscovery of extra-domestic work', and women's work has also been central to the historiography of women in the USA. What kinds of work did women do, inside and outside the household? Did they get paid or not? Who worked? At what ages and for what purposes? How does this change over time and as women move into cities?

3   What was the nature of women's religiosity? Did elite women in both souths play significant roles in religious and benevolent societies, and with similar consequences? If, as seems to be the case, only in the USA did such participation lead fairly directly into overt political activity and demands for suffrage, what accounts for the difference?

4   Did Protestant and Catholic religiosity have different consequences for the perpetuation of patriarchal ideas and norms? Here, the inclusion of Catholic Louisiana in the equation may offer important insights.

5   As recent historiography makes clear, race and gender systems have been intimately intertwined from the foundation of British colonies in North America, with notions of whiteness and blackness on the one hand, and femininity and masculinity, on the other, constantly being used to define one another and legitimate slavery and white supremacy. What is the equivalent, if any, in the language of class in the Mezzogiorno?

6   As Bertram Wyatt-Brown suggested at the London conference, a system of 'honour' has been posed as central to the social and cultural organization of both souths. Wyatt-Brown himself has seen the Mediterranean case as something of a paradigm for his own analysis of the US south's system of honour, but, as Fiume points out, the

stereotypical images of the role of honour in family life are under attack in the Italian historiography itself.

Some of these ideas may prove to be dead ends for research, but others might yield important insights into the national and regional histories. Ultimately, the question of whether comparisons the Italian and American souths will prove as fruitful as earlier comparisons of slavery and race can only be determined by the work of scholars brave enough and skilled enough to master the challenges that all comparative history poses.

Notes

1   W. J. Cash, *The Mind of the South* (New York, 1941; reprint New York, n.d.), pp. 52, 87, 89.
2   Bertram Wyatt-Brown, *Southern Honor: Ethics and Behavior in the Old South* (New York, 1982), p. vii.
3   Joel Williamson, *The Crucible of Race: Black–White Relations in the South since Emancipation* (New York, 1984).
4   Eugene D. Genovese, *Roll, Jordan, Roll: The World the Slaves Made* (New York, 1974), pp. 93, 96.
5   Anne Firor Scott, *The Southern Lady: From Pedestal to Politics 1830–1930*, 2nd edn (Charlottesville, VA, 1995) In the second edition, the text of the original 1970 edition is included unchanged, but added is a fascinating account by Scott of how she came to the subject and wrote about it in an era when women's history was almost entirely invisible in mainstream historical scholarship. A full historiographical account of southern women's history and gender history is well beyond the scope of this chapter; for guides to the literature, see Jacqueline Dowd Hall and Anne Firor Scott, 'Women in the South', in John B. Boles and Evelyn Thomas Nolen (eds), *Interpreting Southern History: Historiographical Essays in Honor of Sanford W. Higginbotham*, (Baton Rouge, 1987), pp. 510–48; and for the antebellum period, Joan E. Cashin, 'Introduction: Culture of Resignation', in Cashin (ed.), *Our Common Affairs: Texts From Women in the Old South* (Baltimore, MD, 1996), pp. 1–41.
6   Jacqueline Dowd Hall, *The Revolt Against Chivalry: Jesse Daniel Ames and The Women's Campaign Against Lynching* (New York, 1979).
7   Catherine Clinton, *The Plantation Mistress: Woman's World in The Old South* (New York, 1982).
8   Jan Lewis, *The Pursuit of Happiness: Family and Values in Jefferson's Virginia* (New York, 1983); Jane Turner Censer, *North Carolina Planters and their Children, 1800–1860* (Baton Rouge, LA, 1984); Suzanne Lebsock, *The Free Women of Petersburg: Status and Culture in a Southern Town, 1784–1860* (New York, 1984); Elizabeth Fox-Genovese, *Within the Plantation Household: Black and White Women of The Old South* (Chapel Hill, NC, 1988); Jean E. Friedman, *The Enclosed Garden: Women and Community in the Evangelical South, 1830–1930* (1985); Sally G. McMillen, *Motherhood in the Old South: Pregnancy, Childbirth, and Infant Rearing* (Baton Rouge, LA, 1990); Marjorie Spruill Wheeler, *New Women*

of the New South: The Leaders of the Women's Suffrage Movement in the Southern States (New York, 1993).

9 Orville Vernon Burton, *In My Father's House Are Many Mansions: Family and Community in Edgefield, South Carolina* (Chapel Hill, NC, 1985); Norreece T. Jones, Jr., *Born a Child of Freedom, Yet a Slave: Mechanisms of Control and Strategies of Resistance in Antebellum South Carolina* (Hanover, NH, 1990); Jacqueline Jones, *Labour of Love, Labour of Sorrow: Black Women, Work, and the Family From Slavery to the Present* (New York, 1985), pp. 11–43; Deborah Gray-White, *Ar'n't I a Woman? Female Slaves in the Plantation South* (New York, 1985). Slave family behaviour and mores had earlier received considerable attention from general studies of slavery such as Genovese, *Roll, Jordan, Roll*, John W. Blassingame, *The Slave Community: Plantation Life in the Antebellum South* (New York, 1972), and especially Herbert G. Gutman, *The Black Family in Slavery and Freedom, 1775–1925* (New York, 1976).

10 Joan W. Scott, 'Gender: A Useful Category of Historical Analysis', *American Historical Review* 91:5 (1986), pp. 1053–75 (quotation: p. 1053).

11 Jim Cullen, '"I's a Man Now": Gender and African American Men', in Catherine Clinton and Nina Silber, (eds)., *Divided Houses: Gender and the Civil War* (New York, 1992), pp. 76–91; James M. McPherson, *For Cause and Comrades: Why Men Fought in the Civil War* (New York, 1997), esp. pp. 77–89; Kenneth S. Greenberg, *Honor and Slavery: Lies, Duels, Noses, Masks, Dressing as a Woman, Gifts, Strangers, Humanitarianism, Death, Slave Rebellions, the Proslavery Argument, Baseball, Hunting, and Gambling in The Old South* (Princeton, NJ, 1996); Ted Ownby, *Subduing Satan: Religion, Recreation, and Manhood in The Rural South, 1865–1920* (Chapel Hill, NC, 1990).

12 Joan E. Cashin, *A Family Venture: Men and Women on the Southern Frontier* (New York, 1991); Betty Wood, *Women's Work, Men's Work: The Informal Slave Economies of Lowcountry Georgia* (Athens, GA, 1995).

13 Scott, 'Gender: A Useful Category', p. 1067.

14 Kathleen M. Brown, *Good Wives, Nasty Wenches, and Anxious Patriarchs: Gender, Race, and Power in Colonial Virginia* (Chapel Hill, NC, 1996).

15 Stephanie McCurry, *Masters of Small Worlds: Yeoman Households, Gender Relations, and the Political Culture of the Antebellum South Carolina Low Country* (New York, 1995); McCurry, 'The Two Faces of Republicanism: Gender and Proslavery Politics in Antebellum South Carolina', *Journal of American History* 78:4 (1992), pp. 1245–64; Peter W. Bardaglio, *Reconstructing the Household: Families, Sex, and the Law in the Nineteenth-Century South* (Chapel Hill, NC, 1995).

16 LeeAnn Whites, *The Civil War as a Crisis in Gender: Augusta, Georgia, 1860–1890* (Athens, GA, 1998); Laura F. Edwards, *Gendered Strife and Confusion: The Political Culture of Reconstruction* (Urbana, IL, 1997).

17 Glenda Elizabeth Gilmore, *Gender and Jim Crow: Women and the Politics of White Supremacy in North Carolina, 1896–1920* (Chapel Hill, NC, 1996); Grace Elizabeth Hale, *Making Whiteness: The Culture of Segregation in The South, 1890–1940* (New York, 1998), pp. 85–119.

18 Nancy MacLean, *Behind the Mask of Chivalry: The Making of the Second Ku Klux Klan* (New York, 1994); Charles M. Payne, *I've Got the Light of Freedom: The Organizing Tradition and the Mississippi Freedom Struggle* (Berkeley, CA, 1995), pp. 265–83 (quotation: p. 271); Belinda Robnett, *How Long? How Long? African American Women in the Struggle for Civil Rights* (New York, 1997).

19   Brenda E. Stevenson, *Life in Black and White: Family and Community in the Slave South* (New York, 1996), p. 221; Marli F. Weiner, *Mistresses and Slaves: Plantation Women in South Carolina, 1830–80* (Urbana, IL, 1998), quotation: p. 129; Leslie A. Schwalm, *A Hard Fight for We: Women's Transition from Slavery to Freedom in South Carolina* (Urbana, IL, 1997).

20   Cynthia A. Kierner, *Beyond the Household: Women's Place in the Early South, 1700–1835* (Ithaca, NV, 1998), p. 2; Elizabeth Varon, *We Mean to be Counted: White Women and Politics in Antebellum Virginia* (Chapel Hill, NC, 1998).

21   Drew Gilpin Faust, *Mothers of Invention: Women of the Slaveholding South in the American Civil War* (Chapel Hill, NC, 1996), quotation: p. 256.

22   Elna C. Green, *Southern Strategies: Southern Women and the Women's Suffrage Question* (Chapel Hill, NC, 1997); Judith N. McArthur, *Creating the New Woman: The Rise of Southern Women's Progressive Culture in Texas, 1893–1918* (Urbana, IL, 1998); Gilmore, *Gender and Jim Crow*; Anastatia Sims, *The Power of Femininity in the New South: Women's Organizations and Politics in North Carolina, 1880–1930* (Columbia, SC, 1997).

23   Evelyn Higginbotham, *Righteous Discontent: The Women's Movement in the Black Baptist Church, 1880–1920* (Cambridge, MA, 1993); Tera Hunter, *To 'Joy My Freedom: Southern Black Women's Lives and Labours After the Civil War* (Cambridge, MA, 1997); the quotation is the title of her ch. 8. See also Cynthia Neverdon-Morton, *Afro-American Women of the South and the Advancement of the Race, 1895–1925* (Knoxville, TN, 1989), for a survey of activities of African-American club women in major southern cities.

24   Victoria E. Bynum, *Unruly Women: The Politics of Social and Sexual Control in the Old South* (Chapel Hill, NC, 1992), quotation: p. 90; Diane Miller Somerville, 'The Rape Myth of the Old South Reconsidered', *Journal of Southern History* 61:3 (1995), pp. 481–518; Jacqueline Dowd Hall, 'Disorderly Women: Gender and Labour Militancy in the Appalachian South', *Journal of American History* 73:2 (1986), pp. 354–82.

25   Kimberly S. Hanger, ' "The fortunes of women in America": Spanish New Orleans's free women of African descent and their relations with slave women', in Patricia Morton (ed.), *Discovering the Women in Slavery: Emancipating Perspectives on the American Past*, (Athens, GA, 1996), pp. 153–78; Virginia Meacham Gould, ' "If I can't have my rights, I can have my pleasures, and if they won't give me wages, I can take them": gender and slave labour in antebellum New Orleans', in ibid., pp. 179–201; Christie Anne Farnham, *Women of the American South: A Multicultural Reader* (New York, 1997).

26   McCurry, *Masters of Small Worlds*; Varon, *We Mean to be Counted*. See also the review of McCurry's book by Jan Lewis in *Journal of Social History* 30:4 (1997), pp. 988–91.

27   Giovanna Fiume, Chapter 9 below and Peter Kolchin, Chapter 2 above.

9
Making Women Visible in the History of the Mezzogiorno

Giovanna Fiume

I

The distinction has finally been consolidated between the history of the southern question (understood as the history of the cultural and political movements which denounced the causes and modalities of socio-economic imbalances between North and South and the patrimony of ideas about the Mezzogiorno) and the history of the Mezzogiorno (understood as the history of the conditions and the economic and social processes in relation to the comprehensive development of Italian society). This southern tradition has canonized the image of an immobile Mezzogiorno characterized by an eternal plague of the *latifundium*, semi-feudal relations of production throughout the countryside, the absence of entrepreneurial initiatives, the rural peasants squashed by fatalistic passivity or actors of a desperate 'jacquerie'. The concealment of major property changes (proving Sonnino wrong), of democratic municipalism (correcting Salvameni), of the creation of new, open, innovative classes (moving away from Dorso), and of the protagonism of urban centres (arguing against Gramsci) has left much work for the latest generation of historians, who know how to interpret the political and ideological importance of the issue of liberalism in Southern Italy.[1] Piero Bevilacqua has convincingly illustrated the process which led to the reduction of the history of the South to the history of the southern question, perceiving 'southernism' as the construction of a false uniformity within the Mezzogiorno, thus unifying an area strongly marked by differences.[2] Within the southern question lurks a female question as an internal complication, characterized by the same generalizations and stereotypes.[3]

In the decade from 1960 to 1970, prevalent interpretations largely agreed on the backwardness of the condition of southern women in view of their exclusion from work outside the home, the consequent domestic segregation and female submission to husbands and fathers. From this economic and social condition originated an archaic, conservative and superstitious mentality, one particularly resistant to innovations and totally indifferent to interests outside one's own family and the tight circle of blood relatives. The fact is that the foundation of 'amoral familism' was represented by the women of the South. From the countryside this view widened to include all women, according to a semantic elision that at the same time identified the whole South with the countryside and the countryside with the *latifundium*. The anthropological literature regarded women as custodians of traditions and vessels of ancient values, the most typical cultural elements of the peasant world, of the magical and religious South. The backwardness of the South was represented in the stereotype of the peasant woman, illiterate, forever pregnant, a supporter of the Christian Democrats, religious to the point of superstition, custodian of the honour of the men in her family. If in the beginning this stereotype had a conservative matrix, it later significantly joined intellectuals, liberals and Marxists in a common view of women as obstacles to change in a peasant society that was gradually adapting to modernity. In the pages of Carlo Levi and Rocco Scotellaro, as observed by Gabriella Gribaudi, 'the peasants from Basilicata and Calabria [are] made into a symbol of the human condition of pain and oppression'.[4]

Related to this paradox is an embarrassing misunderstanding of Ernesto De Martino's work that ended up creating a gap, still not completely filled, between the history and the anthropology of the Mezzogiorno. The latter has been the prerogative of scholars, the majority of them being Anglo-American, such as Pitt-Rivers, Peristiany, Charlotte Gower Chapman, Edward Banfield, John Davis, Anton Blok and Jane and Peter Schneider, to name a few. Women, here, were relegated to the framework of 'material culture': ritual mourning for the dead, gift exchange, exalted participation in festivities or revolts, fervent religiousness, vigilance over excessive sexuality, and jealous protection of the family's patriarchal values. In this anthropological school, interpretative references could be facts dating back to the Magna Grecia or, as John Dickie put it in another context, an 'obsession with the picturesque'.[5]

De Martino's study of the ritual forms of crying in the Mediterranean is of great persuasive force. The laments of Lucanian women genuinely appear to be at the extreme borders of the historic world and far from conscious action. In the words of the author, these actions symbolize the condition of whoever 'has experienced only the irrationality of natural forces and the overwhelming oppressiveness of social forces';[6] the reaction to this becomes, not conscious historic action, but the ancient technique of the ritual lamentation: a ritual of survival and not a gesture of transformation. Even De Martino feeds the stereotype of women as vehicles of archaic permanence, excluding 'the real gestures of the Lucanian women... freezing them in a forced passivity',[7] when in his book he tries to see the human ability to 'singularize pain', and the 'changing by repetition' of social subjects within the apparent immobility of ritual.

Excluded from relationships of production and monetary exchange, outside the market, denied education, and excluded from the state, women, increasingly tied to their biology, represented a feudal enclave in the nineteenth and early twentieth centuries. While the political and economic history of the Mezzogiorno distanced itself from anthropology, the history of women was obliged, in a sense, to come to terms with such an intense genealogy. The history of women and the history of the Mezzogiorno developed, therefore, on parallel lines, with the latter misunderstanding the interpretative power of gender (a mode of analysis which developed in relation to national and international scholarly and feminist debates and eschewed any sustained engagement with southern Italy). In such a situation we historians found it necessary to carve out niches in a territory defined by others, with the hope of not having left gaps that were too visible.

From this point of view, the generation of scholars to which I belong places itself outside the southern Italian historiographic milieu. Of course, this is partly because many of us study the modern age, but also because our sporadic incursions into the early modern period revealed how many elements of 'southerness' constituted an 'invented' tradition. The often crude description of material and moral backwardness saw women as a critical problem within a public discourse. We were not in the presence of a pre-existing tradition (women became active in the investigations at the beginning of the nineteenth century), challenged by the awareness of modernity: better still, 'tradition' and 'modernity' were produced at the same time and placed in a sequential order. In a 'first' that became atemporal and transcultural, women were inactive, hostile to change, superstitious and corrupt. Tradition became one of the vestiges of the feudal past; women were neither subject nor object, but simply a site upon which to construct 'discourse'. With modernity came the division of property, expanding suffrage and education, teaching women the 'work of affection'; this was an ideological construct in which urban middle-class families seemed to represent the 'natural' context. With the dominance of this interpretive model, incomprehension regarding the role of southern Italian women became complete.

The history of women in Italy in the 1970s and 1980s developed in close symmetry with the women's movement that was fighting bitter civil battles over such hotly contested issues as divorce and abortion rights in a Catholic country. Many in the movement were practising consciousness-raising in small groups and critically discussing the relation between emancipation and liberation, and therefore between feminism and 'socialism'. This dialectic influenced the investigations pursued by the first wave of women's historians. Some of us wrote about rebellious female figures of the past (from women bandits, to leaders of popular insurgencies, to women who participated in the Sicilian *fasci* and the occupation of the land), but this largely meant staying within a political history that already condemned women to a subalternity. The history of women thus risked becoming a ghetto within the larger field of social history, and the 'grassroots' origins of the women's movement produced a conflictual rapport with institutions, especially the university, where women remained confined to the lowest professional levels.[8]

Reaction against these stereotypes and 'tradition' began with the rediscovery of extra-domestic work. An interest in female waged labour, both in manufacturing[9] (indicating low levels of specialization in, for instance, weaving, or revealing the marginality of women workers because of the persistence of corporate prohibitions, as in the case of silk[10]) and in the countryside (where female employment experienced an almost total collapse between 1888 and 1901[11]), sought to demonstrate the capitalist nature of the southern economy and document its development out of and away from earlier feudal relationships. Looking back, one can see that this scholarship with its political urgency and expectant sense of revolution was typical of those years. The overvaluation of banditry, following the lead of Eric Hobsbawm, as an immature, preclass form of rebellion, was posed in this political and cultural climate, together with the 'colonial' explanation of the split between North and South.[12] Research still tied to political history confirmed the low levels of female participation in political movements, except in moments of extreme insurgency such as 1799, 1848, or the *fasci Siciliani*'s occupation of the land. Other investigations into female rebellion that could be considered forms of 'social anomie' faltered, failing to discover much of worth. Thus, exploring multiple types of common criminality, where women appeared in such small numbers in the South compared to other parts of Italy, Michele Amari says that the crimes of women were so rare as to seem to be inside a harem or under the gaze of a sultan.[13] Ironically, the low criminal disposition of southern women became another indicator of backwardness, especially when placed alongside Sicilian population in general with its high levels of political violence and structured consistency of *mafia* organizations.[14]

If history without women reveals itself to be, as E. P. Thompson said, 'futile', the early results obtained were unsatisfactory for the women scholars carrying out the work. These historians were able to illuminate only small spaces in their effort to recover women who had been 'hidden from history', to use Sheila Rowbotham's phrase. Moreover, these first findings pointed to the marginality of the female presence in the Mezziogiorno's past; it was disappointing that they were unable to follow the leads of Louise Tilly and Ester Boserup who suggested that feminist history could overturn or subvert the hierarchy of relevance established by gender-blind politico-economic historiography.

Understanding the importance of the networks and social relations (domestic, solidarity, patronage and so on) that tie together individuals, and therefore systems of kinship, marriage conventions (exogamy, endogamy, monogamy, divorce), rules of residence (virilocality, uxorilocality, matrifocality), lines of descent (patrilineal, matrilineal, bilateral), and mechanisms for the transmission of property (dowries and inheritance) convinced us early on not only of the importance of gender in the comprehension of social systems, but also of the prime relevance of *informal* aspects of social relations. Since these women traditionally were regarded as social actors and manipulators, this development was crucial for the analysis of 'male domination' and patriarchy which it allowed: the flip side, if you will, of 'female oppression'. Further, it identified female subjects in whom an individual sphere could be recognized, a realm of experience not only socially predetermined but allowing conscious action and agency. The social world thus could be represented as a 'forest of contradictory rules and norms that propose themselves in an elastic backdrop requiring continuous personal and group strategies and choices'.[15]

In 1986 an important conference on female patronage attempted to define, in Foucauldian fashion, the 'constellations of unequal relations' that tie together men and women by investigating exchange, interdependence, reciprocal conditioning and complementarity rather than the unrealistic and simplistic opposition between domination and oppression. The choice of patronage as a topic was explicitly intended to focus attention on the asymmetry of relations that are, by definition, unequal relations based upon hierarchy and uneven access to power.[16] This permitted exploration not simply of the opposition between normative discourses and social practices, but of the ample and variegated terrain where subjects manipulate and negotiate social norms.

Of course, still more work is needed on southern women. In particular, we need to pursue even further the observations that these women have always worked, in and outside the home, that they enjoyed a considerable mobility, and that they were formidable mediators in social relations and the transmission of memory, and that they ensured the reproduction of the nuclear family 'in their double role as creators and holders of goods conferring on them strength inside the family and prestige in the society'.[17]

The analysis of the family within the context of the larger social system was furthered by the emergence of exciting new scholarship in demographic history. In particular, this concurrent wave of research extended our understanding of households and kin groups, demonstrating with striking clarity the presence of different forms of co-residence (such as conjugal, extended, multiple family) and questioning the supposed pre-eminence of the nuclear family. Indeed, in the face of these findings much of the historical and anthropological literature that posited a distinctive 'Mediterranean model' of the family does not hold up.[18] In arguing against this model, Franco Benigno pointed out that the 'family seems immersed in a context of social, economic and symbolic relations that seem difficult to ignore'. He went on to suggest that we required, instead, 'a differentiated demographic history, open to the analysis of context': that is, a history capable of explaining the multiple correlations between different types of productive organization and the different characteristics of the households. This must also be, Benigno argued, a project that considered the co-resident domestic group as both a unit of work and consumption.[19]

Within the sphere of family studies it has been relatively easy to highlight the important role of women in relation to a number of measurable phenomena. Some of these have been demographic, such as the age of marriage or the number of children. Others have had a more pronounced social dimension: for instance, the networks that emerge from the parish registers in relation to baptism and marriage or, to choose another example, domestic living arrangements. Other scholarship has focused on domestic work, dowries and, more generally, the evolution patrimony.[20]

Through the family we can analyse values and social behaviour, and by exploring the cultural codes informing these we can contribute towards an explanation of the distinctive nature of the female sphere.[21] This was shown clearly at an international conference, held in Palermo in 1987, where the hypothetical cultural unity of Mediterranean countries was debated. Also noted at this gathering were codes of honour in relation to socio-economic contexts and precise historical periods, where they emerge as idioms expressing social differences.[22] Pursuing the relationship between the crisis of the family and the control of female honour, a number of historians focused attention upon a series of female transgressive figures – for example, prostitutes and unwed mothers [23] – and upon charitable and correctional institutions.[24]

Interest in reproductive roles, inside the family and kin group, has moved into the dangerous territory of female subjectivity and its expressive forms, further developing themes touched upon at the end of the 1970s such as the transformation of social models through the generations.[25] The changes recorded by Renate Siebert in three generations of Calabrian women are relevant in this respect; they concern schooling and the level of instruction, a rise in female age at marriage, fertility control and the reduction of the birth rate, the hospitalization of natal care, and the easing burden of domestic work. Calabrian women seem to have passed, in three generations, from seamless integration into a socially rich and communitarian life world to a fragmented and socially isolating world in which 'urban consciousness' dominates even in rural and suburban settings. In the life stories of the youngest women, however, productive work does not represent an organizing principle; and even though southern society now allows significant female upward mobility, it does not fully recognize women's social rights.[26]

Scholarly interchange with Anglo-American historians (Joan Scott, Louise Tilly, Natalie Zemon Davis) and French researchers (Michelle Perrot, Arlette Farge, Christiane Klapisch) has helped move our work away from women's history *per se* and towards gender history. At the same time the example and comradeship of these historians has served as a tonic against the devaluation of research on women that the southern context induced. One can now study with the same scientific legitimacy as Mistretta or Provence the model of sanctity of an aristocratic nun from Palma di Montechiaro, or the logic of the Parisian masses being pushed to the scholarly margins.

II

The history of the Mezzogiorno has produced important insights into community dynamics, households in relation to marriage and inheritance strategies, the aristocracy and elites, productive systems, the southern countryside in general, markets, migratory chains, social disorder and criminal associations. The debt to sociology is also great, especially with regard to our understanding of the condition of the South today.[27]

In the last few decades, the Mezzogiorno has not been at the centre of the political agenda as it was in the preceding decades. During this period there has been a noticeable shift in the way in which scholars have approached the Italian South. It has been partially reappraised in numerous studies and partially in collective consciousness. The economic-statist orientation towards the Mezzogiorno prevalent from the 1950s to the 1970s – an orientation that focused on development, the social classes, state politics, governing groups and their ideologies – has slowly given way to an approach that has insisted on the centrality of cultures, collective mentality, primary relationships, forms of organization, social identity, traditions and the logic of the local and centralized public apparatus. A new context of 'non-economic conditions' has occupied centre stage.[28] This new wave of scholarship, however, is not exempt from its own excesses, limits and contradictions. These faults and weaknesses have prompted Biagio Salvemini, in particular, to criticize the overproduction of models to insist that historians focus upon:

> analyzing families rather than familism, agricultural workers rather than peasant society, the organization of the Mafia rather than the ethos 'mafioso', the structures and the functions of settlement patterns rather than urban parasitism, the networks of relationships inside and out of the public apparatus instead of clientelism and *transformismo*, production and exchange instead of backwardness.[29]

Salvemini's plea can reconcile a long disagreement, a 'polemic in the family', to use the phrase Anna Kulishoff utilized a century ago against the Italian socialists who were still opposing female suffrage, on the condition that we are speaking not about a generic appeal for concreteness as opposed to generalization in cultural analysis, but a call to contextualize single aspects in a dense social and cultural universe. This discussion becomes possible in the context of the general renewal of historiographical paradigms of the last decade.

Gérard Delille, studying the peasant family in diverse areas of Italy, suggests that we should not be limited to an approach that favours the parameters of the nuclear family and warns against explanations that are too summary. He suggests, rather, that we launch problematics that are richer and more complex – and which must be fully reintegrated into the study of the history of the family – including the mechanisms of female dowry, the transmission of inheritance, marriage exchanges, the control of the land market, and so on.[30] His contribution consists not in simply stressing the importance of the family next to that of the economy and demography of the Mezzogiorno, but also in considering how closely linked in any analysis are the family, kin groups, alliances and the economy. In fact, the family, the kin group and the alliances seem to be 'fundamental economic facts in the functioning of the social system'.[31] Studying the complex situation in the Kingdom of Naples, Delille isolates two different systems: in the cereal-growing region of Puglia, characterized by extensive cultivation, low work productivity, seasonal movements of agricultural workers and low age at marriage, male mortality is high, the transmission of goods is through hereditary division or dowry, and property passes through the dowries of women who often marry outsiders. In the wheat producing part of Sicily, there is a high mortality for working-age males (20–50 years) due to the work-related difficulties on the *latifundium* where the men are far from home and are exposed to a bad diet, illness, and so on.[32] The *latifundium* uses up the male work force, but through uxorilocality and the transmission of property via the women that 'attract' males, these men then become available in moments of work-force deficit.

In areas of intensive cultivation in Campania, with high work productivity, better conditions for life and work on the small peasant-owned properties and among the rural artisans allow for a lower level of mortality. Sons are under paternal authority and gain possession of their inheritance on the death of the parent; subsequently, they marry later. The males receive land and property; the dowry of the women consists of linen, money and jewellery, and residence is patrilocal. Here we see male lineages and neighbourhoods of male residences. Both systems obey the rules of matrimonial reciprocity being structured around collateral branches, well outside the ecclesiastical prohibitions regarding degrees of consanguinity (and economic reciprocity) that regulate the land market according to mechanisms that are foreign to those of supply and demand.

Giovanni Levi has observed that for the Piedmont region of the *ancien régime*, as in areas still largely feudal, where:

> the economy is only partially mercantilized and where the primary objective is not exchange but self-consumption . . . the prices are determined by need. It is not the market in general that determines the

price of land, but the needs of each individual peasant family in a specific moment of its life cycle that defines how much one is willing to pay and when one is willing to buy and sell land.[33]

The prices, therefore, also define the relations that unite the contracting parties and change depending on whether they are relatives, neighbours or strangers. Paradoxically, the most active market is that which is dominated by small peasant proprietors, oriented towards self-consumption, and where property is often female, either in the form of dowry or inheritance. Economic exchange and marriage exchange are therefore 'two spheres closely linked to each other'[34] and their erosion in the contemporary period, partly in a free land market and in the equal division of inheritance, produces forms of resistance (falling back on more restricted family groups, and increasingly strong consanguinity) which lead, in the end, to 'a slower and more difficult transition'.[35]

This approach has given coherence to fragmented elements – mortality, marriage, natality, fecundity – where the conjugal family does not represent the basic demographic entity. It considers the complete family cycle – matrimony, the birth of children, the death of parents, marriage of children, the birth of grandchildren – and observes these elements in relation to the ecological resources and relations of production. Utilizing this sort of approach, Ida Fazio has studied the 'plurality of factors that generate the forms of the family'[36] in an area of Messina in the nineteenth century. In Cesarò, a community in the Nebrodi mountains characterized by large-scale wheat cultivation, the women – excluded from agricultural work – are at the centre of a system of transmission of property. They marry very young, since it is not necessary for them to remain at home as they only do domestic spinning and weaving and do not contribute to the maintenance of the paternal family. The dowries, transmitting the trousseau and land according to the 'Pugliese system' identified by Delille, are able to attract men; the widows remarry thanks to favourable clauses in the husbands' wills, constituting marital legacies that enrich the dowries of the widows. In the 'silk town' of Santa Lucia, characterized by small and medium properties, and surrounded by sparsely settled farms that are exploited intensively, the women work outside the home in agriculture and this keeps them more closely tied to the family of origin; they marry late, and the dowry consists of valuable goods including jewellery, silk, linens, and so on, while the land is reserved principally for the men. In Taormina we find a intermediate situation: here we see the specialized agriculture of 'gardens' of citrus trees linked to the sea trade and commerce. Marriages are postponed by the need to accumulate the necessary resources. Rapport with the resources is more individualistic and not always organized inside the family; the women work in the citrus groves and the men go to sea, and spousal mobility (both male and female) is high.

Here we find ourselves faced with strong differences of gender in the division of labour and the transmission of property as opposed to a simplification that represents a 'Sicilian family' as characterized by the low female age at first marriage, strong nuclear bonds and neolocality, the 'vigilance of virgins', honour, and patriarchal tendencies.[37] Variables articulated in this manner can permit comparison with other areas and contexts, rather than the creation of compact regional coherencies.

III

However, the relationship between family, demography, social stratification, territorial and socio-productive context, female work and the transmission of property brings us back to the discussion of the 'force of the periphery' and the importance of local cultures and their processes of legitimization, together with the mediation and interconnections between different social spheres. It is here that the concept of politics as jurisdiction, patronage, negotiation and mediation becomes relevant. The local dimension becomes, therefore, densely politicized and local politics organizes itself around competition for the monopoly on mediation. The territorial-political system is thus defined by a series of levels, often in conflict among themselves, that constitute the cardinal points of the political process: from the informal assembly of heads of households who meet in the oratory or piazza, to the town of the parish, to parliament.[38] From here interest goes towards the periphery as 'the heart of the definitions of jurisdiction, possession, sovereignty'[39] and leads to the devaluation of the notion of particularism.

The concept of periphery in the political history of the Mezzogiorno has remained dispersed (*poco disaggregato*). Despite the long tradition of scholarship from Rosario Romeo to Francesco Brancato and Orazio Cancila and the plethora of studies that have shown the complexits of the southern economic fabric, the image of the area remained tied to the countryside; at the same time the scarcity of the 'middle class', lamented first by Leopoldo Franchetti, has led to an underestimation of the existing social articulation and the forms of upward mobility. The identification of the Mezzogiorno with the countryside and of the ruling class with the landed aristocracy – which is responsible for the long resistance to modernization and state centralization – has led to the representation of the historiographic paradigm of the 'historic bloc' and to the idea of social mobility almost exclusively linked to the use of violence.

Marta Petrusewicz has provided a vivid description of the multiple subjects, roles, functions and interests tied to the Calabrian feudal estate of the Barracco family; she has analyzed the tight link between market and subsistence economy, the co-existence of wage payment and exchange in kind within the context of the flexible system of a feudal estate, which became a *latifundium* as it adapted to the economy of the changing nineteenth century.[40] Yet the classical line of studies regarding 'modernization' and the investigation of the southern elites have demonstrated that, by the first decades of the nineteenth century, a very dynamic process of social differentiation began to unfold, one that took advantage of favourable economic trends resulting from the abolition of feudal statutes (in 1806 in Naples and in 1812 in Sicily) and of new instruments placed at the disposal of the new administrative monarchy.

Surveys in some Sicilian communities[41] demonstrate the dissimilar profiles of the new bourgeois class that promoted itself in terms of political and social hegemony, the force of the plots, of the revolts, of the revolution of 1848, and of the support for Garibaldi's activities. The specific weight of the aristocracy, the importance of the *borgesi*, the *civili* or of the merchants, changes in each town in relation to the economic activity of the community, to the networks activated regarding the *intendenze* and the other centres of the monarchy, to the strength of the kin or client networks, and in the last instance, to the capacity to mobilize popular insurgence. This area of research was neglected early on,[42] without furthering the investigation, for example, of the functioning of the communal administrations, before and after unification, the formation of bureaucratic personnel,[43] of the judicial system, and so on. Gabriella Gribaudi's important book has permitted us to correct the stereotypes of both the 'absent state' and the 'foreignness' of southern towns that have figured so prominently in the debates about the Italian South. Seen from Eboli, a large town in the province of Salerno,[44] the state is the chain that unites the centre to the periphery, 'the fabric that regiments political relationships and controls public resources; it loses its reified aspect as impersonal organ and *super partes*, but assumes the semblance of what it personifies'.[45] In reality, it is the state's pervasive presence that perverts the accumulative mechanisms, consolidating the networks of mediation and parasitism.[46] In this scenario, politics becomes the arena where 'the logic of authority of the traditional type competes with acquisitive and contractual dynamics'.[47]

If we consider sociology, we note that the 'Italian case is peculiar among advanced countries because of the relevance of the kin and family system, besides the network of local relations'.[48] The most frequently cited 'national' reasons regarding the importance of the family are as follows: the statist-corporativist tradition of Italy (diffidence regarding the efficiency of the market); the Catholic conception of the family (considered as the centre of social life and the prime resource of social cohesion); the long absence of laws for divorce; and other restrictive pieces of legislation regarding family matters. Despite the relatively recent introduction of divorce, abortion and new rules for adoption, recognition of equal rights for illegitimate children and equal rights for women, the cohesion of the family structure is the same.[49] In fact, the family has been sustained by the state's contributions to small and medium-scale artisanal activities, agricultural enterprise, and small-scale businesses that in the last few decades have become the foundation of a new model of Italian growth benefiting from the effects of family-run economic resources. From the tendency to save and the sense of solidarity, that family is obliged to deal with the inefficiency of the Italian welfare system: 'The Italian family has had a crucial role ... on the level of production and accumulation of capital'.[50] But, while in the North the family has interacted with the re-organization of the local economy, in the post-Fordist years in the South, because of social integration realized in the last decades, it has produced familism. Where politics is freed from the primary traditional structures (family and kin), in order to realize greater solidarity, the role of the family becomes less dramatic. In the Mezzogiorno, however, the 'absence or lack of answers and collective identity has led to an enhancement of the defensive role of the family and kin group faced with threats and uncertainty of social interaction and has placed it in direct relation with the forms of political mediation',[51] intercepting possible development of a larger solidarity. Public intervention in the South, from the end of the Second World War, has favoured as a 'perverse effect' the incomplete emancipation of society from politics, the political weight of family networks, the extension of client networks, and the proliferation of political corruption and criminality. Income has increased but economic development has been blocked.

The involvement of well-known local people inside the system of the redistribution of state resources (agrarian reform, public assistance, pensions and, above all, jobs in the public sector) has simultaneously produced a modernization of consumption and a clientelist regime. The latter guarantees a series of advantages for economic growth of the

Italian state: a reserve work force at low cost, an expansion of the market for consumer goods produced in the North, and a stable base of political consent. The relevant changes here concern the disappearance of the families maintained by the agricultural work of an adult male (due to the abandonment of the countryside and emigration), the strong presence inside the urban working class of workers in the building trades, the persistence of a low level of female participation in the work force (especially among women with little education), and a low level of youth employment. Southern families support a high number of children, making the objective of intergenerational mobility very difficult. In general, both middle-class families (with fewer children and higher levels of education) and impoverished families are both strongly dependent on clientelism.

> In the South the only opportunity to find an acceptable job, as an alternative to organized crime, depends on the client game and on the redistribution of resources by the central state ... In the South, familism ... is the effect of the system of social integration realized in the last decades, rather than the cause of the blocked industrial development of the South.[52]

In this context the concept of 'work of substitution' gains ground, and serves to indicate the versatility of female work, used according to the necessity and the circumstances of the job market and the life cycle in both the private and the public spheres. The 'pragmatism of the southern women', the conception of the world, and the system of understanding, is the base of a cultural attitude that makes it possible for them to enter and exit from social and reproductive roles without formal ascription. This provides the entire social system not only with the flexibility necessary for its reproduction, but also the means to innovate and effect substantial change.[53] The three macro-sociological dimensions of female change in the southern regions can be summarized this way: the contraction of the period of the life cycle devoted to childbirth,[54] the transformation of women from inactive to active (that is, employed looking for work or unemployed)[55], and the growth of secondary and university education. On the other hand, welfare policies and clientelism have favoured types of female employment in not particularly innovative jobs (teaching or the public sector) subordinate to male employment. The model of the 'double presence' of women, at home and at work, represents a consolidated normality in the North but only an aspiration in the South. Indeed, in the Mezzogiorno it has produced consequences regarding reproductive choices: faced with the scarce productive role of women, a disproportionate level of consumption has been observed, such as to suppose 'a mode of social reproduction higher or more advanced than what one might deduce from the development of the relations of production'.[56] The permanent importance of the maternal role, even in one-child families, the long cohabitation of youths with the family, the rise in age at marriage and the search for the 'family income' combine to push large numbers of women into precarious jobs and into competition with males in relation to the client networks. The characteristics of the structures of production, the dependence upon public funds, the persistence of patron–client networks in the distribution of resources, the low quality of life caused by the lack of public services, and the absence of urban mass movements have prompted some scholars to define the Mezzogiorno as a 'reproducing society'. At the same time, these very factors show the kind of difficulties experienced by women in a process of emancipation whose potential appears to be 'intimately connected to the public sphere' rather than being a political matter. Women have renounced emancipation and have refused political representation, except in the local administrations. What will be their role in the collapse of the Mezzogiorno?

> At the beginning of the history of women, the first step concerned the discovery and identification of women's presence in the past. Afterwards an effort was made to improve techniques to analyse this presence, though it was not easy to understand how we were to study it: through the kin and socio-economic structures, or inside a complex system of symbolic production or as active protagonists in strategies of resistance, consciousness-raising etc?[57]

Accompanying the scholarship on subjectivity was an interest in exploring the experience of female religiosity, a field of study already well-grounded in national groups with well-structured international ties, and boasting a secure and long tradition of research.[58] More recently, interest has turned to aspects of the history of religious institutions: for example, convent architecture as a form of making urban space sacred.[59] Similar features characterize studies that have inherited, in a certain sense, an entire body of research on the family, including female social roles in relation to juridical norms and state policies. Finally, scholarship that is just emerging examines female patrimonies and their management, the normative system that guides them, and the role played by property in the construction of personal identities. Taken together, this wave of writing has led to attempts to historicize matrimony, to understand the moral economy of conjugality among the lower urban as well as the middle and aristocratic classes, and to analyse the links and the meaning of male and female roles within the conjugal couple.[60]

In conclusion: in 1987 Louise Tilly, on the occasion of the tenth anniversary of the *Journal of Family History*, lamented the tangential interest in the history of women in relation to the political history of the family.[61] There has not been a systematic reflection in this direction – not even from historians of the family – about the family as a political institution of primary importance. Paul Ginsborg, commenting on this problematic relationship, affirms that the 'marginalization of the political dimension in the history of the family leads to the marginalization of the family from the great history'.[62] In reality, the family has increased in analytic importance, and the analysis of the role of women within it has deep and profound implications. Political history's disinterest here is paradoxical, for we are witnessing the opening of a new paradigms that can add new layers of comprehension to a vitally important aspect of historical reality. Moreover, this approach can lead to a reformulation of the concept of 'the political' as more permeable and open to society. Only if we renounce generalizations, and attend to the 'passion for the differences', will gender find its collocation and will political history stop being a 'particular history'.

Notes

1 G. Barone, 'Il lato inedito dell'altra metà d'Italia', *I viaggi di Erodoto*, A. III, n. 8, 1989, p. 48; J.A. Davis, 'Remapping Italy's Path to the Twentieth-Century', *Journal of Modern History* 66 (June 1994), pp. 291–320; J.A. Davis, 'Casting Off the "Southern Problem": Or the Peculiarities of the South Reconsidered', in J. Schneider (ed.), *Italy's 'Southern Question': Orientalism in one Country* (Oxford, 1998), pp. 205–24.

2 P. Bevilacqua, *Breve storia dell'Italia meridionale dall'Ottocento a oggi* (Rome, 1993); see also the succinct summary in Chapter 3 above.

3 J. Dickie, 'La "sicilianità" di Francesco Crispi. Contributi a una storia degli stereotipi del Sud', *Meridiana* 24 (1995), p. 132.

4 G. Gribaudi, 'Images of the South: The Mezzogiorno as seen by Insiders and Outsiders', in R. Lumley and J. Morris (eds), *The New History of the Italian South: The Mezzogiorno Revisited* (Exeter, 1997), p. 105.

5 J. Dickie, 'Stereotypes of the Italian South, 1860–1900', in Morris and Lumley, *The New History of the Italian South*, pp. 114–47.

6 E. De Martino, *Morte e pianto rituale* (Turin, 1958), p. 358.

7 G. Pomata, 'La storia delle donne, una questione di confine', in *Il mondo contemporaneo*, vol. 10 (Florence, 1983), p. 1435; G. R. Saunders, 'The Magic

Giovanna Fiume 189

of the South: Popular Religion and Elite Catholicism in Italian Ethnology', in Schneider, *Italy's 'Southern Question'*, pp. 177–202.

8 R. Moscati, *Chi governa l'Università? Il mondo accademico italiano tra conservazione e mutamento* (Naples, 1977).

9 G. Fiume, 'Il lavoro della donna nella Sicilia dell'Ottocento', *Nuovi Quaderni del Meridione* 60 (1977), pp. 435–52; G. Fiume, 'Il proletariato femminile in Sicilia prima dell'Unità', *Nuovi Quaderni del Meridione* 61 (1978), pp. 67–95.

10 S. Laudani, 'Le attività tessili delle donne siciliane tra autoconsumo e mercato (secc. XVIII– XIX)', in *Dai mangani alle filande: Trasformazioni produttive e modificazioni colturali in Sicilia (XVIII–XIX secolo)* (Acireale, 1991), pp. 87–104.

11 S. Laudani, 'Trasformazioni agrarie e condizione femminile in Sicilia nell'Ottocento', *Annali dell'Istituto Cervi* 12 (1990).

12 These were, after all, the years of Baran and Sweezy's *Monthly Review*, and a period of intense struggle in the world's anti-colonial movements.

13 G. Fiume, 'Violenza femminile nella Sicilia dell'Ottocento: la criminalità "banale"', *Incontri meridionali* 3 (1984).

14 D. Pompejano, I. Fazio and G. Raffaele, *Controllo sociale e criminalità: Un circondario rurale nella Sicilia dell'Ottocento* (Milan, 1985); G. Raffaele, *L'ambigua tessitura: Mafia e fascismo nella Sicilia degli anni Venti* (Milan, 1993). G. Fiume, *Le bande armate in Sicilia. Violenza e organizzazione del potere (1819–1849)* (Palermo, 1984). A. Blok, *The Mafia of a Sicilian Village, 1860–1960* (New York, 1974); C. Duggan, *La mafia durante il fascismo* (Soveria, 1986); D. Gambetta, *La mafia siciliana. Un'industria della protezione privata* (Turin, 1992); S. Lupo, *Storia della mafia dalle origini ai nostri giorni* (Rome, 1993); P. Pezzino, *Mafia: industria della violenza* (Florence, 1995); M. Marmo, 'Tra le carceri e i mercati: Spazi e modelli storici del fenomeno camorrista', in P. Macry and P. Villani (eds), *La Campania* (Turin, 1990), pp. 691–730.

15 G. Levi, 'Villaggi', *Quaderni Storici* 1 (1981), p. 8.

16 *Ragnatele di rapporti: Patronage e reti di relazione nella storia delle donne* (Turin, 1988).

17 M. Minicuci, *Qui e altrove: Famiglie di Calabria e di Argentina* (Milan, 1989), p. 385; Minicuci, *Le strategie matrimoniali in una comunità calabrese: Saggi demoantropologici* (Soveria, 1981).

18 F. Benigno, *Una casa, una terra: Ricerche su Paceco, paese nuovo nella Sicilia del Sei e Settecento* (Catania, 1985); G. Longhitano, *Studi di storia della popolazione siciliana: Riveli, numerazioni, censimenti (1569–1861)* (Catania, 1988); M. Grillo and S. Raffaele, 'Butera nel '700: dinamica demografica e struttura della famiglia', *Le Forme e la Storia* 1 (1980) S. Raffaele, *Dinamiche demografiche e struttura della famiglia nella Sicilia del Sei-Settecento* (Catania, 1984); S. Raffaele, *Il censimento siciliano del 1831:Viagrande* (Catania, 1993); P. Travagliante, *Il censimento siciliano del 1831: Afferana Etnea* (Catania, 1990); G. Da Molin, *La famiglia nel passato: Strutture familiari nel Regno di Napoli in età moderna* (Bari, 1990); and D. Ligresti, *Catania e i suoi casali* (Catania, 1995).

19 F. Benigno, 'Famiglia mediterranea e modelli anglosassoni', *Meridiana* 6 (1989), pp. 29–61, quotation: p. 60.

20 I. Fazio, *La signora dell'oro* (Palermo, 1987); I. Fazio, 'Trasmissione della proprietà, sussistenza e status in Sicilia (Capizzi, 1790–1900)', *Annali dell'Istituto Cervi* 12 (1990); I. Fazio, 'Valori economici e valori simbolici: il declino della dote nell'Italia dell'Ottocento', *Quaderni Storici* 79 (1992), pp. 291–316;

I. Fazio, 'La trasmissione della proprietà alle donne nel Nord e nel Sud: specificità o coerenze?', in N. Ginatempo (ed.), *Donne del Sud: Il prisma femminile sulla questione meridionale* (Palermo, 1993), pp. 27–34.

21   S. D'Onofrio, 'La vergine e lo sposo legato', *Quaderni storici* 75 (1990), pp. 859–78; S. D'Onofrio, 'Amicizia ed eros nel comparatico siciliano', in *Forme di comparatico italiano, L'homme* 1:11 (1987), pp. 93–135; J. Schneider and P. Schneider, *Festival of the Poor: Fertility Decline and Ideology of Class in Sicily (1860–1980)* (Tucson, AZ, 1996); J. Schneider, *La vigilanza delle vergini* (Palermo, 1987).

22   G. Fiume (ed.), *Onore e storia nelle società mediterranee* (Palermo, 1989).

23   G. Fiume, 'Morale sessuale e igiene sociale: il controllo sulla prostituzione nella Sicilia degli ultimi Borbone', in *Malattie, terapie e istituzioni sanitarie in Sicilia* (Palermo, 1985), pp. 239–59; P. Catalanotto, 'Sulla soglia del disonore. Gravidanze illegittime e infanzia abbandonata nella Sicilia del Sette-Ottocento', in Fiume, *Onore e storia*, pp. 155–64; and G. Fiume, ' "Sotto la Real protezione": l'infanzia abbandonata nella Sicilia del Sette Ottocento', in G. Fiume, *Povertà e beneficenza tra rivoluzione e restaurazione* (Naples, 1990), pp. 63–78; L. Guidi, 'Onore e pericolo. Il valore di una donna secondo il sistema di carità napoletano dell'Ottocento', in Fiume, *Onore e storia*, pp. 165–80; G. Fiume, 'Condizione femminile e istituzioni a Napoli nel decennio francese', in Fiume, *Povertà e beneficenza*, pp. 183–96; G. Fiume, ' "Ragazzi discoli": Famiglia e ordine pubblico nella Napoli postunitaria', in *Storia e paure: Immaginario collettivo, riti e rappresentazioni della paura in età moderna* (Milan, 1992), pp. 246–54; S. Raffaele, 'Essendo Real volontà che le donne badino all'onore: Onore e status nella legislazione meridionale (secc. XVI–XVIII)', in Fiume, *Onore e storia*, pp. 143–54; G. Fiume, 'Infanzia abbandonata: la normativa del decennio francese', in Fiume, *Povertà e beneficenza*, pp. 79–94.

24   L. Guidi, *L'onore in pericolo: Carità e reclusione femminile nell'Ottocento napoletano* (Naples, 1991); L. Valenzi, *Poveri, ospizi e potere a Napoli (XVIII–XIX secc.)* (Milan, 1995); S. Raffaele, *Dalla beneficenza all'assistenza: Momenti di politica assistenziale nella Sicilia moderna* (Catania, 1990).

25   A. Arru and M. T. Chialant (eds), *Il racconto delle donne: Voci, autobiografie, figurazioni* (Naples, 1990); S. Piccone Stella, *Ragazze del Sud* (Rome, 1979).

26   R. Siebert, *E' femmina, però è bella: Tre generazioni di donne al Sud* (Turin, 1991). It is important to note that in contrast to the Marxist approach practised a decade ago, study of women's work has assumed a marked ethno-anthroplogical shape. See, especially, L. Guidi, 'Maestre e imprenditrici nell'industria manifatturiera meridionale dell'Ottocento', in P. Nava (ed.), *Il lavoro delle donne nell'Italia contemporanea, continuità e rotture* (Turin, 1992); M. Fiume, 'L'onore femminile nell'agrumeto: Lu spassu di lu lumiaru', in Fiume, *Onore e storia*, pp. 349–76; G. Fiume, 'La tomba di Angelica la ricamatrice', in Ginatempo, *Donne del Sud*, pp. 57–66; M. Fiume, *Vita di Orazia, contadina e guaritrice* (Palermo, 1988); N. Triolo, 'Famiglia, aborto e ostetriche in Sicilia (1920–1940)', in G. Fiume (ed.), *Madri. Storia di un ruolo sociale* (Venice, 1995), pp. 247–66.

27   For specific themes within community studies, see the work by G. Arrighi, F. Piselli, G. Gribaudi and G. Civile; on marriage and inheritance, see the work by G. Delille and P. Macry; on aristocracy, see the work by D. Ligresti

and G. Montroni; on the elites, see the work by G. Barone, E. Iachello and A. Signorelli; on productive systems, see the work by O. Cancila and M. Petrusewicz; on the southern countryside, see the work by P. Bevilacqua; on markets and migratory chains, see the work by B. Salvemini and F. Piselli; on social disorder and crime, see the work by J. Davis, S. Lupo, P. Pezzino and M. Marmo; on sociology, see the work by B. Meloni.

28   See B. Salvemini, 'Sulla nobile arte di creare le peculiarità nel Mezzogiorno', in B. Salvemini, *L'innovazione precaria. Spazi, mercati e società nel Mezzogiorno tra Sette e Ottocento* (Catanzaro, 1995), p. 187.

29   See Salvemini, 'Sulla nobile arte', p. 203.

30   See G. Delille, 'La famiglia contadina nell'età moderna', in P. Bevilacqua, *Storia dell'agricoltura italiana in età contemporanea*, vol. II: *Uomini e Classi* (Venice, 1990), p. 534.

31   G. Delille, *Famiglia e proprietà nel Regno di Napoli, XV–XIX secolo* (Turin, 1988), p. 11.

32   See F. Benigno, 'I dannati del primo sole. Ipotesi sulla mortalità di genere in Italia meridionale tra XVI e XX secolo', *Meridiana* 26–27 (1996), pp. 277–310.

33   G. Levi, 'Economia contadina e mercato della terra nel Piemonte di Antico Regime', in Bevilacqua, *Storia dell'agricoltura italiana*, pp. 538–9.

34   Delille, *Famiglia e proprietà*, p. 346.

35   Delille, *Famiglia e proprietà*.

36   I. Fazio, 'Famiglia, matrimonio, trasmissione della proprietà: ipotesi di lavoro a partire dal caso siciliano', in B. Meloni (ed.), *Famiglia meridionale senza familismo* (Rome, 1993), p. 4.

37   See Fazio, 'Famiglia, matrimonio, trasmissione della proprietà'.

38   See E. Grendi, *Il Cervo e la Repubblica. Il modello ligure di Antico Regime* (Turin, 1993), p. 28.

39   O. Raggio, 'Visto dalla periferia. Formazioni politiche di Antico Regime e Stato moderno', in M. Aymard (ed.), *Storia d'Europa*, vol. IV: *L'Età moderna. Secoli XVI–XVIII* (Turin, 1995), p. 512.

40   M. Petrusewicz, *Latifondo. Economia morale e vita materiale in una periferia dell'Ottocento* (Venice, 1989), published in English as *Latifundium: Moral Economy and Material Life in a Nineteenth-Century Periphery* (Ann Arbor, MI, 1996).

41   G. Giarrizzo, *Un Comune rurale della Sicilia etnea. Biancavilla (1810–1860)* (Catania, 1963); E. Iachello, *Il vino e il mare. 'Trafficanti' siciliani tra '700 e '800 nella contea di Mascali* (Catania, 1991); P. Pezzino, 'Monarchia amministrativa ed élites locali: Naro nella prima metà dell'Ottocento', in P. Pezzino, *Il paradiso abitato dai diavoli. Società, élites, istituzioni nel Mezzogiorno contemporaneo* (Milan, 1992); A. De Francesco, *La guerra di Sicilia. Il distretto di Caltagirone nella rivoluzione del 1820–'21* (Acireale, 1992); G. Fiume, *Le regole del gioco. Riorganizzazione dell'amministrazione civile e liste degli elegibili a Marineo (1819–1859)*, forthcoming.

42   A. Spagnoletti, *Storia del regno delle Due Sicilie* (Bologna, 1997).

43   R. Romanelli, *Sulle carte interminate. Un ceto di impiegati tra privato e pubblico: i segretari comunali in Italia, 1860–1915* (Bologna, 1989).

44   See also G. Civile, *Il comune rustico. Storia sociale di un paese del Mezzogiorno nell'Ottocento* (Bologna, 1990).

45   G. Gribaudi, *A Eboli. Il mondo meridionale in cent'anni di trasformazioni* (Venice, 1990), p. 291.

46   L. Musella, *Individui, amici, clienti. Relazioni personali e circuiti politici in Italia Meridionale tra Otto e Novecento* (Bologna, 1994).

47   Gribaudi, *A Eboli*, p. 90.

48   E. Mingione and M. Magatti, 'Strategie familiari e sviluppo: una comparazione Nord-Sud', in Meloni, *Famiglia meridionale senza familismo*, p. 139.

49   See C. Saraceno, *Anatomia della famiglia: strutture sociali e forme familiari* (Bologna, 1976); and M. Barbagli, *Provando e riprovando* (Bologna, 1990).

50   Mingione and Magatti, 'Strategie familiari', p. 139.

51   C. Trigilia, *Sviluppo senza autonomia. Effetti perversi delle politiche nel Mezzogiorno* (Bologna, 1992), p. 91; G. Gribaudi, 'Familismo e famiglia a Napoli e nel Mezzogiorno', *Meridiana* 17 (1993), p. 14; S. Lupo, 'Usi e abusi del passato. Le radici dell'Italia di Putnam', *Meridiana* 18 (1993), p. 167.

52   Mingione and Magatti, *Strategie familiari*, p. 153.

53   A. Signorelli, 'Il pragmatismo delle donne. La condizione femminile nella trasformazione delle campagne', in Bevilacqua, *Storia dell'agricoltura*, vol. II, pp. 625–60; and Signorelli, 'Ancora sul pragmatismo delle donne', in Ginatempo, *Donne del Sud*, pp. 67–77.

54   The birth rate in the South in 1964 was 3.31 per cent; in 1977, 2.49 per cent, and in 1989, 1.60 per cent (national rate 1.30); ISTAT (*Institute Italiano di Statistica*) 1993.

55   The size of the female work force active in South Italy in 1993 was 25.5 per cent, as opposed to a national level of 30.8 per cent; ISTAT 1993. C. Leccardi, 'Il lavoro come piacere. Il nuovo sguardo sul lavoro delle giovani donne del Mezzogiorno', in D. Barazzetti and C. Leccardi (eds), *Fare e pensare* (Turin, 1995); idem., *Futuro breve. Le giovani donne e il futuro* (Turin, 1996).

56   F. Piselli, 'Donne e mercato del lavoro: il caso della Calabria e del Portogallo', in *Donne del Sud*, p. 118.

57   P. Di Cori, 'Soggettività e storia delle donne', in Società Italiana delle Storiche, *Discutendo di storia. Soggettività, ricerca, autobiografia* (Turin, 1990), p. 40; L. Passerini, *Storia e soggettività* (Florence, 1988).

58   S. Cabibbo and M. Modica, *La santa dei Tomasi. Storia di suor Maria Crocifissa (1645–1699)* (Turin, 1989); S. Cabibbo and M. Modica, 'Identità religiosa e identità di genere: scritture di famiglia nella Sicilia del Seicento', *Quaderni Storici* 83 (1993), pp. 415–42; S. Cabibbo, *Il Paradiso del Magnifico Regno. Agiografi, santi e culti nella Sicilia spagnola* (Rome, 1996); S. Cabibbo, 'Religiosità femminile', in *Dizionario di storiografia* (Milan, 1997); S. Cabibbo, 'Catene d'inventioni. Cittadine sante a Palermo tra XVI e XVII secolo', in G. Fiume (ed.), *Il santo patrono e la città* (Venice, 2000), pp. 199–216; M. Modica, 'La scrittura mistica', in L. Scaraffia and G. Zarri (eds), *Donne e fede. Santità e vita religiosa in Italia* (Rome, 1994); M. Modica, '"Figlio in Christo". La maternità spirituale tra ortodossia ed eterodossia nella cultura cristiana post-tridentina', in *Madri*, pp. 205–20; G. Palumbo, 'L'archetipo oscuro e dimenticato della sorella: Calmana, sorella di Caino', *Quaderni Storici* 87 (1994), pp. 669–700.

59   M. Campanelli, 'Monache in provincia. Le canonichesse lateranensi di Arienzo', in G. Zarri (ed.), *Il monachesimo femminile in Italia* (Verona, 1997), pp. 369–97; H. Hills, 'Iconography and Ideology: Aristocracy, Immaculacy and Virginity in Seventeenth-Century Palermo', *The Oxford Art Journal* 17:2 (1994), pp. 16–31; Hills, 'Monasteri femminili aristocratici a Napoli

e Palermo nella prima età moderna e la "conventualizzazione" della città', in Fiume, *Il santo patrono e la città*, pp. 68–78.

60 M. Pelaja, *Matrimonio e sessualità a Roma nell'Ottocento* (Rome, 1994); M. De Giorgio and C. Klapish (eds), *Storia del matrimonio* (Rome, 1996); G. Fiume, 'Cursing, Poisoning and Feminine Morality: The Case of the "Vinegar Hag" in Late Eighteenth-Century Palermo', *Social Anthropology* 4:2 (1996), pp. 117–32; L. Accati *et al.*, *Padre e figlia* (Turin, 1994); G. Calvi, *Il contratto morale. Madri e figli nella Toscana moderna* (Rome, 1994); M. d'Amelia (ed.), *Madri; Storia della maternità* (Rome, 1998); L. Accati, *Il mostro e la bella. Padre e madre nella educazione cattolica dei sentimenti* (Milan, 1998); *Donne e proprietà. Una analisi comparata* (Naples, 1996), vol. I; A. Groppi, 'Femmes, dots et patrimoines', *Clio* 7 (1998); 'Gestione dei patrimoni e diritti delle donne', *Quaderni Storici* 98 (1998); G. Calvi and I. Chabot (eds), *Le ricchezze delle donne. Diritti patrimoniali e poteri familiari in Italia (XIII–XIX secc.)* (Turin, 1998); I. Fazio, 'Le ricchezze e le donne', *Quaderni Storici* 101 (1999), pp. 539–50.

61 L. Tilly, 'Women's History and Family History: Fruitful Collaboration or Missed Connection?', *Journal of Family History* 12 (1987).

62 P. Ginsborg, 'Famiglia, società civile e stato nella società contemporanea: alcune considerazioni metodologiche', *Meridiana* 17 (1993), p. 180.

Part IV
Connections

10

Radicalism and Nationalism: Northern 'Liberators' and Southern Labourers in the USA and Italy, 1830–60

Enrico Dal Lago

The Liberals of Italy...are to a man, philanthropists, or 'friends of humanity' by profession. Accordingly, we find that they are fanatical *Negrophiles*, abolitionists of as a deep dye as their friend and panegyrist, Horace Greely, or any other of our northern fanatics...They tell us boldly that they intend to act, that it is their duty, in virtue of the 'solidarity of the people', to make all men free. As soon as they will gain their own freedom, they will offer their aid for the establishing of freedom in America. Italian Liberals and American Abolitionists form but one army, fighting under the same banner in the same cause.[1]

This excerpt is taken from one of the foremost literary reviews in late antebellum America: *Russell's Magazine*. Since the appearance of its first issue, in 1857, *Russell's Magazine* had quickly established itself as a periodical which – in the words of the editor, Paul Hamilton Hayne – represented 'the opinions, doctrines and arguments of the educated minds of the South'.[2] At the same time, the magazine's contributors, who included celebrated planter and poet William Grayson, were wholeheartedly committed to the support and defence of Southern institutions, and especially of slavery.[3] Therefore, the author of the excerpt had captured the opinion of a considerable part of the southern slaveholding elite towards the movement for National Unification in Italy; more to the point, he had made an interesting connection between Italian Democrats, whom he called 'liberals', and American abolitionists.

Studies undertaken by a handful of historians – notably Giorgio Spini, Howard Marraro and Joseph Rossi – have shown that there were, indeed, connections between the two movements.[4] It is well-known that Giuseppe Mazzini was very popular in American anti-slavery circles both because of his 'conviction in favor of the holy cause of abolition-ism'[5] and because of his personal acquaintance with William Lloyd Garrison and other important abolitionists.[6] However, Mazzini was only the most illustrious of a large number of political refugees who, by teaching in universities and writing in newspapers, helped to shape the positive attitude of American public opinion towards the Italian *Risorgimento*. Indeed, in a recent study, Matteo Sanfilippo has argued that Italian refugees who ended up as university professors in the USA and Canada were instrumental in forming a pro-Italian and anti-Bourbon and anti-Austrian opinion among upper-class North American students who were bound to become high civil servants and diplomats.[7]

Whilst mentioning some of these important connections, the main objective of this chapter will be to explore the possibility of comparing the development of the American anti-slavery movement and of the Italian movement for National Unification between 1830 and 1860, with specific reference to the two souths. In this respect, the parallel made by the *Russell's Magazine*'s excerpt about two related struggles is the starting point of our comparison. American anti-slavery and the Italian movement for National Unification strove to achieve an ideal of freedom in different national contexts and under different circum-stances. The fact that this struggle was perceived as '*one single cause*, not only in principle, *but in the means of success*'[8] is remarkable and invites us to reflect upon the meaning of categories such as liberty and oppression in nineteenth-century Europe and America.

In general terms, anti-slavery and Nationalist ideologies were linked by a strong belief in progress. David Brion Davis has shown how at the end of the eighteenth century slavery had started to be considered retrogressive and consequently emancipation stood as a symbol of pro-gress.[9] Nineteenth-century abolitionism, therefore, was a progressive movement and its advocates held the belief that slavery was an injustice against which each person of conscience had to fight.[10] Nationalism started to be linked with the idea of progress when the idea of a modern nation spread in Europe at the end of the eighteenth century, as a consequence of the French Revolution. Nineteenth-century nationalists believed that the fight for the recognition of oppressed nationalities led humankind into an increasingly progressive path.[11]

To be sure, the nineteenth-century idea of progress also had clear connections with the rise of Romanticism, whose language of 'natural rights' – originally an idea of the Enlightenment – appealed to both abolitionist and Nationalist rhetoric. Individual freedom was a central concept in Romanticism and its denial either in the form of slavery or in the form of oppression of patriotism was rejected with horror as highly immoral.[12] The liberation of slaves from bondage and the liberation of patriots from oppression clearly had some points in common that romantic intellectuals were keen to stress. A passage from Mazzini brilliantly illustrates this link and also its relation to the romantic notion of freedom:

> Blessed be your efforts [*he is addressing Rev. Dr Beard, chairman of the antislavery committee in England*], if they start from this high ground of a common faith; if you do not forget, whilst at work for the emancipation of the black race, the million of white slaves, suffering, struggling, expiring in Italy, in Poland, in Hungary, throughout all Europe: if you always remember that free men only can achieve the work of freedom, and that Europe's appeal for the abolition of slavery in other lands will not weigh all-powerful before God and men, whilst Europe herself shall be desecrated by arbitrary, tyrannical powers, by czars, emperors, and popes.[13]

Progress and Romanticism were incompatible with slavery and oppression of nationality in any form and for romantic intellectuals such as Mazzini the fight against these two evils constituted the 'national problem' of those countries where either of them was present. There is no question that the USA and Italy in the nineteenth century provided the most dramatic examples of successful struggles against slavery and against national oppression. However, what makes them comparable cases is also the fact that the way the two struggles were handled and the way the two 'national problems' were resolved contributed to the creation of a permanent difference between the northern and southern part of the two countries.

In the case of the USA, since slavery was a southern institution, the struggle of the forces of progress against evil was organized in the northern states and involved a glorification 'of northern society... by isolating slavery as an unacceptable form of labour exploitation';[14] the presence of slavery in the South was seen by northern reformers both as an evidence of institutionalized tyranny and as a threat to the very foundations of republican life.[15] In the case of Italy, the oppression of national feeling was diffused throughout the peninsula, but progressive intellectuals and revolutionary ideologues based themselves in the northern states of Piedmont and Lombardy, from which they looked increasingly, especially after 1848, at the Bourbon Kingdom in the South as the negation of the idea of progress, both because of its systematic denial of basic political rights and because of an oppressive social system which was based on the exploitation of the peasantry.[16]

American slaves were exploited in a very straightforward way: they were stripped of their freedom, they were brutally beaten and over-worked in the plantations and they were racially discriminated against on the grounds of their race. On the other hand, southern Italian peasants were mostly landless labourers or tenants on the large landed estates called *latifondi*, on which they were tied to the landowners by particularly usurious contracts. Although their particular conditions differed greatly, both slaves and peasants provided progressive reformers with two powerful examples of exploitation of agrarian labourers, an exploitation which both abolitionists and Democrats considered as the most evident symptom of the presence of unjust and tyrannical societies in the souths of the USA and Italy.[17]

However, whereas American abolitionists put the exploitation of slaves in the American south at the centre of the American national problem, Italian Democrats viewed the exploitation of southern Italian peasants as part of the Italian national problem only because of the oppressive nature of the Bourbon regime in the Mezzogiorno. Still, in the minds of both abolitionists and Democrats, slaves and peasants became the symbols of repressive societies which stood in the way of national progress. Therefore, the achievement of national progress had to pass through the emancipation of the slaves in America and through the destruction of the Bourbon state and the improvement of conditions of the southern peasantry in Italy.

Between 1830 and 1860, the two souths became the object of powerful attacks by abolitionists and Democrats, both through public opinion and through direct action. The aim in both cases was to overthrow a reactionary regime, which was denying individual freedom to a considerable part of the population in one way or another. In both cases there were several plans to achieve this aim through armed revolt of the masses of agrarian labourers. The 'liberation' which would have followed would have merged with the formation of a new republican nation, which would have guaranteed basic rights and some degree of social justice. Throughout this 30-year period, there grew a conviction that a change in the two souths' oppressive regimes could only come from external forces located primarily in the North. Long before the Union Army arrived in the American South and Garibaldi landed in Sicily, southern labourers in the USA and Italy were thought to expect 'liberators' from the North to bring the change they longed for.

American abolitionists and Italian Democrats shared a deep moral commitment in the realization of their goals. Their best-known representatives – William Lloyd Garrison and Giuseppe Mazzini – were convinced that the two national problems were first and foremost moral problems. Consequently, abolitionism and the Democratic movement were utopian movements, which saw the practical solutions to problems of social injustice as being necessary for the moral regeneration of society.

Garrison, who in 1831 had started a campaign for immediate abolition through his own newspaper, *The Liberator*, based his moral crusade against slaveholding on the idea that slavery contaminated the whole of southern society and made it profoundly unequal and therefore un-American.[18] This moral judgement was in large part derived from the influence of Evangelicalism, according to which men had to repent for their sins; and slavery was the greatest sin of all.[19] Democracy, for Garrison, was based on personal recognition of freedom and equality as the true laws of God. The crusade against slavery was a battle to win the souls of Americans, to persuade them to take responsibility for their actions and to recognize the sin of maintaining a republic which allowed the existence of unfree labourers.[20] In Garrison's mind, the great abolitionist aim of immediate emancipation of the slaves in the South was subordinated to the conversion of ministers, editors, and of the whole American public opinion through 'moral suasion'; the 1833 foundation of the American Anti-Slavery Society, whose Declaration of Sentiments talked about 'abolition of slavery by the power of repentance', marked the high tide of Garrisonian abolitionism and its non-violent approach to slavery.[21]

Several influential abolitionists thought the same way as Garrison and rather than becoming involved in violent actions to free the slaves, they tried to shake public opinion by any non-violent means, particularly propaganda. Wholly committed to the strategy of 'moral suasion', between 1833 and 1840 the American Anti-Slavery Society covered the USA with a flood of publications which included descriptive eye-witness accounts of the effects of slavery accompanied by images, pamphlets denouncing the horrors of slavery in a particularly graphic manner, and recurrent appeals to the conscience of Americans. Anti-slavery pamphlets and speeches showed how slavery was evil because it reduced labourers to things, deprived them of free will and exposed them to acts of brutal violence. However, as Don Doyle has pointed out, the abolitionist campaign did not draw 'so much on the audience's sympathy for the slave as it did on condemnation of slaveownership as a sin'.[22]

In this respect, the abolitionist crusade – especially as symbolized by Garrison – was a highly utopian enterprise. Winning the battle for 'moral suasion' would have automatically guaranteed freedom and equality to the slaves. The resolution of the American national problem was left to the good conscience of northerners.[23] As Ronald Walters has shown, abolitionists sought to redeem the nation by spreading south-ward northern ideals of morality. This kind of 'cultural imperialism' tended to present northerners as 'hardworking, educated, prosperous, freedom-loving' persons.[24]

At the same time, in the anti-slavery pamphlets, slaves were presented as helpless victims of southern brutality who were patiently waiting for a rescue which would be brought about by northern public opinion. The liberation of the slaves would have been achieved when northern pres-sure on the National Government could force southerners to give up slaveholding.[25] While not ruling out the possibility of spontaneous slave revolt, Garrisonian abolitionists helped to build the idea of slaves as not being capable of looking after themselves and therefore in need of help from the North. Although committed to the establishment of racial equality in America – to which they contributed in a major way – Garrisonian abolitionists could not help but think that they were des-tined to fight for the liberation of an unhappy race.[26]

The idea, inspired by abolitionists, that slaves were gentle and patient in the midst of oppression, unlike 'vengeful and liberty-loving' Anglo-Saxons, was a powerful engine of racial prejudice. Slave revolts in the American South were surprisingly few; almost all of them – except for Nat Turner's rebellion in 1831 – had been discovered and repressed before any action could take place. Why, people asked, do the slaves not revolt against their bondage like any white man would do? Aboli-tionists invariably answered this question by invoking Christian virtues and asserting that 'the negro's heart, spite the maddening influence of oppression, is too kind, too full of tenderness and love . . . the white man seeks vengeance, but not he'.[27]

This attitude has been called by George Fredrickson 'Romantic Racial-ism' and was best represented by Wiliam Ellery Channing, who wrote in 1835 that 'we are holding in bondage one of the best races of the human family. The negro is among the mildest and gentlest of men.' Because slaves belonged to a gentle race, they could not rise in arms against their oppressors; this logic justified early forms of northern racial discrimin-ation against southern blacks and at the same time it constructed the idea of slaves as being dependent on the help of northerners to break free from their oppression.[28]

In 1831, while in exile in France, Mazzini founded the association called *Young Italy* for the promotion of Italian National Unification; Denis Mack Smith describes it as an 'apostolate', a quasi-religious movement calling its members to a life of political conspiracy and self-sacrifice'.[29] Truly, there was in Mazzini as much of a moral commitment and a religious sense of mission as there was in Garrison.[30] According to Roland Sarti, Henri de Saint-Simon's 'view of a future society based on the principle of association, religious faith, and faith in progress became an essential part of the Mazzinian creed'.[31] Mazzini added to this messianic background his particular views on democratic nationalism; his central idea was that the nation was a product of the work of the people and at the same time the fulfilment of God's plans for humankind. Repeatedly, Mazzini wrote phrases such as 'where God wanted the existence of a nation, there were the means to create it'; every man had a mission and the most important mission was to bring the nation to existence.[32]

Unlike Garrison, Mazzini believed in the realization of his mission through revolutionary insurrection; the people, which he called 'the largest and poorest class', were to be guided by the intellectuals on the road to liberation from oppression. However, since Mazzini looked for collaboration – rather than conflict – between different classes, his whole idea of achievement of national unification through revolution ended up being as utopian as non-violent abolitionism.[33] Much like Garrison, Mazzini believed that the people could be led to 'the discovery of their collective mission and hence...the establishment of a new moral...order'. Therefore he was against any revolutionary plan involving class conflict as potential generator of violence and civil war.[34]

In the mind of the Democrats, who were primarily Mazzini's followers, the liberation of the masses from oppression meant simultaneous achievement of national unity and social justice. In the document in which he outlined the main ideas behind his programme, Mazzini wrote that '*Young Italy* does not want national unity to be based on *despotism*, but rather on the agreement and free consent of everybody.'[35] All Democrats agreed on the incompatibility of the institution of monarchy with these premises; therefore, the resolution of the Italian national problem had to pass through the destruction of the monarchies throughout the peninsula, and first and foremost of the Bourbon Kingdom in the South, which was the largest and most reactionary state.[36]

Mazzini turned his attention to the Bourbon Kingdom at different times in his attempts at provoking the revolution which would have freed the people from national oppression. Several Democrats considered the South as a place which had the potential for insurrection. The idea was that the exploited southern peasantry would rise against Bourbon oppression and would be guided by the leaders of Mazzinian organizations trained in the north.[37] The peasants of the South were seen by Mazzinian Democrats as representing a kind of spontaneous and primitive insurrectionary force, which needed to be directed and guided by properly northern-trained revolutionary leaders. The liberation of peasants from exploitation and Bourbon oppression could be achieved only after preliminary work to introduce ideas and set up networks which had to start outside the southern kingdom. Like slaves in the American South, southern Italian peasants were constructed as helpless victims of an oppressive regime patiently waiting for rescue brought by northern-trained revolutionaries.[38]

Revolts among peasants in the Bourbon Kingdom were frequent and their cause, rather than being the fulfilment of an abstract idea of freedom or nationality, was usually the hunger for land. Failure to address the land problem among Mazzinian Democrats meant that their carefully planned revolutionary insurrections could never succeed. Moreover, to follow Antonio Gramsci's thought, the fact that Democrats never elaborated a programme capable of fulfilling the peasantry's expectations over land distribution in the end made them subordinate to much more successful moderate political forces in the construction of the Italian nation.[39] However, in Mazzini's view, to address the land problem meant to spark class conflict; this would have inevitably led to a degeneration of social relations into violence and anarchy, whereas the fundamental tenets of his political programme talked about harmony and consent as ideal foundations of the Democratic nation.[40]

Perhaps most important of all was the fact that the construction of the southern peasantry as waiting for a spark coming from outside to start a general insurrection was, in the words of Paul Ginsborg, a true 'romantic myth'. This myth had its highest moment with the failure of the expedition of the Bandiera brothers, who were killed in Calabria whilst trying to start a revolution in the southern countryside in 1844.[41] The two brothers sacrificed their lives in a highly symbolic expedition in which they knew that they could count on little military support, but they still had complete faith in the revolutionary potential of the Calabrian peasants; in fact, according to Ginsborg, 'the peasants of Calabria were considered by the Bandiera as endemic rebels and as ready to answer to the patriots' call to arms'.[42]

Southern Italian peasants were not the object of 'romantic racialism', like slaves in America; however, in an equally powerful kind of 'romantic myth' they were seen as needing guidance and education before they could realize their own condition and make a decisive contribution to the improvement of their own lives. As in the case of American slaves, this view led dangerously to the idea of southern masses as being dependent upon northern help, since they were seen as incapable of successfully fighting Bourbon oppression on their own.

Both American abolitionism and the Italian Democratic movement had extremist fringes, which were characterized by a more radical approach to the national problem. Radical leaders were both more pragmatic and more committed to using violent means to achieve their aims. Revolution for them had to be sparked by an initial armed revolt, which would serve as an example and which would eventually lead to a general insurrection.

In the USA, radical abolitionists were the most active in advocating a general armed revolt of southern slaves; the 1850s saw a crescendo of attempts at provoking it. On one hand, this was a result of the basic failure in achieving the objectives of the highly utopian enterprise of 'moral suasion'. On the other hand, the increasingly violent atmosphere of sectional conflicts after 1848 prompted a redefinition of abolitionist means and aims. Jane and William Pease have argued that the failure of the anti-slavery politics of the Free-Soil Party and the passage of the Fugitive Slave Act of 1850 – by which fugitive slaves were made to return to their masters – forced the new generations of abolitionists to change strategy and move towards direct action against the slavery system.[43] In the words of James Brewer Stewart, 'abolitionists who endorsed non-violence for practical reasons would obviously feel free to discard the tactic whenever desperate circumstances seemed to justify doing so. For some Abolitionists, the pro-slavery triumphs of the early 1850s were such a compelling reason.'[44]

Among the most active radical abolitionists was James Redpath, a leading propagandist of slave insurrection from the mid-1850s up to the Civil War. Being in contact with other radical abolitionists – notably John Brown – Redpath undertook several trips in the southern states in order to see for himself the conditions of the slaves and the possibilities of slave insurrection.[45] He stated clearly his view of the American national problem when he proclaimed: 'let the abolitionists of the North not be deceived. The South will never liberate her slaves unless compelled to do so.'[46] In line with what he wrote – 'I do not hesitate to urge the friend of the slave to incite insurrection'[47] – he was willing to initiate the enterprise himself and to resort to guerrilla warfare. The idea of northern 'liberators' going to rescue oppressed southern labourers had never before been as clear as in Redpath's prediction that 'a general stampede of the slaves' could make Virginia and North Carolina free states 'if the Abolitionists would send down a trustworthy band of "Liberators" provided with compasses, pistols, and a little money for the fugitives'.[48]

When advocating slave insurrection, radical abolitionists such as James Redpath looked to Haiti, where the only successful slave revolt had occurred, as a source of inspiration. Haiti stood as a permanent warning to slaveholders and as permanent symbol of hope for slaves.[49] However, when referring to practical means of sparking slave insurrection through guerrilla warfare, radical abolitionists (such as John Brown) seemed to have had in mind the example of Napoleonic Spain. There are speculations that John Brown might have known and applied the insurrectional theories of the Italian Bianco di Saint-Jorioz, who had fought in the Spanish War.[50]

John Brown was certainly the symbol of slave insurrection in America. In the words of Herbert Aptheker, he was 'the apotheosis of revolutionary commitment' of the last generation of abolitionists. Together with a fanatical religious belief, John Brown held the view that 'physical resistance by or on behalf of the slaves was not only just, but necessary'.[51] In Brown's view, the liberation of slaves and the solution to the American national problem were to be achieved by sparking insurrection through acts of guerrilla warfare directed at the heart of southern slave-ocracy. These actions would have achieved the double aim of prompting a general revolt of the slaves in the south and shaking public opinion in the north. It was this conviction that pushed John Brown to organize the 1859 raid at Harpers' Ferry and to die for the cause for which he had fought so determinedly.[52]

However, John Brown marked a departure from earlier abolitionist attitudes in an important way, since 'his hatred of slavery reflected a rejection of both racism and elitism. He repeatedly insisted that he was a partisan of the slave and of the poor.'[53] In the words of William Phillips, a reporter for the *New York Tribune*, 'he thought society ought to be reorganized on a less selfish basis . . . and thought there was an infinite number of wrongs to right before society would be what it should be, but that in our country, slavery was the "sum of all villainies"'.[54] In his emphasis on social justice and elimination of poverty, as linked to a much wider idea of moral reform, John Brown placed the American national problem in a new perspective. In his view, the way to

American national progress passed not only through the abolition of slavery, but also through the abolition of social inequality and class conflict.

Still, like James Redpath, John Brown firmly believed in the liberation of slaves as a process whereby a few committed northerners could have rescued the masses of oppressed southern blacks. His conviction that guerrilla acts such as Harpers' Ferry were needed in order to spark slave insurrection only reinforced the abolitionist construction of slaves as helpless victims who belonged to a submissive race. Indeed, all radical abolitionists carried as far as possible the idea of northern 'liberation' of southern slaves by asserting the necessity of resorting to immediate violent action given the fact that the slaves themselves were meant to be waiting for it.

Plans for revolutionary insurrection were constantly made by Democrats in Italy. Guerrilla warfare was especially suited for countries such as Italy which were occupied by reactionary regimes. The methods of guerrilla warfare and their possible application to the Italian case were popularized by the writings of Bianco di Saint-Jorioz. Like some Radical abolitionists, Italian Democrats looked at Napoleonic Spain as a successful example of insurrection through guerrilla warfare. They believed that between 1808 and 1814 most of the Spanish population had participated in the struggle to achieve national independence from the Napoleonic army. The war had been organized through small bands of partisans (*guerrillas*) trained in the countryside and used for sudden attacks against the enemy.[55]

The key factor, stressed by Bianco in his writings, was the participation of the people, particularly of peasants in the countryside. Bianco saw peasants as an ideal reservoir of guerrilla forces, because the fact that they were accustomed to intolerable living conditions made them able to stand the cruelty of guerrilla warfare much better than the urban masses. However, in Bianco's view, peasants' participation in a war of liberation from national oppression could have been guaranteed only by the promise of equal distribution of lands. Therefore, to him, the war of liberation assumed the character of a class war in which peasants could have fought a revolution to bring about national unity with the prospect of receiving a portion of the land of their former landlords.[56]

The idea of guerrilla warfare involving peasant participation appealed particularly to those Democrats who believed in the possibility of a revolutionary movement starting from the southern countryside. Whereas Mazzinian Democrats held a highly utopian view of the necessity of educating the southern masses to revolution – and became increasingly sceptical about the possibility – other Democrats, such as Nicola Fabrizi, thought in practical terms about the organization of guerrilla groups among southern peasants. Starting from 1839, Fabrizi organized a clandestine revolutionary structure, called *Legione Italica*, which was intended to be in charge of organizing a general insurrection of southern peasants through the constitution of guerrilla units.[57]

The *Legione Italica*, which was based in Malta, succeeded only in causing minor problems for the Bourbon regime rather than overthrowing it, but its example proved far-reaching in its consequences. Fabrizi contributed more than any other Democrat before 1848 to showing that the way to the resolution of the Italian national problem had to pass through the organization of the peasants in the South and the overthrow of the Bourbon monarchy. In his view, the idea of a 'liberation' of the southern masses coming from outside the South was subordinated to the practical organization of warfare, which he thought was the key element of a future general insurrection.[58]

The year 1848 marked a watershed in the Italian Democratic movement. The revolutions that occurred in 1848 throughout the peninsula, including Naples and Sicily, failed because of the irreconcilable differences between Democratic and Liberal ideas over the solution of the Italian national problems. While Democrats strove to achieve radical objectives through the constitution of a revolutionary republic, Liberals wanted only limited reforms carried out by a constitutional monarchy. Above all, Democrats failed to address the land question in the countryside and this failure drove the support of peasants away from them. Both in Naples and in Sicily, it was clear that the 1848 revolutionary governments had collapsed when their leaders had retreated from radical programmes involving the distribution of land among southern peasants. As Bianco di Saint-Jorioz had noticed, the solution of the Italian national problem through revolutionary insurrection was tied to the land problem in the countryside; this was particularly true of the southern kingdom, where peasants' exploitation and hunger for land was more acute than anywhere else in Italy.[59]

Keeping in mind the reasons for the 1848 failure, Carlo Pisacane elaborated a theory of insurrection which combined the participation of the people in the revolutionary war and a truly socialist approach to the land problem. Pisacane believed that the revolution would have been brought to life by spontaneous organization of the people, rather than by regulated guerrilla groups; an 'armed nation' would have risen against the tyrant governments and would have outnumbered the oppressors.[60] However, if the people were to spontaneously rise in a revolution, then the objective of the revolution should have involved a radical redistribution of property. In his writings, Pisacane made clear that, unlike Mazzinian utopians, he thought that the birth of a new Italian nation had to go hand in hand with the resolution of class conflict; speaking in socialist terms, he located the potential for a social revolution among the lower classes who were exploited by capitalists and landed proprietors in the cities and in the countryside.[61]

Pisacane repeatedly said that the solution of the Italian national problem was tied to a much more general problem of social justice. In this sense, he was an extremist like John Brown. An exiled southerner himself, he became progressively convinced that the revolution had to start from the Bourbon Kingdom, because the extreme polarization of southern society had brought the masses – especially in the countryside – to a level of poverty that was no longer bearable to them.[62] Consequently, southern peasants only needed a 'spark' to start the fight against their oppressors and then they would have spontaneously continued the battle; the victory of the oppressed over the oppressors would have carried with it the abolition of private property and the establishment of a classless society.[63] It was with this conviction that in 1857 Pisacane embarked on an expedition to Sapri, in the continental south, in the hope of being able to provide the 'spark' that southern peasants needed to start their social revolution; however, he was killed together with his 300 followers and, like John Brown, he became a symbol of martyrdom for the cause of freedom.[64]

Pisacane's attempt reinforced the idea of southern Italian peasants as helpless victims of oppression waiting for 'liberation' to arrive from outside the South. In his view, all oppressed classes had an innate goodness and sense of justice. However, they were unable to start the fight against exploitation by themselves; therefore, they needed an external source of help in order to start a social revolution. In Pisacane's own words: 'I am convinced that a moral revolution is already occurring in southern Italy; an energetic impulse can push the people to start a determinant [revolutionary] movement; therefore, my efforts are directed towards carrying out a conspiracy which will give that impulse.'[65] Pisacane believed that an organized expedition of armed men, just like James Redpath had longed for to start a slave insurrection, would have provided the southern masses with the help they needed. In this sense, his ideas about the possibility of insurrection in the Bourbon Kingdom were similar to the ideas James Redpath and John Brown had about the possibility of insurrection in the slave south.

Between 1830 and 1860, American abolitionists and Italian Democrats sought to resolve two distinct, but related, national problems. In the USA, the focus of the national problem was on the elimination of slavery as incompatible with the ideals of the American republic. In Italy, the national problem was the constitution of a republican nation through the overthrow of reactionary regimes, such as the Bourbon monarchy in the South. In both cases, the emphasis was on the removal of obstacles on the path that led to national progress.

Both through propaganda and direct action, abolitionists and Democrats waged a constant war against the oppressive regimes located in the two souths. In the process, they constructed an image of themselves as 'liberators', while at the same time constructing an image of the southern masses as helpless victims longing for help coming from outside, particularly the North. This construction of northern 'liberators' as opposed to southern labourers had two related effects in the long term: it created a history of dependency of the two souths upon the norths for social change and it contributed to northern discrimination against ex-slaves in the American South and against peasants in the Italian South. Although the actual shape that the discrimination took was different, because of the non-existence of a racial factor in Italy, it contributed in both cases to the creation of a perception of permanent difference between the northern and southern parts of the two countries.

Notes

1   'Prospects of Italy–Italian Liberalism', *Russell's Magazine* 3 (1858), pp. 459–60.
2   *Russell's Magazine* 1 (1857), p. 178.
3   For more information on *Russell's Magazine*, see R. J. Calhoun, 'Southern Literary Magazines, III: The Antebellum Literary Twilight, *Russell's Magazine*', *Southern Literary Journal* 3 (1970).
4   See G. Spini, 'Le relazioni politiche fra l'Italia e gli Stati Uniti durante il Risorgimento e la Guerra Civile', in *Incontri europei e americani col Risorgimento* (Florence, 1986); H. Marraro, *American Opinion on the Unification of Italy* (New York, 1932); J. Rossi, *The Image of America in Mazzini's Writings* (Madison, WI, 1954).
5   Giuseppe Mazzini, quoted in Rossi, *Image of America*, p. 124.
6   See H. Mayer, *All on Fire: William Lloyd Garrison and the Abolition of Slavery* (New York, 1998), pp. 378–9.
7   See M. Sanfilippo, 'Il Risorgimento visto dal Canada e dagli Stati Uniti', *Il Risorgimento* 47:1/2 (1995), pp. 490–3.
8   This phrase is taken from an article written by Giuseppe Mazzini on the *New York Times*, 15 August 1854, and quoted in 'Prospects for Italy', p. 460.
9   See D. B. Davis, *Slavery and Human Progress* (New York, 1985), pp. xvi–xvii.

10 See C. Azevedo, *Abolitionism in the United States and Brazil: A Comparative Perspective* (New York and London, 1995), pp. xviii–xx.

11 See S. J. Woolf, 'Introduction' in S. J. Woolf (ed.), *Nationalism in Europe 1815 to the Present: A Reader* (London, 1996).

12 On Romanticism and Abolitionism see D. A. McBride, 'Romanticism and Abolitionism', in J. P. Rodriguez (ed.), *The Historical Encyclopedia of World Slavery* (Santa Barbara, CA, 1997); on Romanticism and Nationalism with special reference to the Italian case, see A. De Paz, *Europa romantica. Fondamenti e paradigmi della sensibilità moderna* (Naples, 1994), pp. 170–87. See also D. A. J. Richards, *Italian American: The Racializing of an Ethnic Identity* (New York, 1999), p. 116: according to the author, Americans actively supported the Risorgimento, because 'during the nineteenth century [they] took an understandable interest in the developing forms of liberal nationalism in Europe from the perspective of the legitimate aims of revolutionary constitutionalism that had justified their own revolution and the resulting constitutional developments'. However, as David Brion Davis points out, the American radicals' effort in supporting the struggle of oppressed nations in homage to the principles of Republicanism was seriously damaged by the presence of slavery within the borders of the American republic; see D. B. Davis, *Revolutions: Reflections on American Equality and Foreign Liberations* (Cambridge, MA, 1990), pp. 74–5.

13 *Manchester Daily News*, 30 May 1854. In 1860, Mazzini expressed similar ideas when speaking with Theodore Weld, a leading American abolitionist: 'We are fighting the same sacred battle for freedom and the emancipation of the oppressed, you, Sir, against *negro*, we against *white* slavery': quoted in A. De Conde, *Half Bitter, Half Sweet: An Excursion into Italian American History* (New York, 1971), p. 60. See also G. Spini, 'I democratici e la guerra civile americana', *Rassegna Storica Italiana* 11:1 (1965).

14 E. Foner, 'The causes of the American Civil War: Recent interpretations and new directions', *Civil War History* 20 (1974), p. 206.

15 See D. J. McInerney, *The Fortunate Heirs of Freedom: Abolition and Republican Thought* (Lincoln, NA, 1994), pp. 16–17.

16 The influence of northern elites on Italian history since the Risorgimento is reviewed in the introduction to a special issue of the journal *Meridiana* 16 (1993), called 'Questione settentrionale'.

17 The literature on plantation slaves and *latifondo* workers is enormous; for specific issues of comparison related to the elites' ideology of power and treatment of labourers, see E. Dal Lago, 'Southern Elites: A Comparative Study of the Landed Aristocracies of the American South and the Italian South, 1815–1860', PhD Thesis, University of London, 2000, pp. 69–97 and 116–80. See also M. Petrusewicz, 'Wage-Earners, but not Proletarians: Wage Labour and Social Relation in the Nineteenth Century Calabrian *Latifondo*', *Review* 10:3 (1987), where the author makes a compelling argument for comparison between different examples of exploitation of non-proletarian labour forces – including southern Italian peasants and American slaves – at the periphery of the world economy; and E. Fox-Genovese and E. D. Genovese, *The Fruits of Merchant Capital: Slavery and Bourgeois Property in the Rise and Expansion of Capitalism* (New York, 1983), p. 394, where the authors relate the 'only technically free labour' of the peasantry in Italy, Poland and Hungary to American slavery.

18   See W. E. Cain, 'Introduction: William Lloyd Garrison and the Fight against Slavery', in W. E. Cain (ed.), *William Lloyd Garrison and the Fight against Slavery: Selections from The Liberator* (New York, 1995), pp. 11–13. See also Mayer, *All on Fire*, pp. 88–126.

19   On links between abolitionism, Evangelicalism, and Romanticism, see R. G. Walters, *American Reformers, 1815–1860* (New York, 1997), pp. 81–5; see also J. L. Thomas. 'Romantic Reform in America, 1815–1865', *American Quarterly* 17:4 (1965), pp. 656–81; and A. C. Loveland, 'Evangelicalism and 'Immediate Emancipation' in American Antislavery Thought', *Journal of Southern History* 32 (1966), pp. 172–88.

20   On Garrison's religious views of abolition, see J. B. Stewart, *William Lloyd Garrison and the Challenge of Emancipation* (New York, 1992), pp. 56–78. See also W. L. Van Deburg, 'William Lloyd Garrison and the "Pro-Slavery Priesthood": The Changing Beliefs of an Evangelical Reformer, 1830–1840', *Journal of the American Academy of Religion* 43 (1975).

21   See J. B. Stewart, *Holy Warriors: The abolitionists and American Slavery* (New York, 1996), pp. 54–6.

22   D. H. Doyle, 'Slavery, Secession, and Reconstruction as American Problems', in L. J. Griffin and D. H. Doyle (eds), *The South as an American Problem* (Athens, GA, and London, 1993), p. 106.

23   See W. L. Garrison, 'Guilt of New England', *The Liberator*, 8 December 1832: 'So long as we continue as one body – a union – a nation – the compact involves us in the guilt and danger of slavery.'

24   R. G. Walters, *The Antislavery Appeal: American abolitionism after 1830* (New York, 1978), p. 141.

25   Non-violent resistance and anarchist principles prompted Garrisonian abolitionists to encourage slaves to be patient and wait; see L. Perry, *Radical abolitionism: Anarchy and the Government of God in Antislavery Thought* (Ithaca, NY, 1973). On Garrisonian Abolitionists' non-violent fight for equality, see A. S. Kraditor, *Means and Ends in American Abolitionism: Garrison and His Critics on Strategy and Tactics, 1834–1850* (New York, 1969).

26   Correcting this basic historical distortion, which was the fruit of a consistent part of abolitionist propaganda, Herbert Aptheker has written in *Abolitionism: A Revolutionary Movement* (Boston, MA, 1989), p. 59: 'if the slaves had embraced their 'natural' status, there would have been no abolitionist movement. Slavery induced slave unrest, and slave unrest induced abolitionism.' On Garrisonian Abolitionism's struggle against racial prejudice, see P. Goodman, *Of One Blood: Abolitionism and the Origins of Racial Equality* (Berkeley, CA, 1998), pp. 233–60.

27   A. Phelps, *Lectures on Slavery and its Remedy* (Boston, MA, 1834).

28   See G. Fredrickson, *The Black Image in the White Mind: The Debate on Afro-American Character and Destiny, 1817–1914* (New York, 1971), p. 106.

29   D. Mack Smith, *Mazzini* (New Haven, CT, 1994), p. 16; see also E. Morelli, *Giuseppe Mazzini, quasi una biografia* (Rome, 1984).

30   Garrison, who knew Mazzini, spoke of his 'love of liberty unlimited by considerations of race or clime': quoted in E. Hinkley, *Mazzini: The Story of a Great Italian* (London, 1924), p. 80.

31   See R. Sarti, 'Giuseppe Mazzini and his Opponents', in J. A. Davis (ed.), *Italy in the Nineteenth Century* (Oxford, 2000), p. 81.

32 S. J. Woolf, 'La storia politica e sociale', in R. Romano and C. Vivanti (eds), *Storia d'Italia*, Vol. III: *Dal primo settecento all'Unità* (Turin, 1973), pp. 311–12.

33 On Mazzini's utopianism, see L. Perini, 'Gli utopisti: delusioni della realta', sogni dell'avvenire', in Romano and Vivanti, *Storia d'Italia*, Annali 4: *Intellettuali e potere* (Turin, 1981), pp. 409–12.

34 C. Lovett, *The Democratic Movement in Italy, 1830–1876* (Cambridge, 1982), pp. 48–52.

35 Quotation in F. Della Peruta, 'Risorgimento e identità nazionale italiana', in F. Della Peruta, *Politica e società nell'Italia dell'Ottocento. Problemi, vicende e personaggi* (Milan, 1999), p. 18.

36 Although Mazzini was much more interested in the urban artisans than in the peasants, his ideas on social justice in this famous excerpt applied to all classes: 'There must not be on this earth either *masters* or *slaves* but only *brothers* in the same faith, associated, each according to his calling, in a task to which all must contribute': in 'Agli italiani, e specialmente agli operai italiani', quoted in Lovett, *Democratic Movement* p. 56.

37 Several important pages on the relation between northern democrats and the Bourbon South can be found in F. Della Peruta, *Mazzini e i rivoluzionari italiani. Il partito d'azione, 1830–1845* (Milan, 1974); see also the important study by G. Berti, *I democratici e l'iniziativa meridionale nel Risorgimento* (Milan, 1962).

38 See G. Galasso, *La democrazia da Cattaneo a Rosselli* (Florence, 1982), pp. 20–3.

39 See Della Peruta, 'Risorgimento e identità nazionale', pp. 12–13.

40 See Della Peruta, *Mazzini e i rivoluzionari italiani*, pp. 30–40.

41 See P. Ginsborg, 'Risorgimento Rivoluzionario', *Storia e Dossier* 6:47 (1991), pp. 78–80; see also G. Candeloro, *Storia dell'Italia moderna*, Vol. II: *Dalla Restaurazione alla Rivoluzione nazionale* (Milan, 1958), pp. 380–3.

42 Ginsborg, 'Risorgimento Rivoluzionario', p. 80.

43 J. H. Pease and W. H. Pease, 'Confrontation and Abolition in the 1850s', *Journal of American History* 58:4 (1972).

44 Stewart, *Holy Warriors*, p. 155; see also M. L. Dillon, *The Abolitionists: The Growing of a Dissenting Minority* (New York, 1974), pp. 219–43.

45 On James Redpath, see J. R. McKivigan, 'James Redpath, John Brown, and Abolitionist Advocacy of Slave Insurrection', *Civil War History* 37:4 (1991).

46 J. Redpath, *The Roving Editor; or, Talks with Slaves in the Southern States* (New York, 1859), pp. 129–30.

47 Redpath, *Roving Editor*, pp. iii–iv.

48 *National Anti-Slavery Standard* (11 November 1854).

49 See A. N. Hunt, *Haiti's Influence on Antebellum America: Slumbering Volcano in the Caribbean* (Baton Rouge, LA, 1988).

50 See G. Schenone, 'John Brown e il pensiero insurrezionale italiano', in *Atti del I congresso internazionale di storia americana: Italia e Stati Uniti dall'Indipendenza americana ad oggi (1776–1976)* (Genoa, 1978), pp. 356–60. According to Raimondo Luraghi, John Brown's ideas on guerrilla warfare and slave insurrection show an acquaintance with the theories and writings of contemporary European radicals and, in particular, Italian revolutionaries, such as Mazzini and Bianco di Saint-Jorioz; see R. Luraghi, *Storia della Guerra Civile Americana* (Milan, 1966), pp. 132–3.

51 Aptheker, *Abolitionism*, pp. 123–4.

52   On John Brown, see B. Wyatt-Brown, 'John Brown's Antinomian War', in
     B. Wyatt-Brown, *Yankee Saints and Southern Sinners* (Baton Rouge, LA, 1985).
     See also responses to Harpers' Ferry in Europe in P. Finkelman, 'Servile
     Insurrection and John Brown's Body in Europe', P. Finkelman (ed.), *His Soul
     Goes Marching On: Responses to John Brown and the Harpers' Ferry Raid* (Char-
     lottesville, VA, 1995).
53   Aptheker, *Abolitionism*, p. 131.
54   W. A. Phillips, quoted in Aptheker, *Abolitionism*, p. 131.
55   See Ginsborg, 'Risorgimento Rivoluzionario', pp. 67–9.
56   See C. Bianco di Saint-Jorioz, *Della guerra nazionale d'insurrezione per bande
     applicata all'Italia* (Turin, 1830).
57   See V. Douglas Scotti, 'La guerriglia negli scrittori risorgimentali italiani
     prima e dopo il 1848–1849', *Il Risorgimento* 27:3 (1975), pp. 106–10; see also
     Candeloro, *Storia dell'Italia moderna*, Vol. II, 367–70.
58   See F. Della Peruta, 'La guerra di liberazione spagnola e la teoria della guerra
     per bande nel Risorgimento', *Il Risorgimento* 40:3 (1988), pp. 156–7.
59   On the 1848 watershed among Italian revolutionaries, see Scotti, 'La guerri-
     glia negli scrittori risorgimentali', pp. 96–8. On the reasons for failure of the
     1848 revolutions in the Bourbon Kingdom, see A. De Francesco, 'Ideologie e
     movimenti politici', in G. Sabbatucci and V. Vidotto (eds), *Storia d'Italia I. Le
     premesse dell'unità* (Rome and Bari, 1995), pp. 270–94; see also L. Riall,
     'Garibaldi and the South', in J. A. Davis (ed.), *Italy in the Nineteenth Century*
     (Oxford, 2000), pp. 133–7.
60   On Pisacane and other Italian revolutionaries in the 1850s, see the seminal
     work by F. Della Peruta, *I Democratici e la rivoluzione italiana. Dibattiti, ideali e
     contrasti all'indomani del 1848* (Milan, 1958); and N. Rosselli, *Carlo Pisacane
     nel Risorgimento italiano* (Turin, 1977).
61   See Ginsborg, 'Risorgimento Rivoluzionario', pp. 75–6; see also Candeloro,
     Storia dell'Italia moderna, Vol. IV: *Dalla Rivoluzione nazionale all'Unità* (Milan,
     1964), p. 252.
62   See Perini, 'Gli utopisti', pp. 412–13. See also Candeloro, *Storia dell'Italia
     moderna*, Vol. IV, pp. 258–60; and S. J. Woolf, *A History of Italy, 1700–1860.
     The Social Constraints of Political Change* (London, 1979), pp. 430–2.
63   Lovett, *Democratic Movement*, pp. 64–5.
64   See Ginsborg, 'Risorgimento Rivoluzionario', pp. 80–4.
65   C. Pisacane, *La Rivoluzione*, quoted in Ginsborg, 'Risorgimento Rivoluzio-
     nario', p. 84. In his *Storia della Guerra Civile Americana*, p. 141, Luraghi has
     compared John Brown's raid at Harper's Ferry with Giuseppe Garibaldi's
     expedition and with Carlo Pisacane's and the Bandiera brothers' attempts
     at provoking a revolution in the Mezzogiorno: 'in truth, the enterprise
     started by the 'One Thousand' did not differ substantially from the ones
     carried out by John Brown, the Bandiera Brothers, and Pisacane: the men
     and the arms that Garibaldi had at his disposal were as unequal to the task of
     overthrowing the well-defended Bourbon Kingdom as the ones his unlucky
     predecessors had.' However, Garibaldi left for Sicily when there was a real
     chance of revolutionary insurrections, while John Brown, like Pisacane and
     the Bandiera brothers, operated according to his own distorted idea of the
     oppressed classes waiting for him to start a social revolution in the South; see
     again Luraghi, *Storia della Guerra Civile Americana*, p. 143–4.

11

Two Great Migrations: American and Italian Southerners in Comparative Perspective

Donna Gabaccia

While certainly innovative, the comparison of the 'Two Souths' that the organizers of the 1999 Commonwealth Fund Conference have proposed is not in itself controversial. The comparison respects the conventions of the national historiographies of both Italy and the USA. Historians in both countries make regionalism a key theme, and see it as a source of pluralism and political tension in the process of nation-building.

Comparison of Italy's and America's southerners as migrants, however, immediately opens controversy about the validity of comparison. The largest group of migrants from Italy's south between 1870 and 1930 – roughly 3.5 million of them – went to the USA. Their migrations peaked in the years between 1900 and 1914, when large numbers settled in the industrializing cities of the north and north-east. Although their migrations to the USA remained impressive, even after restrictive legislation passed in the 1920s, this great migration to the urban north-east was over by 1930.[1] During the first 30 years of the twentieth century, the cities of the American north and north-east also became magnets to migrants from the American South. Among them were 1.5 million African-Americans who looked for work and a release from 'Jim Crow', especially after 1915, when the First World War temporarily cut off the flow of immigrant workers.[2] Two groups of southerners thus converged in some of the same northern cities – Chicago, Pittsburgh, Philadelphia, Cleveland and New York – before immigration restriction and depression intervened. But their migrations were not completely simultaneous: as migration from Italy's South waned, during and after the First World War, migration from the American South burgeoned. More important, the migration of Black southerners

northward resumed, and grew larger during and after the Second
World War.

Does it make sense to compare these two migrations or two groups of
migrants? Most historians today would not automatically think so. Italy's
southern migrants find incorporation into the American national narrative as 'immigrants' that quickly became part of the multiethnic American mainstream. Recent studies suggest they joined the nation after a
period of uncertainty about their racial status, as they became unambigu-
ously 'white'.[3] America's southern migrants instead find their place in the
national narrative as an oppressed, 'black', racial group denied access to
the American dream.[4] The immigrant paradigm of American history
celebrates the assimilative power of American pluralism, and the democratic promise of a nation of immigrants. The racial paradigm instead
reminds Americans of the limits that racism imposed on American
democracy and pluralism.[5] The histories of immigrants and of blacks
thus suggest two national narratives, at odds with each other.

For 30 years, most American historians have tended to agree with Nell
Irvin Painter, writing of the earlier period of US history, that to use the
word immigrant for enslaved Africans 'strips language of symbolic
meaning'.[6] Most have also dismissed out of hand Glazer and Moynihan's 1963 portrait of black migrants in New York as 'the last of the
immigrants' for ignoring the difference that informal and formal discrimination imposed on them.[7] As Allan Spear, writing a few years after
Glazer and Moynihan, noted, the Chicago experience 'tends to refute
any attempt to compare northern Negroes with European immigrants'
because 'the Negro ghetto was unique among the city's ethnic
enclaves'.[8] Only a handful of recent studies directly compare Italian
and African-American migrants.[9] In American historiography, white
immigrants and blacks have become the apples and oranges common
sense chides us not to compare.

The 1999 University College London conference on the 'Two Souths'
offered me, as a historian of migration, an opportunity to rethink this
truism and also to contemplate comparative methods in fresh ways.
'Convergent comparison' of two migrant groups arriving in one city is
a common comparative method in the histories of race and ethnicity.
Scholars generally use it to identify differences in culture or to locate the
origins of groups' differing rates of progress (whether economic, educational or structural) into the American mainstream.[10] But the vast
differences of southern blacks and southern Italians are already obvious; racial prejudice convincingly explains their differing histories of
inclusion and exclusion. While it is easy to justify an exploration of the

interactions between these two groups in northern cities – indeed such explorations may hold keys to understanding the racial dynamics of the twentieth century – comparing them still requires careful justification.

It makes sense to compare black southerners and southern Italians if our intention is to understand regionalism and its complex meanings better. In this study, I change the usual unit of analysis in comparative studies of race and ethnicity to compare the two groups not as blacks and as whites, or as natives or foreigners, but rather as migratory southerners. Comparing southerners of differing origin we have an opportunity to explore how regionalism has shaped historians' interpretation of their migrations. The comparison also allows us to tease out how regional identities – which by definition are spatially generated – travel spatially within and across national boundaries along with migrants. Finally, comparison reveals how regionalism shaped racial and ethnic dynamics and created national groups in the two countries. Comparison thus allows me to sidestep the iron cages of both racial and immigrant paradigms of American history while simultaneously viewing Italy's southern problem from a diasporic perspective.

*   *   *   *   *

Americanists call the migration of black southerners to northern cities between 1910 and 1930 the great migration. For Italianists, the comparable term is the mass emigration (*emigrazione di massa*) of southerners between 1870 and 1914. No standard history of either country dares completely ignore these migrations. By examining how two nations have understood the greatness of their southern migrations, however, we quickly see how differently Italy and the USA have understood the place of the South in their two histories.

The greatness of black migration to the American North before 1930 does not originate in its volume. Approximately 8 million blacks lived in the USA in 1900. Roughly 1.5 million left the South for northern cities between 1900 and 1930; migrations after 1940 were more than twice as large. Nicholas Lemann sees the latter migration as 'one of the largest and most rapid mass internal movements of people in history'.[11] But in the first 30 years of the century, when the great migration first earned its label, immigrants from Italy (3.8 million) and Jews from eastern Europe (1.8 million) were far more numerous than black southern migrants to American cities. German and Polish immigrations just about equalled them in numbers.[12] Put into comparative perspective even the latter, and larger, 'great migration of the post-war era' runs the risk of looking less great. The migration of Italian southerners to Italy's and Europe's north after 1945 surpassed the American great migration of black southerners both in absolute and relative numbers.[13] Furthermore, it now appears that more white than black migrants left the American South between 1910 and 1960, although migration rates among blacks southerners probably exceeded those of white southerners.[14] Obviously, something other than numbers makes the early twentieth-century movement of black southerners a 'great' migration.

The greatness of this migration originates in the sharp and symbolic break it represents in both the history of black Americans and of the USA generally. In most recent interpretations, black Americans became masters of their own destinies by migrating. By doing so, they proclaimed their independence from the legacy of plantation slavery and the reality of sharecropping and the South's oppressive racial etiquette. While acknowledging the disappointments migrants encountered in northern cities such as Chicago, historian Jim Grossman nevertheless describes the great migration of the early twentieth century as a 'second emancipation'.[15]

Like the first emancipation of blacks from slavery in 1865, the great migration changed not only black lives, but also the American nation as a whole, and the place of the American South within it. In 1900, more than 90 per cent of all black Americans still lived in the South; over 80 per cent were rural dwellers. Northern cities, by contrast, housed populations that were largely of foreign extraction: fully 80 per cent of Chicago residents had at least one foreign-born parent, and New York and Pittsburgh were not significantly different. By 1970, however, 50 per cent of all black Americans instead lived in the North, and 75 per cent were urbanites. (In the intervening decades, by contrast, foreigners were as likely to migrate to the suburbs – where the descendants of earlier European immigrants also now lived – as to the cities of the north-east.) The great migration signalled the beginning of a century-long transformation that made urban into a euphemism for black, transforming a centuries-long association of African-Americans with rural and southern life and ending a shorter, but firm, association of urban life with foreigners and immigrants. The great migration made racism into a national and American, rather than a distinctively southern, problem. The great migration thus provides the historical foundation for an ongoing, great twentieth-century debate about the causes, consequences and cures of the contemporary, and overwhelmingly black and urban, 'underclass'.[16]

In contrast to the numerically rather unimpressive great northward migration from the American South, Italy's *emigrazione di massa* constitutes one of the largest and most dispersed international migrations of the nineteenth and twentieth centuries. Italy's roughly 27 million migrants (1870–1970) just about equalled the population of Italy in 1861, and people from Italy may have formed as high a proportion as 10 per cent of global migrants from 1830 to 1930.[17] But while Italian southerners are usually the only migrants that appear in general histories of modern Italy (apart, in some cases, from pioneer Ligurians and Genovese mariners in the early nineteenth century), they were not the largest group of mobile Italians.[18] The greatness of the Italian mass emigration of 1870–1914, too, rests on something other than the numbers of southern migrants.

Emigration was not a distinctively southern response to the economic crises, poverty or disadvantaged place of the Mezzogiorno in the newly unified Italy. Before 1890, and after 1920, rates of emigration were higher from northern than southern Italy. In the intervening years, provinces such Piedmont and Veneto had higher rates of emigration than southern provinces such as Sardinia or Apulia. Between 1876 and 1914 – when 14 million migrants left Italy – southerners made up only one-third of this total. Only after 1945 did southerners become a slight majority (52 per cent) among Italy's emigrants. And these southern emigrants, numbering somewhat under 4 million, were outnumbered by the 7–8 million southerners who moved internally in the post-war era to northern and central Italy.[19]

The only truly distinctive characteristic of mass emigration from Italy's South was its orientation towards the USA, especially in the years between 1876 and 1914 (see Table 11.1). During these years, one-third of Italy's migrants went to the USA, while one-quarter went to Latin America (mainly Brazil and Argentina) and over 40 per cent to other European nations. Many northerners went to Latin American destinations, and they formed a sizeable majority migrating to Europe. By contrast, three-quarters of Italian immigrants in the USA before the First World War were southerners.

If historians of the USA have inaccurately viewed migration from the American south in racial terms – as a black migration – historians of Italy have viewed mass emigration inaccurately in regional terms, as a southern and US-centred phenomenon. Studies of the American great migration identified racism as a central problem of the American nation, rather than as a regional phenomenon. The migration of blacks revealed how racial prejudice united the two sections of the nation. Italianists' understanding of mass emigration reflects instead a national preoccupation with the Italian South as a distinctive region, attached to, yet somehow apart from, the Italian nation. Lack of recognition in mass

Table 11.1   Percentage of all migrants going to the USA by regional origin, 1876–1914

	%
North	
Piedmont	10
Lombardy	6
Veneto	3
Liguria	23
Emilia	12
Centre	
Tuscany	17
Marche	20
Umbria	19
Lazio	71
Abruzzi-Molise	59
South	
Campania	64
Apulia	57
Basilicata	53
Calabria	48
Sicily	72
Sardinia	12

Source: *Annuario statistico*, table III.

emigration from Italy's North (oriented largely towards northern Europe) is telling in the national historical narrative of Italy for it suggests that northern Italy, unlike the South, was itself part of Europe in a way that the South was not. Histories of Italy tend to tie mass emigration from the Italian South to the far-off USA, thus separating southerners further from the Italian nation and from modern Europe. Historians of Italy do not see in mass emigration important clues to the evolution of the modern Italian nation in the same way that historians of the USA see the great migration and American racism as being critical moments in nation-building.

*   *   *   *   *

Despite the importance of race in defining the America's great southern migration, America's black migrants had a more pronounced – if also ambivalent – sense of their identities as southerners than did their migratory Italian counterparts. Few migrants left Italy's South thinking of themselves as southerners, while almost all historians of Italy now think of them that way. By contrast, almost all participants in the

American great migrations were aware of themselves as blacks and as southerners before they left their homes for the industrial cities of the north-eastern USA.

For most of its residents, the Mezzogiorno was as much a 'geographic expression' as was 'Italia' in 1861. Indeed, the northern rulers of Italy seemed unsure about where the South started: Was it south of Piedmont and Lombardy? Or in the former Papal States? Was it south of Rome in the former Bourbon Kingdom of the two Sicilies, with its capital in Naples? No matter how defined, the southern provinces of Italy shared no common language. They did not acknowledge the collective leadership of a single regional elite, and neither did traditional ties of marriage, common agricultural practices, or commercial exchange bind the southern provinces into a single region. Regional identities meant *siciliani* and *napolitani*, not *meridionali*.[20] The contrast to the American case, with its Mason–Dixon line, its shared history of plantation agriculture, of slavery, of secession, of military defeat, and of occupation and its self-consciously southern white elite could not be sharper.

In the years following Italian unification – and notably among Italy's governing classes – the definition of a Mezzogiorno, or south, somewhat apart from the Italian nation was a gradual one. John Davis and others have described the political chaos that erupted after unification in many territories of the former Papal States and Kingdom of the Two Sicilies. Davis calls the new Italian government's military campaign against brigandage and crime in the 1860s a civil war of northern government and occupied southern territories.[21] Other scholars have traced notions of a 'barbarian' South to these early post-unification years. Italy's new governors 'racialized' Italy's southerners as something other than Italians and Europeans, as they linked southerners' location, 'two steps from Africa', to their barbarism and dismissed their political violent opposition to incorporation into the new state as criminality.[22]

Still, as late as 1877 when Italy's 'historic left' government sought to study, and thus to solve, the problems creating widespread political disorder in the new nation, it saw the problems of Italy as agrarian and rural in origin, not as a distinctively southern problem. Thus the agrarian inquest headed by Stefano Jacini explored unrest, economic crisis and emigration in all of Italy's many rural regions in the 1870s and 1880s with equal attention to that given to South, centre, North, and islands.[23] The inquest sharply distinguished for the first time what it called the disciplined and orderly migrations of northerners (usually under sponsorship of *padroni* and labour contractors) from the disorganized (and threatening) migrations from southern districts. While noting the many directions migrants travelled, the investigators recognized mass emigration as a concomitant of rural poverty throughout Italy, not just in the South.[24] They did not yet see emigration as a southern problem, or distinguish between southern migrations directed towards the USA from others.

Twenty-five years later, during the first decade of the century, however, a second governmental inquest into rural economic problems focused exclusively on Italy's South, calling all its southern provinces '*il Mezzogiorno*', the South.[25] From the late 1880s, discussions of national laws to regulate emigration focused increasingly on migration as a southern phenomenon. Both secular and religious efforts to provide social services to migrants created differing programme for transoceanic migrations (predominantly from the South) and those within Europe and the Mediterranean (predominantly from the North).[26] Indeed, some insisted that the term emigrant should be limited to those travelling to the Americas.[27]

Italy's southerners thus existed mainly in the minds of those who thought of themselves as northerners, Italians and Europeans. Those who resided in the south of Italy identified themselves instead as the poor, as Christians or as residents of their hometowns or (occasionally) of their region (*siciliani, calabresi,* and so on.) The terms Italy, Italian, Mezzogiorno and southern do not even appear in the peasant and plebeian proverbs, songs and stories collected by Sicilian folklorist Giuseppe Pitrè in the years between 1880 and 1910.[28] When they described their oppression, residents of southern Italy clearly identified the urban, governing classes, and their local landowners, not 'Italians' or 'northerners', as their enemies. They portrayed emigration, furthermore, as an escape from the 'gentlemen' who, as landowners and office-holders, ruled their lives in their home villages. These gentlemen, furthermore, did not share the identification of peasants with their home village. Even this latter group hesitated to think of themselves as southerners; they identified with the Italian nation, and sought inclusion and leadership within it. They were Italian, not southern, nationalists.

In very sharp contrast, residents of America's South had created their own identities as southerners well before the great migration. Historians and anthropologists today generally describe the southern culture of the USA as a creole, or amalgam, of African, Native American and European traits. This was of course, not the view of white southerners in the late nineteenth and early twentieth centuries. Myths of a cause lost to Yankee or federal aggression, of whites' rescue of the South from black rule and of white southerners' burden of paternal responsibility for blacks instead sought to make black subordination a defining component of southern identity even after slavery's end.[29]

Many newly emancipated blacks nevertheless claimed positive identities as southerners. No one argued more vehemently than Booker T. Washington and his followers for the South as the best homeland, and best training ground, for black-initiated and voluntary 'boot-strap' efforts, from education to business.[30] Black writers often described a strong sense of attachment to a regional home place they called 'the great Southland'. Atlanta's black newspaper, *The Independent*, insisted that the Negro 'prefers to be here. He loves its traditions, its ideals and its people', and it concluded: 'the Southland belongs as much to the Negro as to the white man'.[31] In the useful distinction explored by Italian political philosopher Maurizio Viroli to describe Italian localism,[32] black southerners were southern patriots. They loved their birthplaces and felt attached to their home places in a region they themselves conceived as the South. To this day, transplanted male southerners refer to their close friends as their 'home boys' or 'homeys'. Black southerners were not southern nationalists, however. They did not feel themselves part of a bi-racial southern people or of a nation united by blood or fellow feeling. No myths of a confederate 'lost cause' stirred their emotions. But they were southerners, and thought of themselves as such.

Jobs in cities such as Chicago and Philadelphia strengthened black identities as southerners. Migrants were very aware that they travelled north to urban work, just as fugitive slaves had followed the 'north star' north to freedom. Long before they migrated, blacks viewed the north as a place fundamentally different from the south. Trainloads of migrants sometimes cheered when they crossed a state boundary or river that symbolized to them the Mason–Dixon line.[33] Blacks, and white observers, spoke of migrants having caught northern fever. If the great Southland was the beloved home place of southern blacks, then the north became their promised land.[34]

The equivalent disease caught by Italy's southerners was instead 'America fever.' America fever developed in much the same way that northern fever appeared in the American South. Returners brought news of high wages, and good work opportunities back home, inspiring envy, fantasy and desire.[35] Choosing '*l'America*' did not require a migrant to leave 'the South' but instead to depart from Italy and Europe. Indeed, '*l'America*', to most Italians did not necessarily mean the USA, but any transoceanic destination. Migrants travelling north across the Alps or to

North Africa did not claim to go to '*l'America*' but a woman who went to Melbourne before the First World War noted, 'I migrated to "*l'America*". It did not occur to me that Australia was not in fact "*l'America*" '.[36]

Southern migrants from both Italy and the USA have been portrayed as feverish in their pursuit of economic and personal freedom. Migration meant a release from the hierarchies and restraints of home, whether the migrants defined the promised land as the North or as '*l'America*'. 'If you can freeze to death in the north and be free, why freeze to death in the south and be a slave?', one migrant in Chicago argued.[37] Meanwhile, in Italy, a peasant taunted his landlord, 'Hey, mister, better dead in America than alive in Italy', and another explained to a visitor that 'in Italy we lived like beasts', but abroad a man felt civilized.[38] Both groups seemed equally attached to their home places, which Italians called their *paese* or patria, and to their 'homeys' or '*paesani*'. Somewhere between 40 and 80 forty and per cent (depending on region and decade) of Italy's migrants to the USA returned home. Black New Yorkers took advantage of cheap fares to travel back to the Carolinas for holidays and reunions but permanent return was probably rarer.[39] Still, comparable dreams of freedom, and attachments to home places, could not make travelling north and travelling to '*l'America*' equivalent definers of regional identities. However ambivalently, blacks arrived in American cities as southerners while those from Italy's South came with identities shaped by their home province and hometown, and a strong awareness that they had left only Italy and Europe – not 'the South' – behind.

*   *   *   *   *

Life in northern American cities had complex effects on the southern identities of both black Americans and southern Italians. Wherever they settled, migrants from the American South seemed southern primarily in the eyes of their northern black neighbours, while other northerners instead viewed them as black. In sharp contrast, migrants from southern Italy more often found themselves classified as southerners in their interactions with long-time Americans, rather than with each other.

Due to the huge literature on black and Italian migrants in the industrial cities of the USA, I base my discussion here on three cities: Pittsburgh, Chicago and New York. Chicago, in particular, and to a lesser extent, Pittsburgh and New York already had sizeable populations of native black residents in 1890.[40] By contrast, only New York had a sizeable population of Italians before 1880, and most of those early migrants were from Italy's North.

Some scholars have attributed the growth of northern black populations before the First World War to a northward migration of the black 'talented tenth' from the upper south. Racial prejudice condemned them to ghetto life in Chicago well before the great migration, while an emerging ghetto in New York's Harlem soon made unhappy neighbours of older upper-south migrants and more recently arrived southerners from the deep south. The disdain of respectable old-timers and native northern blacks for the newly arrived southerners was palpable: in New York, one black observer addressed the southern migrant aggressively: 'You talk too loud, look too black, don't get anywhere.'[41] Arrival in the North reinforced black migrants' sense of identity rooted in the great Southland.

While migrants from the black South experienced their difference as southerners on a daily basis, they did so mainly in relationship to other blacks and within the black ghettoes forming in all three cities. Tensions of culture and history divided mainstream Protestant from migrants' storefront churches (with their unrestrained and expressive southern modes of worship).[42] Some scholars believe they shaped differing understandings of morality and family life, too, with marital instability and female-headed households more characteristic of the southern migrants.[43] Regional differences even marked the evolution of black strategies for confronting racial prejudice in their new northern homes. Particularly in Chicago, southerners were more likely than long-time natives to support the 'shadies' (businessmen who succeeded in becoming 'race men', representing a black constituency as part of the political machines of the city).[44] In New York, new arrivals from the American South and from the Caribbean were more likely to support Garvey's black nationalism than the interracial cooperation that had been pioneered by the respectable and long-time natives, the 'New Negroes', in the pre-war years.[45]

On the job, and beyond their ghettoized, if divided, communities, migrants from the American South became blacks – not southerners – in white eyes. Neither respectability nor deep northern roots protected blacks who sought jobs or homes outside the ghetto from white scorn. Neither did it protect them from the racial violence of New York's 1905 riot or Chicago's riot of 1919.[46] Opposition to black mobility soon united older and newer white migrants to these cities. Accounts of both New York and Chicago riots suggest Irish immigrants – not the more recently arrived and racially 'in-between' immigrants from southern Europe – played central roles in the early years of the century. But evidence of interracial violence between blacks and Italians in New York is plainly visible by the 1930s, when an Italian-American mayor, depression and Italy's invasion of Ethiopia exacerbated competition for housing in Harlem (a district that was home to large numbers of both groups). Apparently, by the 1930s, Italian 'in-between' immigrants had developed a surer sense of their whiteness, along with the blackness of their black migrant neighbours.[47]

White prejudice in the North made 'black' a northern synonym for 'southern' before it became a national synonym for 'urban'. Northern whites viewed the distinctive cultural forms of black southerners – whether food, dance, music, an individualism that translated into hostility to labour unions, or marriage and family patterns – as black, not as southern, characteristics. Ironically, at the same time in the mid-west, long-time residents and new immigrants alike came to recognize poor white southerners (who shared the foods, religious enthusiasms and individualism of black migrants) as a distinctive cultural group they called hillbillies.[48] But among black migrants, only New York's West Indians attracted much attention from white observers for their distinctive culture, as they did also within Harlem and among northern and southern blacks alike.[49]

Unlike their black, respectable and native counterparts, the northern Italians who preceded and accompanied southern Italian migrants to the USA could and usually did move away from neighbourhoods flooded by southerners; they could, and did, form their own enclaves, separating northern from southern Italians in a single city.[50] In New York, for example, Piemontesi and Lombardi clustered in the West 20s in the years before and after the First World War, while southerners of many backgrounds settled in East Harlem and west of the Bowery in the Fourteenth Ward.[51] Regional differences separated Italian migrant northerners from southerners in American cities rather than creating a regional division within immigrant ghettoes comparable to their black counterparts.

Regional conflict among migrants from Italy did occur, however. Most of the missionary Italian priests who ministered to national parishes in Chicago and in New York were northerners who railed against the primitive or paganism folk Catholicism represented by southern Italian *feste* celebrating patron saints.[52] Radicals and labour leaders from the Italian north also sometimes disparaged the lack of discipline, the restlessness, and the violence of southern workers.[53] Still, this evidence suggests mainly that southerners continued to exist mainly in the minds of those from northern Italy, now transplanted to the USA.

Migrants from the Italian South almost never called themselves southerners in the USA. By contrast, immigrant institutions sometimes
defined themselves, and their members, as national and Italian. Still,
the largest group of immigrant institutions perpetuated the local and
regional distinctions prevalent in Italy. For example, despite strong
dialect differences, there were no northern or southern Italian-language
newspapers in New York, Chicago or Pittsburgh, although immigrant
New Yorkers for a time published a *Corriere Siciliano* (it was written,
however, in standard Italian). Neither were southern or northern self-
help and fraternal organizations common. The Sons of Italy welcomed
all those of Italian background, and southerners joined it, and other
national organizations too, alongside northerners. In fraternalism, older
forms of localism more often prevailed. Migrants in Chicago organized a
Unione Siciliana, while New York claimed 400 *paese* societies that facilitated mutual aid among immigrants from a particular village.[54] The
tension among immigrant institutions was between 'national' and
local groups, not between northerners and southerners.

Nevertheless, migration to the USA helped to re-create a divide
between northern and southern Italians found in Italian discourse by
the turn of the century. While accepting both groups as potential citizens (in sharp contrast to migrants from Asia), Americans quickly
adopted the racialized regional categories developed by Italy's governing
classes to distinguish northerners from southerners. Between 1899 and
1924, migrants entering the USA through Ellis Island found themselves
classified members of either the northern Italian race or the southern
Italian race. Social Darwinist theories about racial differences between
Alpine (northern Italian) and Mediterranean (southern Italian) peoples
became part of US government publications and public records.[55] Eng-
lish-speaking journalists and social scientists regularly characterized
Little Italies as settlements of southern Italians. Already in 1900, in
Chicago and in New York, journalists worried about the special propen-
sity to criminality they claimed to find in such settlements.[56]

Subsequently, during the 1920s, American government abandoned the
language of race for that of nationality in categorizing differences among
European immigrants. Restrictive laws passed in 1921 and 1924 to limit
the numbers of new arrivals from southern and eastern Europe no longer
distinguished northern from southern Italians. The restrictive quotas
imposed by these laws were 'national origins' quotas, applying uniformly
to 'Italians'. Still, discussions of immigration restriction in the post-war
years reveal that stereotypes of southern Italians as a racial group, constructed in nineteenth-century Italy and adopted initially by Americans,

now applied to all migrants from Italy. Nativist fears of Italian criminality, political and cultural backwardness and radicalism shaped how migrants from Italy became white and became American, discarding a southern identity most had never claimed in the first place.

*   *   *   *   *

For the past 30 years, scholars have been hesitant to compare black and foreign-born migrants. Faced with the conflicting paradigms of a successful nation of immigrants and a nation still divided by racism, historians have rejected comparative approaches. Comparison threatened to explore structural origins for blacks' and immigrants' differing experiences of American cities rather than focus on the overwhelming importance of racism in determining differing experiences for the two groups. With this chapter, I attempted to re-establish the usefulness of comparative approaches by changing the units of analysis from racial to regional ones. My goal was to ask how regional identities travelled with migrants to their new homes and shaped their interactions with their new neighbours.

Not surprisingly – although in surprising ways – the role of regionalism in black and Italian migrants' lives differed fundamentally at every phase in their migration. The Italian and American souths were not exact equivalents. America's south was created, at least in part, by southerners, which is why it remained (even as a 'mental map') both racially divided and contested. Italy's South was instead created by outsiders, who viewed southerners through the racial lens of social Darwinist thinking as a distinctive and troublesome group both attached to, yet apart from, the Italian nation. In Italy, racial prejudice created a unified group of southerners that residents themselves did not perceive or embrace. In the USA racial prejudice divided black from white southerners, and gave each group of southerners different understandings of their relationship to the North and to northerners. Black Americans' sense of connection to 'the Great Southland' preceded, and remained strong during, their migrations north. Migrants from the south of Italy, by contrast, lacked an internal sense of connection to a place called '*il Mezzogiorno*' prior to migration. They seem not to have developed a southern identity during migration to '*l'America*', or as a result of life in northern US cities.

Although historians of the USA have preferred racial terminology and historians of Italy regional terminology in interpreting the greatness of each great southern migration, in fact each migration revealed the connectedness of race and region in each national history. Both black migrants from the American South and migrants from Italy's South experienced racial transformations as they entered northern cities, as they sought interaction beyond the boundaries of their migrant communities, and as they claimed membership in the American nation. Northern whites, representing the American nation, rarely distinguished between blacks of northern and southern origin. All that mattered was the colour of their skin. Yet white northerners also conflated poor southern with poor black culture so completely that they deemed it necessary to invent new disparaging terms for whites who exhibited poor southern (or, as northerners saw it, 'black') cultural traits. Regionalism remained salient within black communities, and within a white American nation. The same American nation that required the subordination of blacks as a racial group made room for regional distinctions among whites, either as 'hillbillies' in the North or elite 'rebels' still mourning their lost national cause in their home region. As southern migrants became black Americans in the North, whites in the South became southerners within the nation.

Migrants from Italy's South experienced a parallel transformation in which the conflation of regional and national characteristics left them with identities as hyphenated Americans for two, and sometimes more, generations. Hoping to leave behind the stigma attached to poverty in rural Italy, emigrants to the USA learned that Americans viewed them negatively because of their southern origins, and that they had borrowed from Italy's rulers and scientists a racialized understanding of southern Italian criminality and violence. Worse, as Americans abandoned their concern with migrants' southern origins, they attached the negative qualities Italians had assigned to southerners to all Italians, regardless of background, broadening what had been a racialized regional to a racialized national stigma. Italy's migrants found they could become Americans, but they could not so easily abandon a stigma that had become so firmly associated with origin. What had begun with the assignment of inferiority to Italy's southerners became, in the USA, the assignment of national inferiority to Italians wishing to become Americans. What had begun as the racialization of an Italian regional group became the ethnicization of a plural American nation still viewed as firmly white.[57]

Notes

1   For an introduction to the large literature on Italian migration to the USA, see G. E. Pozzetta, 'Immigrants and Ethnics: The State of Italian-American Historiography', *Journal of American Ethnic History* 9:1 (1989), pp. 67–95. To place

US-focused historiography in perspective, see D. R. Gabaccia, 'Italian History and *gli italiani nel mondo'*, Parts I and II, *Journal of Modern Italian Studies* 2:1 (1997), pp. 45–66 and 3: 1 (1998), pp. 73–97.

2   The best introduction to this literature is J. W. Trotter, Jr, *The Great Migration in Historical Perspective: New Dimensions of Race, Class and Gender* (Blooming-ton, 1N, 1991).

3   J. R. Barrett and D. R. Roediger, 'In-Between Peoples: Race, Nationality and the New Immigrant Workers', *Journal of American Ethnic History* 16 (1997), pp. 3–44.

4   Authors often place 'white' and 'black' in quotation marks to problematize these categories rather than to treat them as natural or timeless. While I share this stance, I prefer not to litter every page with quotation marks.

5   See G. Sanchez, 'Race, Nation, and Culture in Recent Immigration Studies', and J. Gjerde, 'New Growth on Old Vines: The State of the Field of the Social History of Immigration to and Ethnicity in the United States', *Journal of American Ethnic History* (1999); see also D. R. Gabaccia, 'Do we Still Need Immigration History?' *Polish American Studies* 55:1 (1998), pp. 45–68.

6   N. I. Painter, 'Foreword', in Trotter, *Great Migration*, p. viii.

7   N. Glazer and D. P. Moynihan, *Beyond the Melting Pot: The Negroes, Puerto Ricans, Jews, Italians, and Irish of New York City* (Cambridge, MA, 1963).

8   A. H. Spear, *Black Chicago: The Making of a Negro Ghetto, 1890–1920* (Chicago, 1L, 1967), pp. 228, 229. For his dispute with Glazer and Moynihan, see p. 225.

9   N. Venturini, *Neri e italiani ad Harlem: Gli anni trenta e la guerra d'Etiopia* (Rome, 1990); J. Bodnar, R. Simon and M. P. Weber, *Lives of Their Own: Blacks, Italians, and Poles in Pittsburgh, 1900–1960* (Urbana, IL, 1983); S. Model, 'The ethnic niche and the structure of opportunity: Immigrants and minorities in New York City', in M. B. Katz (ed.), *The 'Underclass' Debate: Views from History* (Princeton, NJ, 1993), pp. 161–92; E. Pleck, 'A mother's wages: Income earn-ing among married Italian and Black women, 1896–1911', in *M. Gordon (ed.), The American Family in Social Historical Perspective*, 2nd edn (New York, 1978), pp. 367–92; T. L. Philpott, *The Slum and the Ghetto: Neighborhood Deterioration and Middle-Class Reform, Chicago, 1880–1930* (New York, 1978).

10   N. Green, 'The comparative Method and Poststructural Structuralism: New perspectives for Migration Studies', *Journal of American Ethnic History* 13:4 (1994), pp. 3–22.

11   N. Lemann, *The Promised Land: The Great Black Migration and How it Changed America* (New York, 1991), p. 6.

12   T. Archdeacon, *Becoming America: An Ethnic History* (New York, 1983), table V-3.

13   P. Ginsborg, *A History of Contemporary Italy; Society and Politics, 1943–1988* (London, 1990), table 21.

14   J. Jones, *The Dispossessed: America's Underclasses from the Civil War to the Present* (New York, 1992), p. 205.

15   J. R. Grossman, *Land of Hope: Chicago, Black Southerners, and the Great Migra-tion* (Chicago, IL, 1989), p. 19.

16   Key recent works include C. Murray, *Losing Ground: American Social Policy, 1950–1980* (New York, 1984); Lemann, *The Promised Land*; W. J. Wilson, *The Truly Disadvantaged: The Inner City, the Underclass, and Public Policy* (Chicago, IL, 1987). See also Katz, *The 'Underclass' Debate*.

17   D. Gabaccia, *Italy's Many Diasporas* (London, 1999).

18 The best summary of numbers for the modern, national, period is G. Rosoli (ed.), *Un secolo di emigrazione italiana, 1876–1976* (Rome, 1978)

19 Besides the numbers in Rosoli, see Gabaccia, *Italy's Many Diasporas*, ch. 7; Ginsborg, *History of Contemporary Italy*, ch. 7; F. Romero, *L'emigrazione e integrazione europea, 1945–1973* (Rome, 1991).

20 R. Lumley and J. Morris (eds), *The New History of the Italian South; The Mezzogiorno Revisited* (Exeter, 1997). See also D. M. Smith, 'Regionalism', in , E. R. Tannenbaum and E. P. Noether, (eds), *Modern Italy* (New York, 1974); and C. Levy (ed.), *Italian Regionalism: History, Identity and Politics* (Oxford, 1996). See also G. Levi, 'Regioni e cultura delle classi popolari', *Quaderni storici* 15:2 (1979), pp. 720–73.

21 J. A. Davis, *Conflict and Control: Law and Order in Nineteenth-Century Italy* (London, 1988).

22 G. Gribaudi, 'Images of the South: The Mezzogiorno as Seen by Insiders and Outsiders', and J. Dickie, 'Stereotypes of the Italian South, 1860–1900', in Lumley and Morris, *The New History of the Italian South.*

23 A. Caracciolo, *L'inchiesta agraria Jacini* (Turin, 1973).

24 Gabaccia, *Italy's Many Diasporas*, ch. 2.

25 *Inchiesta parlamentare sulle condizioni dei contadini nelle provincie meridionali e nella Sicilia* (Rome, 1909).

26 Gabaccia, *Italy's Many Diasporas*, ch. 6.

27 P. Verdicchio, *Bound by Distance: Rethinking Nationalism through the Italian Diaspora* (Madison, W1, 1997).

28 G. Pitrè, *Proverbi siciliani* (Palermo, 1978, orig. pub. 1870–1913), 4 volumes.

29 D. Goldfield, *Black, White and Southern: Race Relations and Southern Culture, 1940 to the Present* (Baton Rouge, LA, 1990), ch 1.

30 B. T. Washington, 'The Rural Negro and the South', *Proceedings of the National Conference of Charities and Corrections* 41 (1914), pp. 121–7.

31 *The Independent*, 19 and 26 May 1917, quoted in Grossman, *Land of Hope*, p. 61.

32 M. Viroli, *For Love of Country: An Essay on Patriotism and Nationalism* (Oxford, 1997).

33 Grossman, *Land of Hope*, ch. 5.

34 The use of biblical metaphors for the migration northward was general: 'land of hope', 'promised land'. See also L. R. Rodgers, *Canaan Bound; The African-American Migration Novel* (Urbana, IL, 1997).

35 G. Rosoli, 'From "Promised Land" to "Bitter Land": Italian Migrants and the Transformation of a Myth', in Dirk Hoerder and Horst Rössler (eds), *Distant Magnets: Expectations and Realities in the Immigrant Experience, 1840–1930,* (New York, 1993), pp. 222–40.

36 M. Triaca, *Amelia: A Long Journey* (Richmond, VA, 1985), p. 35, quoted in R. Bosworth, *Italy and the Wider World* (New York, 1996), p. 134.

37 Spear, *Black Chicago p. 135.*

38 *Inchiesta parlamentare sulle condizioni dei contadini*, vol. IV, p. 614 and vol. V, p. 711.

39 B. B. Caroli, *Italian Repatriation from the United States, 1900–1914* (New York, 1973). Interest in black return migration is more recent. See C. Stack, *Call to Home: African Americans Reclaim the Rural South* (New York, 1996), or, for a quantitative perspective, I. Robinson, 'Blacks Move Back to the South', *American Demographics*, 8 (1986), pp. 40–3.

40 For Chicago, my main sources on blacks have been Grossman, *Land of Hope*; Phillpott, *The Slum and the Ghetto* and Spear, *Black Chicago*. For Italians, see H. Nelli, *Italians in Chicago, 1880–1930: A Study in Ethnic Mobility* (New York, 1970) and R. J. Vecoli, 'Contadini in Chicago: A Critique of "the Uprooted"', *Journal of American History* 51:3 (1964), pp. 404–16. For New York, see G. Osofsky, *Harlem: The Making of a Ghetto*, 2nd edn (New York, 1971); I. Watkins-Owens, *Blood Relations: Caribbean Immigrants and the Harlem Community, 1900–1930* (Bloomington and Indianapolis, IN, 1996). On Italians, besides Venturini, *Neri e italiani ad Harlem*, see T. Kessner, *The Golden Door: Italian and Jewish Immigrant Mobility in New York City, 1880–1915* (New York, 1977); D. Gabaccia, *From Sicily to Elizabeth Street; Housing and Social Change among Italian Immigrants, 1880–1930* (Albany, NY, 1984). For Pittsburgh, see P. Gottlieb, *Making their Own Way; Southern Blacks' Migration to Pittsburgh, 1916–30* (Urbana, IL, 1987); and Bodnar, Simon and Weber, *Lives of Their Own*.

41 Osofsky, *Harlem: Making of a Ghetto*, p. 44.

42 See, e.g., Spear, *Black Chicago*, pp. 174–9.

43 Lemann, *The Promised Land*, pp. 29–32.

44 Spear, *Black Chicago*, ch. 4; Grossman, *Land of Hope*, pp. 129–32.

45 Watkins-Owens, *Blood Relations*.

46 W. M. Tuttle, *Race Riot: Chicago in the Red Summer of 1919* (New York, 1970).

47 Besides Venturini, *Neri e italiani ad Harlem*, see C. Greenberg, *'Or Does it Explode?': Black Harlem in the Great Depression* (New York, 1991).

48 Jones, *The Dispossessed*, ch. 7.

49 Watkins-Owens, *Blood Relations*.

50 R. Juliani, *Building Little Italy: Philadelphia's Italians before the Mass Migration* (University Park, PA, 1998); Nelli, *Italians in Chicago*, pp. 22–3.

51 R. E. Park and H. A. Miller, *Old World Traits Transplanted* (New York, 1921).

52 P. R. D'Agostino, 'The Scalabrini Fathers, the Italian Emigrant Church, and Ethnic Nationalism in America', *Religion and American Culture* 7:1 (1997), pp. 121–59; R. A. Orsi, *The Madonna of 115th Street: Faith and Community in Italian Harlem, 1880–1950* (New Haven, CT, 1985).

53 E. Fenton, *Immigrants and Unions, A Case Study: Italians and American Labour, 1870–1920* (New York, 1975); E. Fenton, 'Italians in the Labour Movement', *Pennsylvania History* 26 (1959), pp. 33–143. More recent work suggests that southerners came to dominate among radical and labour activists in the USA; see R. Vecoli and Bruno Bezza, (eds), *Gli italiani fuori d'Italia: Gli emigrati italiani nei movimenti operai dei paesi d'adozione* (Milan, 1983), pp. 257–306.

54 Sicilians, again, sometimes joined together as a pan-ethnic group; see Nelli, *Italians in Chicago*, pp. 173–4; see also S. L. Baily, *Immigrants in the Lands of Promise: Italians in Buenos Aires and New York City, 1870 to 1914* (Ithaca, NY, 1999), pp. 203–5.

55 M. F. Jacobson, *Whiteness of a Different Colour: European Immigrants and the Alchemy of Race* (Cambridge, MA, 1998), pp. 78–80.

56 Nelli, *Italians in Chicago*, pp. 126–7; Gabaccia, *Italy's Many Diasporas*, ch. 8.

57 E. Morawska, *Insecure Prosperity: Small Town Jews in Industrial America, 1890–1940* (Princeton, NJ, 1996), ch. 4.

12
Modernity, Backwardness and Capitalism in the Two Souths

Bruce Levine

The attempt to compare the southern regions of Italy and the USA is a huge and ambitious undertaking. The present collection, like the conference out of which it grew, addresses important aspects of such a comparison. Many others could easily be suggested, including religion, regional identities, political ideology and political action, and relationships with central governments. Rather than presume to offer a global evaluation of the project as a whole or even to comment upon all the contributions included in the present volume, the present essay will restrict itself to highlighting and briefly discussing a few themes running through the volume that strike a student of the US nineteenth-century South as especially interesting.

The dichotomies of 'old/new', 'backward/modern', 'capitalist/non-capitalist' are necessarily central to this broad-ranging discussion. The southern sections of both societies were long perceived and described as being qualitatively different from their respective norths. In each case, such inherited views have subsequently come under heavy fire. One question to be answered, thus, is whether and how the two souths really were in some significant way different from their respective norths, or whether they were simply 'constructed' as such by interested contemporaneous observers.

In the present discussion, the US 'South' under examination is principally the South as it was during the nineteenth century, and especially during the antebellum, Civil War, and Reconstruction eras. That era is also the focus of many of the liveliest discussions among historians of the USA. The institution of slavery and its aftermath are necessarily at the centre of such discussions, just as they were at the centre of economy, society, culture and politics in the nineteenth-century South.

Studies of slavery in the US have been menaced by opposing dangers – a Scylla and a Charybdis, if you will – in attempting to characterize its social system, especially in weighing the degree to which it was 'modern' or 'capitalist'. On one side is the tendency to regard that bondage as thoroughly pre-capitalist and therefore as qualitatively distinct from the North in that way. Note that such an approach could carry either a negative or a positive connotation, depending on the sensibilities and political agenda of the observer. In the hands of romantic-minded champions, the old South's distance from a capitalist norm (and a capitalist North) testified to the more traditional, organic, benevolently paternalist, reciprocal – and less materialist, less impersonal – nature of social relations below the Mason–Dixon line. In the eyes of detractors, in contrast, a pre-capitalist South was an effectively inert, stagnant, impoverished society insulated from outside influence by a protective shield of medievalism and provincialism.

To embrace either version of the view of the old South as pre-capitalist was to risk overlooking the decidedly modern origins of the formally antique social relation of slavery actually fashioned in the South as well as the motives behind its introduction and the use to which it was put. It often meant slighting the fact that New World slavery was the product of a trial-and-error search for a source of especially cheap and malleable labour with which to produce commodities specifically destined for a booming world market. By extension, it usually required neglecting the ways in which the need to respond to the changing requirements and pressures of that market influenced not only the practical functioning of the southern macro-economy but also the contours and rhythms of everyday personal life. In short, it meant missing the ways in which the ancient institution of slavery was reconfigured in the Americas when it was (as Marx put it) 'drawn into the whirlpool of an international market dominated by the capitalistic mode of production'.[1]

The opposite tendency in evaluating New World slavery was to treat it as simply one more in a wide and diverse array of capitalist forms of productive systems. This approach risked eclipsing those characteristics that distinguished slave-based commodity production from production based on legally free wage labour. Over time, nevertheless, this approach gained added legitimacy from an increasingly fashionable rejection of 'essentialism', 'teleologies' and 'meta-narratives' and the accompanying assertion that it was not permissible to 'privilege' one form of capitalism or capitalist development over another. (Ironically, but predictably, this repudiation of allegedly super-historical categories and generalizations in favour of an assumption-less empirical openness often led in practice to falling back upon considerably cruder categories and generalizations than those rejected out of hand.)

Understanding modern slavery as being effectively capitalist could also signify different things to different observers, depending upon their view of how capitalism works. To some, slavery's capitalist character helped explain its brutality. To others, it accounted for the system's putative efficiency, flexibility and ability to enlist the cooperation of its labourers. But whether carrying positive or negative associations, this approach has tended to elide (or at least reduce the emphasis on) the peculiar consequences of pursuing capitalistic economic goals through formally pre-capitalist means.

Clearly, then, all questions are by no means answered when we acknowledge that US slavery was capitalist in *some* sense. Neither are all questions answered when we acknowledge that one or both of those systems were capable of creating great wealth. Such acknowledgements leave major issues still to be addressed, including exactly how the unfree status of labour influenced the way in which wealth was produced and reinvested; how it retarded rates of urbanization, industrialization, mechanization[2] and literacy; and how the market's influence was refracted through the prism of bound labour. Analytically displacing slavery from the centre of southern society also made it difficult to account for the specific evolution within the free white population of various other social relationships as well as of cultural, ideological and political phenomena (including race and racism, gender definitions, honour and paternalism), all of which fed an increasingly distinctive regional self-identification that ultimately crystallized in southern nationalism.

The route to safety though these opposing perils (viewing the South as either non-capitalist or as merely 'another' form of capitalism) could not be found by taking refuge in a merely rhetorical declaration that 'truth lies somewhere in between'. It led instead through a determination to understand slavery in this specific time and place as a social relationship that *combined* capitalist and pre-capitalist elements in a novel manner, and then to determine (as Richard Follett urges in Chapter 4 above) the specific way in which these elements interacted with each other, thereby laying bare the system's actual dynamics.

To an outsider, some aspects of the fascinating discussion now under way about the nature of society in Italy's nineteenth-century Mezzogiorno bear a striking resemblance to the debates about American slavery referred to above, especially in the former's attempt to specify the *latifondo*'s economic character and its relationship to the development of capitalism in Italy.

Some critics of received notions of southern 'backwardness' at times seem to deny that the Mezzogiorno's economy was any less efficient or 'rational' than that of the Italian North, and that this would become clear once culturally-imposed prejudices are discarded.[3] In this respect, their argument follows in the footsteps left by Robert Fogel and Stanley Engerman, whose then-revisionist studies of the antebellum US South are often cited approvingly in the new Italian literature.[4] A host of questions are thereby provoked. Of what, exactly, did the *latifondo*'s 'rationality' consist? Was it successfully sustaining itself from year to year? Was it yielding a profit to its owner? If it accomplished the latter, just how did it do so? Did profitability reflect a favoured position on the market (as it did at least in part in the case of the antebellum southern cotton culture)? Did it reflect success in squeezing more effort out of a very low-cost source of labour? Or did the big landowners utilize their resources in a manner that promoted the kind of steady increase in broad-based economic development and diversification and an increase in productivity derived from a continual improvement in productive technique and technology of the kind more commonly associated with (for example) the antebellum American North?[5]

Is it even possible, moreover, to answer such questions about the Mezzogiorno as a whole? Or must we supply different answers about different sub-regions and time-periods?[6] The Sicilian and Neapolitan *latifondi* that Marta Petrusewicz and Lucy Riall describe seem to differ in important respects, which obviously complicates an attempt to gauge the *latifondo*'s internal organization and relationship to the external market.[7] Was it a large capitalist farm producing agricultural commodities in a relatively efficient manner? Was it a collection of peasant or semi-peasant enterprises preyed upon by parasitical rentiers? Did both kinds of *latifondi* co-exist with each other in time and place? Did different places support different types of enterprise all called by the same name? Or are we looking at one social formation as it appeared at different stages of its history?

To say that *latifondi* were capable of sustaining themselves and yielding a profit for some still leaves larger issues about their impact on the southern economy and their development unanswered, just as parallel assertions about American slavery could not conceal the US South's undeniable underdevelopment compared to the North. That such underdevelopment had profound practical consequences was demonstrated there by both the origins and outcome of the sectionally-defined American Civil War. The northern economy supported a larger and more rapidly growing population, a more diverse type of commercial agriculture, far bigger urban and industrial sectors, higher average living standards, and – especially through the application of technology – a much more rapidly escalating increase in the productive capacity of a given unit of human exertion (a rather good and basic gauge of economic development).[8]

These and other expressions of economic difference (and inequality) between the US North and South underlay the decline of the latter's political fortunes within the federal union by 1860. When the planter leadership sought to change the terms of the competition from economic and electoral to military, the extent of the North's economic superiority was ultimately revealed with even greater clarity. Meanwhile, it swiftly became apparent that the North's core labour force (small farmers, artisans, and wage-earners) felt considerably greater loyalty to their region than slave labourers did to the South. When General Robert E. Lee finally advised Jefferson Davis in late 1864 that 'the inequality is too great',[9] he was thus accurately describing not only the relative size of two opposing armies but also much, much more.

Some evidence of regional inequality in Italy may be found in the repeated attempts by various elite forces (local and otherwise) to 'modernize' economy and society in the *Mezzogiorno*. References to such plans arose repeatedly during the London conference, and both Marta Petrusewicz and Lucy Riall tell us a good deal about some of them. Petrusewicz found such reformist attempts in Campania inspired by a variety of concerns, including the influence upon large landholders and their allies of the Enlightenment, military setbacks (the Napoleonic invasion), and a sincere desire to increase 'public happiness' and 'improve the lot of the peasantry'. Riall attributes land reform's failure in Sicily to errors and miscalculations of various kinds on the part of the initiators and administrators (as the title of Chapter 7 above suggests), including a failure to take into account the social identity and interests of the most influential groups in the South.

Further investigation into this subject might benefit from conclusions reached in studies of land reform and the end of servitude in central and eastern Europe and the end of slavery in the western hemisphere. Especially relevant to Petrusewicz's subject may be discussions of 'revolutions from above', especially in eastern Europe, where deliberate attempts to preserve as much as possible the wealth and power of established elites through modifications in social and political systems still left a large class of dependent, impoverished and legally disadvantaged direct producers available for exploitation. They were designed, in other words, to make the minimum necessary concessions to powerful pressures for change without losing control over the process of change or over post-reform society.

This phenomenon is most closely identified with Prussia, whose Karl August von Hardenburg may well have coined the term 'revolution from above'. Prussian chancellor Chancellor Heinrich von Goldbeck explained the logic behind it: 'It is better to give up something voluntarily than to be forced to sacrifice everything.' Serf emancipation east of the Elbe, despite the considerable variation in the way it occurred there, drew upon the same logic. As Russia's Tsar Alexander II reasoned, 'It is better to abolish serfdom from above than to await the day when it will begin to abolish itself from below.'[10]

Elsewhere I have suggested that an eleventh-hour offer by a beleaguered Confederate government in 1865 to grant a partial form of freedom to any slaves willing to take up arms against the US represented a parallel case B a kindred attempt to save what could be saved as threats to slavery both from within and without palpably mounted.[11] Did similar considerations inspire any of the plans to reform land tenure and related aspects of Mezzogiorno society described in the present volume?

Other kinds of land-reform attempts, undertaken not by representatives of the *ancien régime* but by true bourgeois liberals, sought to emancipate unfree rural producers from legal fetters while still leaving them property-less (or at least property-poor) and hence available to perform day labour for others. This was, in fact, the programme of the Republican Party mainstream immediately following the US Civil War.[12] Explicit comparison with that experience might illuminate further some of the reform attempts in Sicily which were discussed in Chapter 7 above.

It would be useful to know to what degree reform thought in general was influenced by familiarity with changes attempted in land-tenure systems elsewhere in Europe. What role, moreover, did local agrarian unrest play in the formulation of such reform projects? Were at least some of those projects intended to deflect peasant discontent while also providing landowners with an available work force? Perhaps, in other words, the fact that after so many reform initiatives southern peasants remained land-poor and dependent reflected not the failure of reform but (in the eyes of some reformers, at least) success.

More insight into the values of southern Italian peasants, sharecroppers and day labourers – and into the extent and effectiveness of peasant mobilization – would also illuminate the origins and goals of those who initiated attempts at reform. Steven Hahn's study of mobilization among emancipated slaves in the American South, it seems to me, offers a fine model for such explorations.[13] Further study of the southern peasants' aspirations and powers of self-assertion during the reform era might also help account for the economic woes of the *latifondi* during the late nineteenth century. These have been attributed to the effects of trade wars, destabilizing legal struggles within the elite over land titles, and a resulting 'parasitic' mind-set on the part of the 'new men' taking over the estates. But Riall's account suggests the possibility that peasant recalcitrance and resistance may also have played a role in limiting the rural elite's economic options. If true, this would represent another parallel with developments in the US South, where former slaves' increased freedom of action allowed them to block attempts to re-impose gang labour on plantations, to compel landowners to settle for the less profitable sharecropping system, and in a range of other ways to reduce their own rate of exploitation.[14] That phenomenon may serve as a general reminder that the study of subordinated groups is critical not only in its own right but also as part of any larger understanding of historical eras, geographical regions, and the thought and actions of their social and political elites.

Notes

1 Karl Marx, *Capital* (Moscow, n.d.), Vol. 1, p. 226–7.
2 In this respect, Richard Follett's Louisiana sugar planters seem exceptions among slaveholders as a whole. See Chapter 4 in this volume.
3 Marta Petrusewicz, *Latifundium: Moral Economy and Material Life in a European Periphery* (Ann Arbor, MI, 1996), pp. 4–5. This viewpoint was more forcefully expressed by some participants in the London conference than in the contributions reproduced here.
4 Robert William Fogel and Stanley L. Engerman, *Time on the Cross: The Economics of American Negro Slavery* (Boston, MA, 1974); Robert William Fogel, *Without Consent or Contract: The Rise and Fall of American Slavery* (New York, 1989).
5 Fogel's *Without Consent or Contract* seems to grant as much, or, at least, not to shut the door on this interpretation. See, for example, pp. 78–9, 99–101, 105, 108–9.
6 Jonathan Morris, 'Challenging *Meridionalismo*: Constructing a New History for Southern Italy', in Robert Lumley and Jonathan Morris (eds), *The New History of the Italian South: The Mezzogiorno Revisited* (Exeter, 1997), pp. 3, 16–17.
7 Marta Petrusewicz, Chapter 5 above, and Lucy Riall, Chapter 7 above.
8 Paul David, Herbert G. Gutman, Richard Sutch, Peter Temin and Gavin Wright, *Reckoning with Slavery: A Critical Study in the Quantitative History of American Negro Slavery* (New York, 1976); James M. McPherson, 'Antebellum Southern Exceptionalism: A New Look at an Old Question', in McPherson, *Drawn with the Sword: Reflections on the American Civil War* (New York, 1996), pp. 3–23.

9   R. E. Lee to Jefferson Davis, 2 November 1864, in *The Wartime Papers of Robert E. Lee*, edited by Clifford Dowdey and Louis H. Manarin (1961; reprint, New York, 1987), p. 868.

10 Hans Rosenberg, *Bureaucracy, Aristocracy and Autocracy: The Prussian Experience, 1660–1815* (1958; rpt, Boston, MA, 1966), pp. 202–28; Terence Emmons, *The Russian Landed Gentry and the Peasant Emancipation of 1861* (Cambridge, 1968), p. 51 (Tsar Alexander quotation); Alfred J. Rieber, 'Alexander II: A Revisionist View', *Journal of Modern History* 43 (1971), pp. 42–58; Boris N. Mironov, 'When and Why Was the Russian Peasantry Emancipated', esp. pp. 338–9, in M. L. Bush (ed.), *Serfdom and Slavery: Studies in Legal Bondage* (London, 1996); and the work of Jerome Blum, especially *Lord and Peasant in Russia from the Ninth to the Nineteenth Century* (Princeton, NJ, 1961), pp. 536–600, and *The End of the Old Order in Rural Europe* (Princeton, NJ, 1978), pp. 357–66 (quotation from Goldbeck on p. 361). See also Shearer Davis Bowman, *Masters and Lords: Mid-19th Century US Planters and Prussian Junkers* (New York, 1993), pp. 103–11.

11 B. Levine, 'What Did We Go to War For? Confederate Emancipation and Its Meaning', in Susan-Mary Grant and Brian Holden Reid (eds), *The American Civil War: Explorations and Reconsiderations* (London, 2000), pp. 239–64.

12 Willie Lee Rose, *Rehearsal for Reconstruction: The Port Royal Experiment* (New York, 1976); William S. McFeeley, *Yankee Stepfather: General O. O. Howard and the Freedmen* (New Haven, CT, 1968); Eric Foner, 'Thaddeus Stevens, Confiscation, and Reconstruction', in Eric Foner, *Politics and Ideology in the Age of the Civil War* (New York, 1980); Ira Berlin, Barbara J. Fields, Steven F. Miller, Joseph P. Reidy and Leslie S. Rowland, *Slaves No More: Three Essays on Emancipation and the Civil War* (New York, 1992), esp. ch. 2.

13 Steven Hahn, Chapter 6 in this volume.

14 See especially James L. Roark, *Masters without Slaves: Southern Planters in the Civil War and Reconstruction* (New York, 1977); Lawrence N. Powell, *New Masters: Northern Planters during the Civil War and Reconstruction* (New Haven, CT, 1980); Harold D. Woodman, 'Economic Reconstruction and the Rise of the New South, 1865–1900', in John B. Boles and Evelyn Thomas Nolen (eds), *Interpreting Southern History* (Baton Rouge, LA, 1987), pp. 254–307; and Julie Saville, *The Work of Reconstruction: From Slave to Wage Laborer in South Carolina, 1860–1870* (Cambridge, 1994). Roger L. Ransom and Richard Sutch estimated that while the slave got back only about 20 per cent of the value of his labour (in the form of the cost of food, clothing, and shelter), black sharecroppers and tenants by the late 1870s were receiving more than 50 per cent of the value of their output: See Ransom and Sutch, *One Kind of Freedom: The Economic Consequences of Emancipation* (Cambridge, 1977), pp. 4–5, 203–16.

Index